CULTURES IN COLLISION

*Sponsored by
Syracuse University,
the University of Toronto,
and the Americas Society*

*with the assistance of
the William H. Donner Foundation*

CULTURES IN COLLISION

The Interaction of Canadian and U.S. Television Broadcast Policies

A Canadian-U.S. Conference on Communications Policy

PRAEGER SPECIAL STUDIES • PRAEGER SCIENTIFIC

New York • Philadelphia • Eastbourne, UK
Toronto • Hong Kong • Tokyo • Sydney

Library of Congress Cataloging in Publication Data
Canadian-U.S. Conference on Communications Policy (1983 :
   New York, N.Y.)
   Cultures in collision.
   Includes index.
   1. Television broadcasting policy—United States—
Congresses. 2. Television broadcasting policy—Canada—
Congresses. I. Title.
HE8700.8.036 1983   384.55'43   83-19232
ISBN 0-03-069533-3 (alk. paper)

Published in 1984 by Praeger Publishers
CBS Educational and Professional Publishing,
a Division of CBS Inc.
521 Fifth Avenue, New York, NY 10175 USA

456789 052 9876545321

Printed in the United States of America
on acid-free paper

ABOUT THE SPONSORS

The Americas Society is a national organization established to coordinate the activities of leading institutions in the United States and abroad that are concerned with Western Hemisphere affairs. The society's objectives are to improve understanding in the United States of the political, economic, and cultural values of other hemispheric nations. Its chairman is David Rockefeller.

The Canadian Affairs division of the Americas Society was formed in 1981. It seeks to inform an influential constituency of Americans on all important aspects of Canada as well as problems of major concern to the Canada-United States relationship.

The University of Toronto was founded by royal charter in 1827 as King's College, and its present constitution was formulated by the government of Ontario in the University of Toronto Act of 1971. Canada's largest university, it includes 50,000 students in nine undergraduate colleges and an extensive variety of graduate programs. It is a major research institution, and is federated with a number of other Canadian universities. It is one of two Canadian universities to be chosen for membership in the Association of American Universities.

Syracuse University was founded by the Methodist Church in 1871 as a small liberal arts college. It has grown to be a major nonsectarian academic community of 15 fully accredited colleges and schools, and a leader in graduate education. Syracuse is also one of the select group of 50 North American universities elected to the Association of American Universities.

The William H. Donner Foundation, established in 1962 and based in New York City, is a national philanthropy dedicated in part to the advancement of knowledge and understanding of Canada in the United States. The foundation has supplied funds for scholarly re-search, publication costs, and other expenses connected with this conference.

CONTENTS

INTRODUCTION

Goodwin Cooke

No other two countries in the world have so complex and extensive a relationship as Canada and the United States. They are linked by countless personal, academic, cultural, professional, business, governmental, and other ties; and most contacts between individuals and institutions across the border occur without publicity, happily unencumbered by either government. Areas of disagreement or friction between the two nations are remarkably few given the extent of the relationship—they are sometimes referred to as "irritants" to suggest that, while troublesome, they should not affect the totality of relations. When these irritants become particularly vexing, or when the debate they engender becomes increasingly strident, relations are said to be deteriorating. It is thus a generally understood objective of both governments to isolate individual problems and, to the extent possible, to keep from souring the overall harmony between two great and friendly countries.

One such irritant, which has proved singularly resistant to resolution over the past decade, has been the question of U.S. television broadcasting received by Canadian audiences. In 1976 the Canadian Income Tax Act was amended to discourage Canadian firms from advertising on U.S. stations and thus to enhance the use of Canadian television outlets. U.S. television firms filed a complaint with the U.S. Trade Representative in 1979, imputing injury to U.S. commerce. Canada has accused U.S. broadcasters of commercial and cultural overreach, while U.S. interests have charged Canada with supporting unfair competition and interference with what should be a legitimate and open market. Legislation has been proposed to the Congress that would "mirror" or retaliate against the Canadian action by gaining advantage or inflicting injury in some other, perhaps disparate, area. A relatively minor "irritant" has thus been permitted to fester, and, in a period of economic difficulty for both countries, to have a disproportionate effect on the relationship as a whole.

The source of this dispute is not simply protectionism or chauvinism on the Canadian side, nor is it commercial greed or imperialism on the U.S. side. The dispute derives from profound differences, legal, historical, and philosophical, in the two countries' approaches to communications policy. The innumerable similarities between the two nations often conceal these differences. But, for example, U.S. interpretation of the First Amendment, however admirable, does not necessarily play a basic role in Canadian jurisprudence, and Canadian dedication to multicultural development, however central to its national purpose, is frequently irrelevant to U.S. economic concepts. The resolution, or at least the containment of the broadcasting dispute, will require mutual appreciation of the differences in communications law, practice, and policy; in the absence of such appreciation the dispute could lead to a futile and eventually damaging cycle of retaliations.

CANADIAN AND U.S. COMMUNICATIONS POLICIES

Canadian and U.S. regulatory policies differ primarily in the degree to which each relies on market mechanisms, as opposed to government regulation, to determine program content and industry economic structure. Current U.S. policy is skeptical of traditional regulatory assumptions and increasingly willing to trust profit motives to reflect consumer demand. Canada, however, has traditionally emphasized government control rather than market competition to determine industry structure and programming, and broadcast policy seeks to enhance Canadian culture and national identity. Canadian authorities tend to regard public and commercial interests as antagonistic. The inclination of commercial interests (in many instances from south of the border) to ignore Canadian cultural objectives is thus to be controlled by federal regulation.

These differences have varied over time, and, on occasion, policies have appeared to criss-cross in response to social and political pressure. For example, the United States has in the past used content regulation to ensure responsiveness to minority interests, and PBS was established in some measure to compensate for what were seen as failures of the commercial networks. Canada, in time, has become more reliant on advertising revenue and thus more dependent on mass appeal programming.

Although U.S. broadcast policy is more concerned with economic consequences and Canadian more with political or cultural effects, neither country's policy is based purely on one set of concerns or the other. The U.S. preference for competitive markets in goods and services has its counterpart in the First Amendment desideratum of an open, robust marketplace of ideas. The United States has long championed, sometimes alone, the principle of free flow of information and ideas across international borders. However, the U.S. free flow policy serves U.S. economic interests, since the U.S. lead in television software and programming ensures greater input into, and profits from, the international free flow of television.

Likewise, Canada's concern for cultural identity in the face of a potential American television tidal wave has an economic counterpart. To the extent that Canadian broadcast markets can be made secure for Canadian stations and programs, Canada's broadcast industry can grow unchallenged domestically and compete more effectively internationally. Success in international television markets, as with sports and films, brings national pride and recognition, as well as financial profit.

Demographic differences and geography are also pertinent to communications problems. The United States is approximately ten times the size of Canada and a much more profitable market for both U.S. and Canadian programmers. Secondly, over 90 percent of the Canadian population lives within range of U.S. terrestrial broadcast signals. These immutable facts must be accounted for in reaching an accord on the border broadcast dispute, and both countries may find it necessary and desirable to make trade-offs between their concerns for equity and efficiency in broadcast services.

IMPACT OF NEW TECHNOLOGIES

Dramatic changes are occurring in techniques for distributing programming to U.S. and Canadian audiences. Consumers can purchase programs directly through tapes or discs, or select special programs through subscription or pay cable transmission. Direct broadcasting from satellites and optical fiber transmission will vastly expand channels for distribution, giving consumers increased choice and control over what they view. The trend in the United States is toward narrowcasting, identifying audiences with special interests and either charging for programming or finding advertisers who wish to reach that audience. Television is coming to resemble the book, magazine, and movie industries in offering greater diversity and specialization.

These new techniques rely heavily on control by the distributor over reception, offering opportunities for pirating and illegal access schemes and posing new problems for government control, particularly across the U.S.-Canadian border. Canadian efforts to ensure that television promotes national objectives, either in terms of cultural identity or stimulating Canadian production, will be made increasingly difficult as a huge new array of specialized programs becomes available. Canadian advertisers will seek ways to use the new technologies to reach their own audiences, perhaps leading to charges of pirating from U.S. producers. As new methods of transmission are introduced, they will likely bring fresh accusations from Canadian authorities that U.S. interests are undermining Canadian policies, and from American producers that Canada is infringing on property rights.

At the recent Canadian-U.S. Conference on Communications Policy, held in New York in March 1983, four principal areas were addressed: a historical comparison of Canadian and American approaches to broadcast policy; sovereignty and television—who can or should control what is broadcast; the impact of new technologies on Canadian-U.S. broadcasting relationships; and the border-broadcasting dispute itself. Contributions on each of these topics are included in this book, as well as several of the responses to these primary presentations. The conference also profited from presentations by The Honorable Allan E. Gotlieb, Canadian Ambassador to the United States; John Meisel, chairman of the Canadian Radio-Television and Telecommunications Commission;* Stephen Sharp, a commissioner of the Federal Communications Commission; and Leslie G. Arries, Jr., who spoke on behalf of the American border broadcasters. These discussions are singularly pertinent to the issue, and have been included here.

The conference has by no means resolved the problem, but it may represent a starting point for future negotiations, and it is hoped that this volume will be a useful introduction for those wishing to study this complex issue.

---

*The commission began as the Canadian Radio-Television Commission (CRTC) and became the Canadian Radio-Television and Telecommunications Commission (CRTTC) in 1976. The two names are used interchangeably throughout this volume.

CULTURES IN COLLISION

1

WORDS AND SPACE: CULTURE AND COMMUNICATIONS IN THE 1980s

Allan E. Gotlieb

When this conference was first organized, no one could have foreseen how timely it would be. The minister of communications, Francis Fox, announced a new broadcasting policy for Canada on March 1, 1983. I plan to discuss this policy and to place it within the context of Canadian government concerns over broadcasting and similar cultural issues.

These subjects are important, for the ways in which we organize our different mass communications systems reflect in a very real way our different societies.

Here in the United States a free market philosophy has applied to the production of cultural products as easily and successfully as it has applied to the production of any other consumer product. The United States has produced and marketed a popular culture that is the most extensive and attractive in the world. The U.S. cultural industry, while enormously accelerating the traditional pace of cultural evolution, has still been able to produce its own classical schools—from the Marx Brothers and vaudeville through the film musical, photojournalism, the situation comedy, Sesame Street, and the styles and formats of TV news—all this energy, all these prototypes have sprung from U.S. soil and set down roots throughout the world.

The very size of the market here, and the vitality of the entrepreneurial drive that feeds it, have made an open market approach to mass culture highly profitable and of enormous social importance here and around the world. U.S. culture, warts and all, dominates popular culture in all but the most closed societies of the world.

While the United States has left largely to the marketplace how it sees itself and how it is seen abroad, other no less convinced democracies have taken other routes in organizing their mass communications systems.

Most—Britain, Canada, Germany, and France, to name a few—have adopted other approaches, which reflect their traditions and philosophies. Hence, West Germany has a highly decentralized broadcasting system in which no one organization can easily dominate. France has a very carefully expanded state system, until recently highly centralized, as is the country itself. Britain probably has the most independent public system in the world, coupled with a limited private system that matches the public organization program for program in quality and sense of public service.

Broadcasting has traditionally been a critical point in Canadian cultural life. Let me suggest a few of the real challenges we face. First, we are a small population distributed widely and unevenly across a huge land mass. It is a fundamental political imperative that we have the means to speak to one another as Canadians. In some respects this is primarily a technical challenge, and we have developed technical solutions to meet our requirements. Canada has been a pioneer in such areas as microwave, cable, and broadcasting technologies.

Second, we require a thriving cultural sector capable of producing products to reflect ourselves to one another accurately and creatively. This, however, requires a certain "critical mass" of support, measured in terms of creative people, audiences, venues, financial backers, and so on. With the exception of certain major centers, this mass is hard to find in Canada. This is as true of broadcasting as other areas, and so the governments in Canada have historically played a critical supportive role in our cultural life. For example, the Canadian government created the Canadian Broadcasting Corporation, or CBC, in 1932 and charged it with the responsibility for meeting our broadcasting requirements. Over the years, the private sector has also devoted the resources necessary for the development of a thriving private alternative to the CBC.

There is a third challenge that requires special treatment. I refer to the overwhelming presence of the United States and the vast and creative resources devoted to U.S. broadcasting. The linguistic and cultural similarities between Canada and the United States have historically provided Canadians with a wide range of U.S. programming to choose from. We have not hesitated to exercise this choice. But the sheer weight of U.S. broadcasting has often threatened to overwhelm its much smaller Canadian counterpart.

In the days of radio this challenge was acute. However, radio has developed primarily as a local medium and Canadians have chosen to listen to and support local radio stations, whether they be CBC or private. In fact, Canadian radio is diverse and strong. With the advent of television, however, all of this dramatically changed.

Most Canadians live within a narrow band stretched along the Canadian-U.S. border. Most of us are able to pick up over-the-air broadcasting from U.S. border stations with little difficulty, often with an inexpensive rooftop antenna. As our demand for U.S. programming increased, Canada developed a thriving and technologically advanced cable industry. From its inception, the main selling point of cable has been its ability to transmit U.S. television signals into Canadian homes as clearly as signals produced by local Canadian stations.

While this provided Canadians with a wide choice of television programming, it also threatened to destroy our ability to produce our own programming. Canadians like U.S. programming and tune in U.S. stations easily and cheaply. To compete with U.S. stations for advertising revenues, Canadian stations, both public and private, are forced to purchase U.S. programming from U.S. producers.

There is a special wrinkle to this practice that is worth noting. U.S. producers make their programs with the intention of recovering their costs and making their profits through U.S. domestic sales. Sales to broadcasters in other countries are "gravy." As a consequence, U.S. producers sell a program in Canada for a fraction of the cost incurred in producing that program. Canadian producers, however, run into costs roughly equivalent to those encountered by their U.S. counterparts. For example, a U.S. program costing $250,000 to produce may be sold in Canada for as little as $25,000. Canadian producers must also spend $250,000 to produce equivalent programming but are faced with competition from a foreign product selling for one tenth the cost of their production. The economics of this situation are self-evident.

It is estimated that in the peak evening hours on English-language television, foreign programs account for 85 percent of viewing; they represent 75 percent of total viewing throughout the day. Drama programs account for 66 percent of peak viewing time, and only 5 percent of these programs are Canadian. Canadian drama represents only 2 percent of total viewing time. English Canadian children spend 83 percent of their viewing time watching foreign programs.

This is more than just a dilemma. It is a cultural crisis.

It is a crisis because television is the primary medium of cultural expression in our time. If Canadians lose creative access to this medium they will lose the opportunity for cultural self-expression. I believe the loss to Canada would be tragic, with enormous repercussions for our cultural, social, and political life.

There are economic stakes as well. More than $2 billion in revenues are generated by the Canadian broadcasting system, which at the present time includes 1,312 stations, networks, and cable systems and 1,886 rebroadcasters. The Canadian program production and broadcasting industries employ approximately 75,000 Canadians. More than 30,000 Canadians make their living in the independent television production and film industry, and another 10,000 are self-employed performers, writers, directors, and technicians. A significant number of these jobs would disappear if we were to allow our broadcasting industry to wither.

In the past, the government has taken steps to try to protect the Canadian broadcasting industry. The Canadian Radio-Television and Telecommunications Commission, or CRTTC—our regulatory agency—has restricted cable companies to importing no more than three commercial and one noncommercial U.S. stations. In practice, this has meant that most Canadian cable subscribers receive the three U.S. commercial networks and the Public Broadcasting System. The CRTTC also imposed minimum Canadian content regulations on Canadian broadcasters. The content requirements differ according to the viewing time, but at no point are Canadian broadcasters responsible for providing more than 60 percent of their programming from Canadian sources.

The content requirements generated a new and controversial policy. Canadian broadcasters complained they did not have sufficient revenues to produce the programming required by the CRTTC. In an effort to correct this situation, the government amended the Income Tax Act. Canadian advertisers are not now allowed to write off the costs of advertising when that advertising is placed on a foreign station and directed to a Canadian audience. There was no restriction placed on advertising abroad as such, but the government decided it would not subsidize this revenue outflow through the fiscal system. The objective of this policy was to direct more revenues to Canadian broadcasters from Canadian advertisers.

Canadian-U.S. broadcasting relations have often been troubled by misunderstandings or misperceptions. To us it appears that Canadian cultural policies, once they cross the border, become hard economic issues to the United States. We feel that our cultural situation—our aspirations and our fears—are either misunderstood or ignored.

In the United States, we are regarded as unduly restrictive, imposing arbitrary controls on what our population is permitted to see. When we point out that well over 50 percent of the programming seen in Canada comes from the United States while the U.S. commercial networks collectively show less than 2 percent foreign programming from around the world, we are told that this is a marketplace decision. (This U.S. philosophy, of course, does not extend to consumer preferences in automobiles, but that is another matter.) The free flow of information may be perfectly consistent with U.S. First Amendment principles, but I am not at all confident that the founding fathers would stretch the Constitution to include the free flow of advertising dollars.

And so it has gone, back and forth, for a number of years. We began with policies to defend relatively modest cultural goals and ended up being defensive. Relatively minor disputes erupted and seriously detracted from an overwhelmingly positive bilateral telecommunications and communications relationship—the most extensive such relationship in the world and one that, in economic terms, is overwhelmingly in favor of the United States.

As if things were not bad enough, the new communications technologies exacerbated the situation. Communications satellites have greatly expanded the programming possibilities for broadcasters. More than 50 new television programming services are now being delivered by satellite to the U.S. consumer via a rapidly expanding cable industry. By 1986, direct broadcast satellite services will be launched in the United States. Direct broadcast services will be high-powered transmissions capable of being received by home owners with a $300 rooftop satellite dish. Teletext and videotex technologies are now a reality, and the consumer market for these and similar nonprogramming services is expected to grow enormously within the next ten years.

Canadians have watched with interest the proliferation of new services, especially pay television, south of the border. Our appetites have been whetted for more and improved broadcasting. As satellite technology developed, the cost of television receive-only satellite dishes plummeted. For an investment of $10,000 or less many Canadians, either private individuals or commercial establishments, have purchased their own private dishes and now receive programming direct off U.S. satellites.

Canadian broadcasting policy had reached another crossroads.

The government decided that a comprehensive policy response was necessary. An ad hoc approach could remedy specific problems but, ultimately, would fail to meet our overall strategic objectives. A task force on broadcast policy was established by the government to develop a comprehensive policy.

As a result of its studies, the task force established three broad objectives. First, it was decided that the Canadian broadcasting system must be maintained and strengthened if it were to remain an effective vehicle of social and cultural policy. Second, Canadians wanted more and better Canadian programming in all programming categories. Third, Canadians wanted a significantly increased choice of programming of all kinds in both official languages in all parts of Canada.

The goals appear straightforward enough, but they pose interesting and intricate problems. A restrictive approach to the introduction of new technologies and new services would, perhaps, shore up the Canadian broadcasting industry but it would deny Canadians the programming choice they demanded. An "open skies" approach would provide Canadians with a wide variety of programming but at a potentially grave cost to the domestic industry.

The new technologies unquestionably create new challenges to Canadian broadcasting, not all of which are negative. They also create new, perhaps unprecedented, opportunities for Canadian broadcasters and program producers.

For many years we have been told by the United States to produce our programming for the North American market. "Let the marketplace decide whether Canadian broadcasting should survive." A fine theory, but the practice is something else. The economics of traditional U.S. broadcasting are such that the major networks have been afraid to touch foreign programming. Appeals to consumer tastes must be so wide and so general that foreign programming is considered simply too risky. This is not Canadian sour grapes. We are all familiar with the many excellent British productions that have been shown by the Public Broadcasting System to wide critical acclaim. For PBS, the audiences for those programs are exceptionally high. To a network, the viewing figures would mean death. The networks cannot afford such "specialized" or "minority" programming.

We in Canada are familiar with this thinking. There have been occasions when U.S. producers have used Canadian facilities for production of a show intended for the U.S. market. When this is done, however, the U.S. producers often insist that all references to Canada be expunged. Street signs are changed, French signs are taken down, Canadian taxi cabs are replaced with yellow cabs, and similar measures are undertaken to ensure that the U.S. audience is convinced the location is the United States. While such productions may provide jobs for the Canadian artistic community, it would be hard to defend them as reasonable expressions of Canadian culture.

With the advent of the new satellite and cable technologies, the economics of U.S. broadcasting have undergone an irreversible change. Consumers are now willing to pay to have specialized services delivered to their homes. We have entered the era of narrowcasting as opposed to broadcasting. The highly competitive nature of these new services makes them hungry for new programming. They know they cannot survive if they simply repeat what is already being seen for free on U.S. commercial broadcasting stations. They need alternative quality programming. Movies have provided by far the largest single source of this programming, but even this source is not inexhaustible. For example, Time Incorporated now runs two

24-hour-a-day movie channels—Home Box Office and Cinemax. Time must dredge up 48 hours of movie programming a day to satisfy its pay-television audience.

The potential benefits for the Canadian broadcasting industry are obvious. Canadian programs can now be produced for the Canadian market and then sold to specialized television services for distribution to the pay-TV market. An audience of 2 million Canadians for a CBC-produced drama is considered a major success; sale of such a program to a U.S. pay-TV service could double or triple that audience. The same holds true for Canadian-produced documentaries, public affairs shows, children's shows, and variety programming.

The Canadian government has recognized these new opportunities. The challenge now becomes how to use these opportunities to meet the broad strategic objective of our broadcast policy. The result of the policy review was the production of the document called "Towards a New National Broadcasting Policy." In that document the government outlined four broad policies that have been approved by the cabinet and that will be implemented.

Let me briefly describe these policies.

THE EXPANSION OF PROGRAMMING CHOICE

The government has decided to permit the introduction of a much wider range of programming to Canadians. This programming will become available primarily through the cable system and will be offered on a tiered basis. Cable systems will continue to offer their basic packages of conventional broadcasting but, in addition, they will now be permitted to offer new services for additional charges to the consumer. The CRTTC has already licensed a number of new Canadian pay-TV services. In addition to these, cable operators will be able to offer new, foreign signals. Preferably, these foreign signals will be repackaged to include Canadian material. If such packaging is not feasible, we intend, nevertheless, to permit cable operators to distribute these signals—except for foreign pay-TV signals—subject to the appropriate regulatory approval, the conclusion of contractual arrangements with the signal owners, and the pertinent international agreements.

New, nonprogramming services such as videotex, intrusion alarms, and medic alert, will also be available for distribution. Cable will become a major vehicle for the delivery of new services to Canadian homes. In uncabled areas of Canada, direct satellite reception may eventually provide a range of services similar to the services that will be offered by the cable systems. This policy will not only offer Canadians expanded programming choices but will also provide our cable operators with a much-valued boost. We hope our cable operators will continue to develop their expertise and technological capabilities as these new services arrive.

THE STRENGTHENING OF CANADIAN PROGRAMMING

The government believes that public monies should be available to producers of television programming. This reflects our economic situation and the size of our domestic market. Accordingly, a Canadian Broadcast Program Development Fund will be established to spur private production companies and independent producers. The fund will be administered by the Canadian Film Development Corporation and will rise from a total of $35 million in the first full year of operation to $60 million in the fifth year. Funding will be available to the private sector on a two-for-one basis; that is, one dollar from the fund for every two dollars raised by the private producer. Projects must contain certain minimum Canadian content to receive public funding. In this way we hope that Canadian programming expertise will continue to develop, and quality Canadian programming will not only reach Canadian audiences but also reach out to the world audience.

THE DEREGULATION OF SATELLITE DISH LICENSING REQUIREMENTS FOR INDIVIDUALS

The government has decided that individual Canadians, as well as certain small commercial establishments, will no longer need a license under the Radio Act to operate a television receive-only earth station for reception of radio and television programming from satellites. This policy is intended to benefit Canadians in rural and remote areas who are not now served by cable systems. For those entities such as apartment buildings, condominium complexes, hotels, and motels that have set up master antenna services to bring their residents satellite-distributed television services, the government will revise its licensing requirements. The primary consideration will be whether the proposed master antenna system poses a serious economic challenge to existing licensed cable services. Where this challenge does not exist, the government expects the CRTTC to license the system for distribution of satellite programming. The applicant will, of course, be subject to regulation and will be expected to demonstrate that it has concluded an appropriate agreement with the originators of the satellite programming signals.

DIRECTION OF THE CRTTC ON POLICY MATTERS

The government has decided it must be in a position to quickly adjust its broadcasting policies to meet changing circumstances. Many of the issues raised by the new technologies have an impact, including a direct impact on our international relations, that takes us beyond the traditional scope of broadcasting regulation. There is general agreement that the government should be given the legislative authority to issue directives to the CRTTC on broad policy matters, subject to adequate safeguards and procedures. It is not the intention of the government to enter into specific issues such as licensing, Canadian content requirements, and other regulatory and supervisory tasks now the responsibility of the CRTTC. New legislation will require parliamentary approval to implement these changes in the structure of Canadian broadcasting.

These are realistic policies designed to meet critical challenges. We have provided extensive briefings for interested U.S. parties, including the trade press. So far, the reaction has been very positive. Our U.S. interlocutors have shown an appreciation for the situation in which Canada finds itself and an even greater appreciation for the openness this policy document demonstrates. We have made it clear that we are prepared—indeed, would be pleased— to discuss the entire range of bilateral communications issues.

At a time when many nations are erecting new barriers to trade, Canada is turning toward greater openness. Our decisions are regarded in the United States as having global significance as many other countries grapple with the fundamental issues raised by new communications technologies. I believe our decisions will be studied in detail by other countries and may be reflected in the development of their respective policies.

We have created a new set of tools. Canadians have the talent and imagination to make good use of them. I believe that foreign, primarily U.S., television systems will look closely at the products we produce over the coming years. If our programming is good enough it will find a market and if it finds a market it will continue to expand broadcasting opportunities for Canadians.

This is not an empty hope. We have already been approached by U.S. systems interested in picking up Canadian material directly off our Canadian communications satellites. There is strong interest, for example, in receiving Canadian news and public affairs programming. With the agreement in 1982 between our two governments to permit the use of domestic satellites for transborder communications, we have removed the major legal barriers to direct reception of satellite signals from each other. Cheap transmissions across our border via satellites are now possible. I expect there will soon be progress in concluding appropriate transborder arrangements.

A new broadcasting strategy for Canada has been launched. New policies are in place, new actions will be initiated. To many of us in Canada, we have entered a new era, perhaps the most exciting one in our television broadcasting history.

2

CANADA AND THE UNITED STATES: COMPARATIVE ORIGINS AND APPROACHES TO BROADCAST POLICY

Frank W. Peers

Almost every country in the Western Hemisphere has a broadcasting system based on private ownership and operation, financed primarily by advertising. Canada, the country that in geography, resources, material prosperity, and principal language spoken so much resembles the United States, is the outstanding exception: its broadcasting system is said to serve certain social objectives, spelled out in the governing statute, and a large component of the system, following a British and European model, is publicly owned and operated. What accounts for the divergence of the two countries in theory and practice, and how true to the model supposedly adopted is each system in reality? Do the conflicts that arise between the two countries reflect the differing priorities inherent in each model, or a misunderstanding in one country of the objectives pursued in the other?

To begin our understanding of these questions, I shall try to identify the underlying factors that may explain the divergent paths that broadcasting has pursued in each country, and to weigh the potency of each influence named. I shall do that by reviewing the origins of broadcasting in Canada and the United States, looking at principal stages in broadcasting development, and seeking to discover why modifications in broadcasting policy have occurred, if indeed they have. At that point I may be able to assess the continuing differences and potential conflicts between the two broadcasting systems, as well as their interrelationships.

I hypothesize that in the United States the chief determinant of the broadcasting system was the market system on which the economy is based, but also important were prevailing cultural values, which include the liberal tradition in America, consumerism, and a fear of big government. I hypothesize that in Canada the principal determinants have been geographic location; demographic characteristics, including size of population and linguistic diversity; economic considerations, including the sources of capital and fluctuating levels of prosperity; and the political culture—attitudes toward government, the mixture of ideological strains, and sensitivity about accepting leadership from another people.

At this point, I am not attempting to say which of these determinants was most powerful. Nor do I assign a primary place to the technical attributes of broadcasting, though I expect the changing technologies to limit the influence of any of the other factors mentioned at particular stages in the development of radio and television.

THE UNREGULATED PHASE OF
RADIO DEVELOPMENT

The first phase of radio broadcasting was similar in our two countries: a rapid period of development beginning about 1920, when radio was promoted by manufacturers and sellers of transmitting and receiving equipment; a shift toward the recovery of costs from advertisers; the move toward economies of scale in the formation of networks; and minimal interference from government. In each country an existing statute, intended to serve radio telephony, was used to license the operators of the new broadcasting stations, with indifferent results. [1] The first phase of development, when commercial broadcasting became established and regulation hardly existed, lasted until 1927 in the United States. In Canada, the federal government took five years longer to end the first phase, awaiting the results of a public inquiry and then a jurisdictional challenge posed by certain of the provinces, particularly Quebec. [2]

Until 1928, when Canada's public inquiry began its hearings, there was little reason to suspect that the broadcasting systems in the two neighboring countries would pursue different courses. But that is what happened after Canada passed its first broadcasting act in 1932—legislation that found rare all-party agreement in the Canadian Parliament.

THE 1927 LEGISLATION IN THE UNITED STATES
AND THE 1932 LEGISLATION IN CANADA

The 1927 act establishing the Federal Radio Commission as a body delegated by Congress to regulate broadcasting in the United States had a public purpose, to end the anarchic condition of licensing permitted under the former statute, to reserve for the people the ownership of radio frequencies, and to ensure a service that would be equitable, protected by the First Amendment, and regulated in accordance with the "public interest, convenience, and necessity," with a right of appeal to the law courts.[3] There was no challenge either in the statute or its application by the FRC to the assumption that, in the main, stations and networks would be privately operated for profit or that broadcasting was a business almost like any other, except that the physical limitations of the frequency spectrum made it necessary for operators to apply for and renew licenses. Little elaboration was given on the meaning of the phrase "public interest, convenience, and necessity."

The act did not talk about national purpose or national objectives. As time went on, "public interest" seemed to apply to the interest of the individual citizen as a listener and consumer, not as a member of any social group or collectivity. In making policy at the transmitting end, the FRC (later the FCC) was given little direction in the act as to the size or power of economic units undertaking broadcasting enterprises. Indeed, although networks were firmly established by the end of the 1920s as the dominant force in radio broadcasting, the broadcasting provisions of the 1927 act were left substantially unchanged in the 1934 legislation establishing the Federal Communications Commission, and to this day there is no provision for the FCC to license networks.

In short, broadcasting was expected or allowed to continue in the commercial direction it had taken in the period immediately preceding the 1927 and 1934 acts of Congress. In the very earliest years of broadcasting development, there had been considerable talk of radio as an educational instrument. Witness the short-lived declaration by David Sarnoff that broadcasting was a public service that must do the job of "entertaining, informing and educating the nation." Witness the vow by Secretary of Commerce Herbert Hoover that radio should not be allowed to drown the listener in "advertising chatter," that it was "a public concern impressed with the public trust," and should not be "considered as merely a business carried on for private gain."[4]

These concepts were left at the wayside as radio operators recognized the profits to be made by merchandising goods. By 1928-30, educational stations that had gone on the air with high hopes earlier in the decade were declining rapidly in numbers, and those that were left concluded that "their hope of survival, if there was hope, lay not in the FCC but in political action."[5] All but a few Americans came to accept commercial radio as the norm, as did most members of the federal regulatory commissions. The question of any national interest separate from the interest of private owners and advertisers hardly arose. When radio continued to prosper in the 1930s despite the Depression, the seal of approval of Americans in their guise as consumers was placed upon the whole system.

In Canada, radio broadcasting in the 1920s was developing very much according to the U.S. pattern, but was feebler and less prosperous; as a result, its service was spotty and uneven. The country had a small population, with its towns and cities strung out like beads on a string along a narrow band extending 200 miles or so north of the American border. Most Canadians had unsatisfactory reception from the stations occupying the few frequencies allotted to Canada during the reorganization of the broadcast band by the U.S. Department of Commerce in 1923. Reception of Canadian stations was particularly bad at night, when the more powerful U.S. stations came booming in. It looked as if Canadian radio might go the way of the early Canadian film industry, taken over completely by U.S.-owned distributors who had no interest in any but the Hollywood product.

Farmers, who with village residents made up a large proportion of Canada's population in the 1920s and 1930s, were especially ill-served in 1929-30, as were French-speaking Canadians—a majority in the second most populous province, Quebec. Most radio stations in that province, taking their cue from business, broadcast in English and attempted to secure network affiliation with NBC or CBS (two Montreal stations were successful).

Governments in Canada had always played a more central part in providing the services necessary for the development of the country than was true of the federal government in Washington, at least up to the New Deal. The Canadian reliance on government was no doubt a consequence of Canada's large expanse, its hostile climate, and its widely separated natural resources, but it was a response, too, to the faster pace of economic development in the more favorably situated United States. Canada had been accustomed to taking defensive measures to encourage industrialization and east-west trade: the national policy of its first prime minister, Sir John A. Macdonald, in the late nineteenth century, had included tariff barriers and the public financing of transcontinental railways. Unfortunately, by the 1930s it was evident that the growth of Canadian-owned enterprises was slower than the development of a branch-plant economy, in which Canadian plants manufactured and distributed products devised and promoted by their U.S. parent companies. This situation would limit attempts to establish a separate and distinct Canadian broadcasting system.

Nevertheless, in 1928 the dissatisfaction of Canadian listeners, the agitation of a few newspaper editors and opinion leaders, and the uneasiness of the government about its loose regulation of radio broadcasting led to the appointment of a royal commission (a form of public inquiry) to investigate and report on changes that should be introduced into the radio system. The head of the three-person commission, Sir John Aird, was a banker, well-disposed to private enterprise in most lines of business. As a result of the inquiry, however, he and his fellow commissioners became convinced that Canadians should have their own programs, that they would not get them in any satisfactory quantity under private station ownership and operation, and that a public monopoly was the best alternative. Aird no doubt was influenced by the example of the British Broadcasting Corporation, which had assumed responsibility in January 1927, but we are told that his decisive change of heart took place when he visited New York and found NBC entirely ready to assume the control and direction of broadcasting in Canada in the same way it operated in the United States. [6]

A change of government in Ottawa from Liberal to Conservative and a constitutional challenge from the provincial government in Quebec delayed action on the Aird Report. The issue was reactivated by a citizens' lobby organized by two young men 30 and 25 years of age, Graham Spry and Alan Plaunt, the creators of the Canadian Radio League (renamed in later decades the Canadian Broadcasting League). [7] The result of their tireless and inspired campaign was the passing of two pieces of legislation, the Canadian Radio Broadcasting Act of 1932 and its successor, the Canadian Broadcasting Act of 1936, an improved version of the first.

Although the details of the two acts differ, they were both founded on the same general principles. The radio frequency spectrum was to be considered a scarce natural resource to be managed in the public interest. Broadcasting in Canada was to be federally controlled, partly to protect Canadian identity and sovereignty from the incursion of U.S. interests. There was to be a "mixed system," part public and part private, but the whole was to be controlled by a single public agency that would both provide a national broadcasting service and also regulate all private broadcasting enterprises. This body was to be funded in such a way that it would be free of direct government intervention.

Broadcasting services were to be extended to all Canadians as quickly as possible. The system was to be primarily Canadian in its programming, and it was assumed that it would provide employment for Canadian artists, technicians, and broadcasters. [8]

Although the locus of regulatory control would change in successive broadcasting acts, these principles have remained fundamental to the present day. From 1932 to 1936, the regulatory authority, which was also the operator of the public broadcasting service, was the Canadian Radio Broadcasting Commission. From 1936 to 1958, that body was the Canadian Broadcasting Corporation. Since 1958 the CBC has continued as a public broadcasting service, but regulation became the responsibility of the Board of Broadcast Governors from 1958 to 1968, and since that time the regulatory authority at the pinnacle of the system has been the Canadian Radio-Television Commission (CRTC).

Thus by 1936, both the U.S. and Canadian systems had developed distinctive features that in some measure continue to characterize them. The U.S. system has changed less fundamentally than the Canadian in the intervening years, partly because the United States, by virtue of its size and wealth, is more autonomous than Canada, a country that must always take account of what is happening next door. A comparison of U.S. and Canadian radio in their heyday, from 1937 to 1950, will enable us to see whether the very different legal and institutional arrangements in the two countries provided their peoples with a different kind of service, or whether economic and social similarities were in the long run to provide nearly identical patterns.

THE GOLDEN AGE OF RADIO, 1937 TO 1950

The dozen years or so following 1936 were what Sydney Head and others label "radio's golden age." In Canada this followed the passing of the Canadian Broadcasting Act of 1936, and the policy choice that accorded the CBC the dominant role in the Canadian system, as programmer, network operator, and regulatory authority: a period that included six wartime years, when radio provided a principal means of unifying the country in its war effort and raising hopes for the postwar era. Canadian television did not arrive until 1952, so radio's golden age in Canada was extended three or four years beyond that of its U.S. counterpart.

In the United States, the essential characteristics of its national broadcasting system, which had begun to emerge around 1927, were firmly established after 1937. Sydney Head summarizes those characteristics as follows: (1) a system based on competitive free enterprise dependent on advertising for its economic support; (2) "syndication of programs, primarily by means of national networks—without, however, complete sacrifice of local ownership and programming in favor of monopoly ownership or centralized program control"; and (3) government regulation, serving as a compromise between public and private interests. [9]

That formulation on the whole puts a kindly face on the system and the way it works in practice. As early as 1935 the political scientist Pendleton Herring concluded that "the Federal Radio Commission has interpreted the concept of public interest so as to favor in actual practice one particular group . . . the commercial broadcasters." In 1934, the Wagner-Hatfield proposal would have given protection to noncommercial groups interested in broadcasting, but their amendment was defeated, and the Communications Act of 1934 "established the commercial system as the official system—even though the new law, like the old, sidestepped the issue, and said nothing about commercial sponsorship."[10]

As a symbol of commercial dominance, the programming in this period of increasing prosperity for stations and networks became the direct responsibility of advertising agencies. Yet, as Barnouw points out, in the shelter of the commercial operations were "varied non-commercial ventures, reaching smaller but substantial audiences, and serving diverse interests." Barnouw sums up the existence of the two separate worlds in radio broadcasting with an odd image: "Sponsored broadcasting . . . was often in danger of sliding into prostitution. Educational broadcasting, on the other hand, was in danger of dying an old maid. Their cohabitation was unusual but, for the moment, seemed practical and useful."[11]

During this period also, licensing continued to be the FCC's primary regulatory tool. Krasnow and Longley explain that the emphasis on the licensing function resulted in part "from the fact that the Congress specifically denied the commission the power to regulate the rates or profits of broadcasting stations."[12] In this respect the powers of the FCC were inferior to those of the Federal Power Commission, for example.

The FCC was hobbled not only by its statutory authority, but also by the continuing interest Congress took in its handling of delegated powers and by the close alliance of commercial broadcasters and politicians. John Tebbel says, "From the beginning, the commission was under the thumb of Congress and subject to constant pressure from it, as it is today."[13] Nevertheless, just after the war the FCC did make an effort to establish criteria for the issuing and renewal of licenses in the so-called Blue Book. Although the FCC was careful not to violate the First Amendment by prescribing the nature of programs licensees should be prepared to carry, it did establish the principle that overall performance by a broadcaster would be taken into consideration in the granting of a license or in license renewal. The Fairness Doctrine, although opposed by many broadcasters, was articulated in 1946 and 1949, given subsequent backing by the courts, and entered as an amendment to the Communications Act in 1959.

The FCC also attempted to come to grips with the growing concentration of media ownership, but without much success.

Trafficking in licenses became a general practice; the FCC did not
force licensees to live up to their promises; and in the period of
domination by the radio networks, most stations sought affiliation or
to imitate the formulas by which programs gained the largest audiences. [14] Sydney Head concluded that to a large extent the Communications Act "serves as no more than a facade of pious theories. . . .
No serious investigation of the FCC has offered a favorable diagnosis;
all agree on the need for drastic reforms."[15] To the FCC was commonly applied the familiar observation that a regulatory commission
tends to be captured by the industry it regulates.

In the United States, therefore, the state through law and regulatory practice put very feeble limits to the widespread use of the
radio frequency spectrum for the merchandising of goods, the spread-
ing of the assumption that the electronic media of communication exist primarily to serve commercial ends, and the instruction of the
general population that success is to be measured by the standards
of the market. This was not consciously associated with a national
objective to make the world safe for U.S. capitalism and democracy,
but in the decades to come the international influences exercised by
the media industries would have that effect, or so it was hoped by
the more articulate practitioners, such as William Paley and Henry
Luce.

In Canada, the priorities were rather different, but as time
went on, the U.S. example became more influential. As we have
seen, during radio's golden age the leadership role was entrusted
to the public corporation, the CBC. Although the 1936 act did not
spell out the national objectives, these were thoroughly discussed in
Parliament and were instrumental in achieving all-party agreement.
Essentially, the CBC was to ensure that broadcasting should be un-
mistakably Canadian, private stations could be required to broadcast the programs of the public service, and the CBC would operate
its own stations and networks, carrying both sponsored and unsponsored programs, in English and in French, and serving the needs of
major social groups such as farmers, business, labor, schools,
adult education, and welfare organizations. On the face of it, a
system quite different from that in the United States.

Just below the surface, however, the same commercial interests as in the United States were waiting their turn to assume leadership and control. Although the legislation was written in such a
way that the CBC could legally expropriate privately owned stations,
the government and Parliament clearly intended a mixed system,
part public and part private. Although the CBC was financed (until
1953) with a license fee on radio households designed to afford it in-
dependence from government, Parliament never authorized a license
fee large enough to enable it to operate without commercial revenue.

The large advertisers on Canadian stations and networks were often the same large advertisers who supported radio in the United States. Furthermore, U.S. network programs were overheard in most of Canada and exercised an attraction similar to that in the host country. The CBC thought it the better part of valor to distribute the most popular of these entertainment programs on the Canadian networks, rather than dividing the audience unnecessarily between those who tuned to Canadian stations and those who could pick up U.S. ones. Moreover, the private stations that were licensed on the recommendation of the CBC had ambitions of their own: to establish a private network whenever this should become profitable and to establish an independent regulatory board along the lines of the FCC.

During the war years, national radio served to rally the population behind the war effort, to inform Canadians of international developments, particularly the course of the war, to stimulate recruiting for the armed services, to establish Canada as an arsenal for Britain and the Commonwealth, to explain the need for rationing, and to keep up civilian morale. In those years the CBC seemed an unqualified success story in providing a needed communications service that the print media could not match and a force and direction that a completely private system would be unlikely to provide. During these years, the CBC attracted a corps of dedicated broadcasters who were intent on using radio to propel Canada into a new and better age after the war. These social activists were responsible for initiating news, drama, and discussion programs that were intended to make Canadians a more socially aware and cohesive people.

For example, the CBC used a prime-time half-hour on Monday nights to broadcast National Farm Radio Forum, and in cooperation with the Canadian Federation of Agriculture, the Canadian Association for Adult Education, and their provincial counterparts, study and discussion guides were distributed and discussion groups formed across the country. A similar program, Citizens' Forum, was scheduled on Thursday evenings for residents of the cities and towns. (Its counterparts in the United States, such as the University of Chicago Round Table, tended to be scheduled on Sunday afternoons in what later became known as the "cultural ghetto.") An hour of original and anthology drama, the well-known and inventive Stage series, was scheduled in prime-time Sunday evening and built up a large national following. Wednesday evenings were given over to a whole night of more serious fare—symphonic and concert music, plays, social documentaries. All these programs were unsponsored, as were the news and other public affairs broadcasts. Sponsored programs included light music, variety and comedy, and imports from the United States such as Jack Benny, Lux Radio Theater, and Edgar Bergen and Charlie McCarthy (the Chase and Sanborn Hour).

The programs that were controversial or of social significance were reformist in emphasis, and hardly revolutionary. Still,
their discernible thrust was radical enough to alarm some of the
business leaders and politicians. Toward the end of the 1940s and
in the 1950s, the private broadcasters began to find political allies
in their effort to recast the Canadian broadcasting system more into
the U.S. mold.

TELEVISION'S FIRST TWO DECADES

Television, which had its experimental beginnings in the 1930s,
was given its present-day U.S. standards for monochrome transmission and reception through an FCC decision in 1941. With the
end of the war in 1945, television enjoyed a rapid spurt of development, interrupted in 1948 by a four-year freeze resulting from the
need to redefine channel separation and from steel shortages coinci-
dent with the Korean War. The year 1948 is commonly accepted as
the turning point when TV emerged as a mass medium and the U.S.
networks changed their emphasis from radio to television, responding to audience fascination with the newer and more graphic medium.
The effects on evening radio listening were dramatic. In 1947, Bob
Hope, on radio, had a Hooper rating of 30.2 and Jack Benny of 27.
In 1952, Bob Hope's rating plummeted to 2.5, and Jack Benny's
rating declined to 5.8.[16]
The same networks that had dominated radio in the United
States (except the Mutual chain) were ready to take charge of television. The new start enabled them to wrest control of production
from the advertising agencies that had assumed the responsibility in
radio. For a time, New York and Chicago became the chief production centers, but by 1956 or 1957 nearly all production activity (except for news and quiz shows) had moved to Hollywood, and film,
supplemented soon by videotape, took over from live television. As
Erik Barnouw summed it up, "For stations and networks, the road
was clear. Film salesmen were lining up, and so were sponsors.
Much had been settled, and the boom was on."[17]
Television, however, proved too expensive for single sponsors to carry the costs of entire series or hour-long shows. Soon,
participation formats and spot commercials were the more usual
means for collecting advertising revenue. "When advertising agencies relinquished television programming control to program pack-
agers and networks, spots were sold without sponsorship, and the
two-decades-long relationship between sponsor and program,
amounting to sponsor control of programming, broke down."[18]
This change may have given the news departments a little more

freedom, but the principal objective of most entertainment programs remained the same: to attract the largest audience and to realize the highest revenues for the shareholders of the networks and the owners of affiliated stations.

The 1950s were marked by the blacklisting of performers thought to be sympathetic to the United States' "enemies" and by quiz and payola scandals. These events, however, did not result in stronger curbs on the industry by the FCC. The Landis Report on Regulatory Agencies (of December 1960), commissioned by President-elect Kennedy, summed up the situation in these words:

> The Federal Communications Commission presents a somewhat extraordinary spectacle. Despite considerable technical excellence on the part of its staff, the Commission has drifted, vacillated and stalled in almost every major area. It seems incapable of policy planning. . . . The available evidence indicates that it, more than any other agency, has been susceptible to ex parte presentations, and that it has been subservient, far too subservient, to the subcommittees on communications of the Congress and their members. A strong suspicion also exists that far too great an influence is exercised over the Commission by the networks. [19]

Newton Minow, in his wasteland speech of 1961 and his moves to reduce the networks' control of time on affiliated stations, attempted to shake things up, but later admitted a large measure of defeat:

> We remain [he wrote] the only nation in the world with no rules on how many commercials a broadcaster may run, and our best broadcasters are reduced to the law of the jungle. Yet the FCC is blamed as a spineless tool of the broadcasting lobby, when in fact its efforts to regulate were frustrated by the Congress. [20]

In Canada, the government determined that television would not start haphazardly as radio had 30 years previously. After appointing a commission to survey the public role in cultural expression and development, the government authorized the Canadian Broadcasting Corporation to initiate a television service in English and in French, with studios in Toronto and Montreal. Television was deemed too expensive to rely completely on public appropriations, so once again, as with radio, television broadcasting would be shared by publicly and privately owned stations. Service began in 1952, and for the next nine years the CBC provided the only Canadian network service, coast to coast and eventually to the north, scheduling its own productions as well as imports (mainly in the evening) from the three U.S. networks. Until 1961, Canadian cities had only one television station, either owned by the CBC or a private and commercial affiliate, broadcasting network programs from the CBC, supplemented by their own local programs and a few syndicated features or reruns.

The Liberal government was voted out of office in 1957, and the new Conservative government was determined to provide an alternative network service to Canadian viewers by the licensing of additional stations. It wished also to place the CBC and the private broadcasters on a more nearly equal footing.[21] The first step was to pass new broadcasting legislation, the Broadcasting Act of 1958, to remove the regulatory powers from the CBC and to place these powers with a new public agency, the Board of Broadcast Governors (BBG). At the same time, the act enjoined the BBG to ensure "the continued existence and efficient operation of a national broadcasting system" and "the provision of a varied and comprehensive broadcasting service of a high standard that is basically Canadian in content and character." Unlike the U.S. legislation, the act gave the BBG power to regulate the establishment and operation of networks as well as stations, and to determine relations between the public and private stations.[22]

The new "second stations" licensed in the principal Canadian cities formed a second network, CTV, in the 1960s, while other private stations remained for the most part affiliated with the CBC.

The Board of Broadcast Governors had difficulty ensuring that the program services of the new network would be "basically Canadian in content and character" because it was so much cheaper for CTV and its affiliates to import U.S. programs than to produce their own. The BBG attempted to impose a "Canadian content" quota of 55 percent on the programs carried by all stations, but there were so many exceptions, and the latitude in the definition of a Canadian origination was so wide, that the BBG's attempts to regulate came under increasing ridicule. Its credibility was further compromised by unseemly quarrels between it and the CBC, which had its own board of directors, who continued to report directly to Parliament, rather than through the BBG.

When the Liberals returned to power in 1963, they promised to revise the Broadcasting Act, and after another public inquiry and interminable parliamentary debates, a new act (still in effect) was passed in 1968.[23]

Substantively, the greatest change in the 1968 act was to bring cable television under the regulatory authority for broadcasting, now renamed the Canadian Radio-Television Commission (CRTC).[24] Although all members are appointed by the government of the day, the commission is mostly autonomous and is supposed to maintain an arms-length relationship with government, as is the CBC, which still has its own board.[25] For the first time, the regulatory authority had the complete responsibility for issuing licenses to stations and networks, including licenses to the CBC, but the government retained the authority to give directions on "classes of persons eligible to hold licences." Under this provision, the federal government could limit the amount of foreign ownership in a broadcasting enterprise or the terms under which a license might be issued to a provincial agency.

The obligations and responsibilities of broadcasters were much more explicit and fully described in the 1968 legislation than they had been in 1958. Ten subsections in the act stipulated that the broadcasting system should be effectively owned and controlled by Canadians; pronounced the right to freedom of expression; required balance and quality in programming ("of high quality, using predominantly Canadian creative and other resources"); guaranteed broadcasting services in English and French; placed special obligations on "the national broadcasting service" (the CBC); and reaffirmed that broadcasting undertakings (now including cable) constituted a single system and should therefore be regulated by a single independent public authority (the CRTC).[26]

Until 1958, the quality of Canadian broadcasting and its responsibility for fulfilling nationally determined objectives lay principally with the CBC as much the largest producer of Canadian programs and as the sole operator of national networks. Given these functions, the CBC had been a rather permissive regulatory authority, except in its requirements that the private stations serve as outlets for CBC programs in those areas where the CBC did not have its own transmitters.

After 1958, a large part of the responsibility for ensuring that Canadian broadcasting answered to Canadian interests and needs shifted to the regulatory authorities, the BBG and then the CRTC. Particularly after 1968, the privately owned stations and networks had placed upon them much more stringent demands than their counterparts in the United States.

The great unknown at the end of the decade was how the CRTC would regulate cable television. Would it be controlled in such a way to ensure, in the words of the act, that the Canadian broadcasting system would "safeguard, enrich and strengthen the cultural, political, social and economic fabric of Canada"? Or would it be allowed to place before Canadian viewers the vast quantity of U.S. program output to the point where Canadian productions were engulfed by the tide washing in from the California coast? And if cable companies served as such a conduit, could private broadcasters resist such competition by scheduling Canadian programs in prime time?

The answers were to come in the decade after 1970.

SINCE 1970

By the late 1960s, commercial television in the United States, under the leadership of the three networks, blanketed the land. Indeed, it blanketed most of the North American continent, including Canada, and through syndication was exported to most of the non-Communist world. In 1966, for example, NBC's Bonanza, produced for transmission in color, was syndicated in over 30 countries and in eight languages.[27] At a production cost of about $200,000 per episode, few if any countries could afford television on that scale, although Britain and Japan continued to rely mainly on their own productions. By 1968, according to Barnouw, more than 80 countries were showing Bonanza; and The FBI, Mission: Impossible, and The Fugitive "were not far behind."[28]

The trouble was that while U.S. families undoubtedly found entertainment on the home screen, many people were conscious of a sameness in the television fare, and felt that the networks offered little real choice, that too many of the programs were shoddy. For example, in 1968 a book appeared describing one man's ordeal watching a week of commercial television in New York—Charles Sopkin's Seven Glorious Days, Seven Fun-Filled Nights. Sopkin concluded that television was "dreadful, make no mistake about that. . . . I naively expected that the ratio would run three to one in favor of trash. It turned out to be closer to a hundred to one."[29]

Thoughtful people recognized also that not all important segments of the U.S. population were well served. Nicholas Johnson, a former member of the FCC, observed that two groups in particular did not join "the after-dinner rush to the living room TV": those living in out-of-the-way communities beyond the range of broadcast signals and "the social and intellectual classes whose interests and tastes were ignored or given little more than token service by TV programmers."[30] McGeorge Bundy commented: "Twenty years of experience have made it very plain indeed that commercial TV alone cannot do for the American public what mixed systems—public and private—are offering to other countries, notably Great Britain and Japan."[31]

The recognition of this deficiency led to the establishment of a commission in 1965 sponsored by the Carnegie Corporation, and with surprising speed, to the creation in November 1967 of the Corporation for Public Broadcasting, through an act of Congress given the active support of President Lyndon B. Johnson. Congressional appropriations would henceforth make more viable the noncommercial network of educational stations that against odds had survived for a number of years with the aid of grants from the Ford Foundation. PBS—the Public Broadcasting Service—filled in many of the gaps in American television, providing programs that the three commercial networks found it unprofitable to carry. At last the United States, too, had a semblance of the mixed system McGeorge Bundy had talked about. But as Nixon's White House became more suspicious of the PBS role in television journalism, the public stations looked increasingly to large corporations to underwrite their programs, especially their cultural programs. "By the mid-1970s, 74% of programming supported by corporate underwriters was classified as 'culture.' For public television 'cultural programming' became the dominant feature of prime time—and for sponsors, a significant sphere of influence."[32]

In spite of the accomplishments of public television in providing programs of quality, the road to popular success was not so easy. In the mid-1970s PBS stations were said to reach only 1 or 2 percent of the national audience. In 1983, with the U.S. commercial networks now sharing their audience with numerous rivals through the growth of cable television, the share of the audience attracted to PBS has gained in significance. We are told that 72 percent of U.S. homes watch a PBS station at least once a month and that PBS claims to have doubled its audience recently.[33] According to Sterling and Kittross, commercial stations now view PBS as "competition to be fought rather than as a related public service to be supported."[34]

More costly competition is being offered the U.S. networks by pay TV, cable, and advertiser-supported "superstations" distributing their programs with the aid of satellites. Although the long-range consequences cannot be foreseen, I think this appraisal is not far off the mark:

> What little evidence we have indicates that pay-TV, cable, videocassettes and videodiscs, and similar developments promoted as offering greater diversity of content than broadcast television, will find it most profitable to continue the pattern of mass entertainment programming to get the most buyers at the least per unit cost.[35]

Pay television of course represents an alternative method of receiving programs that is attractive to many viewers dissatisfied with traditional forms of broadcasting on this continent and impatient with the frequent commercial interruptions, especially during movies. By now, HBO and Showtime are financial successes, but it is by no means clear that they represent the wave of the future or a vital threat to advertising-supported forms of television. Satellite and cable may merely provide new forms of delivery for the advertising messages, movies, and sports features of yore, as pioneered, for example, by Ted Turner's superstation in Atlanta. I notice reports that Turner and the cable operators are developing their Washington alliances, potent enough to forestall moves to increase copyright payments for programs they transmit but do not originate.

The system of advertising-supported broadcasting in the United States is unlikely to be displaced without a struggle.

In Canada, cable television, enjoying a head start, grew more rapidly than in the United States and did not depend on pay television to attract its customers. (Pay television was held off by the regulatory authority until 1983.) Canadian television stations were aware that cable was being used primarily as a means through which viewers could have access to the program services of the three U.S. television networks, and later of PBS. After the Broadcasting Act of 1968 made cable television a part of the broadcasting system and subject to the regulatory authority of the CRTC, it was expected that cable development might slow down. It did not. The CRTC established rules to grant Canadian television services a measure of priority on all cable systems, but there were still enough channels in most cities for cable subscribers to receive nearby American stations without the use of a converter.

For a time, the CRTC prevented cable systems in cities remote from the U.S. border (Edmonton, Calgary, Sudbury, Halifax) from importing American signals by microwave. However, this set up a howl of opposition in these communities, whose residents argued that they should have access to the same program services as Canadians living near the border, in Toronto, Montreal, or Vancouver; otherwise, they were second-class citizens. The pressures from public and Parliament were intense enough for the CRTC to cave in, and since the early 1970s cable has entered nearly 60 percent of Canadian homes, and over three quarters of households are now within cable's reach. [36]

The impact on Canadian television stations and networks has been dramatic, much stronger than the influence of the new technologies on the four U.S. networks. Because of the increased competition from U.S. sources, Canadian television stations are reluctant to use prime time for the showing of less elaborate (but more costly) Canadian productions, except for sports. To allow stations and networks extra room to maneuver, the CRTC defines prime time as the hours between 6:00 P.M. and midnight, rather than, say, 7:30 to 11:00 P.M. This means the CRTC requirement of 50 percent Canadian content in prime time is less stringent than it might be. Only the CBC has taken seriously the objective set out in the 1968 act that the programming provided by the Canadian broadcasting system should be "of high standard, using predominantly Canadian creative and other resources."

The result of the increased importation of U.S. network television through cable and the licensing of additional private television stations and regional networks has been that many more U.S. programs are available to Canadians in peak viewing times than Canadian productions. The present situation has been summarized by A. W. Johnson, the former CBC president, as follows:

> Only about one-third of all English-language television available in Canada is Canadian. In peak viewing hours . . . only one-quarter of all programmes available are Canadian. In some areas of Canada the proportions are worse: in Toronto, for example, no more than one-fifth of all English-language television is Canadian, in Vancouver one-tenth. And in some categories of television programming the proportions are equally discouraging. In dramatic productions, for example (including television dramas and films)—the area of programming on which 50 per cent of the viewing time of Canadians is spent—less than 5 per cent of all programmes available are Canadian.[37]

Public authorities recognize the handicaps inherent in the Canadian situation, that its people are next to a country that exports more than twice as many TV programs as all other countries combined; that the advertising world is dominated by Americans; that in Jeremy Tunstall's phrase, the media are American; and that Canadians, having so much free access to U.S. broadcasting, are reluctant to adopt the quota systems characteristic of other English-speaking countries such as Great Britain and Australia.[38] John Meisel, chairman of the CRTC, has commented:

> In the past, the electronic media, and television in particular, have contributed significantly to the loss of regional and national identities; they have been among the principal agents of denationalization and of the Americanization of our climate. . . . The currently

available and newly emerging satellite, micropro-
cessor, and fibre-optic technologies provide threatening avenues for the complete annihilation of what
remains of a distinct Canadian culture, of its regional and other unique components, and, in the
final analysis, of an independent Canadian state.[39]

There are signs that Canadian authorities remain unwilling to
resign themselves to the complete conquest of the broadcasting system by a more powerful and dynamic neighbor. The two traditional
defenses have been (1) public encouragement and financing of Canadian production and distribution, largely through the CBC; and (2)
regulation of the broadcasting industry. The problem is that in the
current period of economic uncertainty, the government may not be
ready to allocate the necessary resources to maintain and enhance
Canadian production capabilities. Regulatory measures alone cannot overcome the gap between the accessibility of thousands of U.S.
programs and the relative scarcity of programs produced by and for
Canadians.

As for the CBC, there is no doubt that it has lost support where
it counts—politically, and the thrust of recent decisions by the CRTC
has been to augment the private sector of the industry rather than to
authorize additional CBC services. A recent report from the Federal Cultural Policy Review Committee has recommended that the
CBC procure all its television programs, except news, from private
or independent producers. (This recommendation is unlikely to be
accepted by the government, but its effect may well be to weaken the
CBC in the public mind as a mainstay and bulwark of Canadian production.)

On the other front, regulation: the head of the CRTC, while
expressing his own views, was probably reflecting governmental
attitudes as well when he argued before a U.S. audience:

Unregulated forces cannot be expected to accomplish
everything that a people may wish to do. . . . For
Canada in particular, extensive deregulation would be
inconsistent with the whole history and purpose of communications policy and would threaten values which
Canadians hold dear. . . .
Our history has been characterized by a much
greater degree of government intervention in the economy than has been the case in the U.S. . . . The distinctiveness of the Canadian approach to public policy
generally has been echoed in regulatory policy.[40]

More recently, a working paper prepared by the minister of communications argued that one reason for encouraging the delivery of new program services through cable systems rather than by direct satellite-to-home transmissions was that cable can be more effectively regulated, and in that way Canadian content can be safeguarded. However, unless the government and the CRTC show more determination to preserve the best and most distinctive features of the Canadian system than they have shown in recent years, the broadcasting pattern is likely soon to be very similar to that in the United States. That has grave implications for all Canadians, including those whose first language is French.

But these are issues for the present and immediate future. I now return to the question with which I started: what does the story of broadcast development in the two countries reveal about the similarities and differences in Canadian and American societies? And how best may we account for such differences as we have observed?

DETERMINANTS OF THE U.S. AND
CANADIAN BROADCASTING SYSTEMS

Looking over the record, it seems to me undeniable that the market economy and the liberal tradition in each country go furthest to explain why broadcasting is carried on primarily in the interest of private entrepreneurs, advertisers, and a consumer society. This rationale has never been questioned seriously in the United States. In Canada it has been questioned and is still being questioned; certain countermeasures have been taken, not because Canada is less committed to liberalism and a capitalist form of mixed economy than the United States, but because Canada, intent on remaining a separate country and preserving a good measure of sovereignty, sees that market forces alone would bring about communications completely dominated by U.S. enterprise.

This national consideration, this desire for political sovereignty, leads to policies and actions that are influenced by other factors: geographic, economic, cultural, and demographic, that in turn lend distinctiveness to the legislation, the types of regulation, and the mixture of public and private ownership so characteristic of the Canadian system. These dissimilarities have never succeeded in dislodging popular U.S. programs from a central place in the fare provided in Canada, nor have the unique features of the Canadian system altogether prevented the U.S. pattern from being accepted in the public mind as the standard by which success is to be measured. The result is that Canada has not succeeded in devising a broadcasting system with coherent principles. A further result is that the system is extremely hard to administer.

Other than the sovereignty impulse, the most concrete factor contributing to a Canadian emphasis on distinctiveness is the existence of an important and geographically concentrated French-language minority. The inability of U.S. programs to reflect Canadian conditions and to meet Canadian needs is most clearly seen in French Canada. On the other hand, the popularity of U.S. programs, reflecting as they do the concerns of another society, explains in part the reluctance or inability of many Canadians to come to terms with the country's duality. How many western Canadians want to concern themselves with the special concerns of Quebec or the Inuit when their eyes are fixed on Dallas?

Market considerations alone would never impel Canadians (or anyone else) to produce the variety of programs French-speaking Canadians feel entitled to if they are to have equal opportunities with the English-speaking majority. The "French fact" in Canada is as important as any other in explaining why the government turned to public enterprise to guarantee parallel French and English program services, and why the CBC to the present remains an important component of the broadcasting system.

The acceptance in Canada of a state-owned institution such as the CBC and of a more powerful regulatory agency than the FCC is explained on other grounds as well. The British example of the BBC had some force in the 1930s, but has little pertinence now, as Canadian-British ties have been loosened. However, there are factors other than economic and linguistic that are significant. Geographic and climatic conditions have had a continuing influence on Canadian notions of what governments should be expected to do. A more positive role for government has been a noticeable characteristic of the Canadian state for many decades. Further, the absence of constitutional guarantees of freedom of the press has made it more acceptable for the regulatory authority to judge the performance of stations and networks in program terms than is permitted in the United States.[41]

It has often been observed that Canada is a more conservative country than the United States, in the sense that Canadians are cautious, pay heed to tradition, and value order as much as they do individual freedom. One political theorist (influenced by Hartz) hypothesized that the dialectic of the liberal and conservative traditions has paved the way for an indigenous socialist movement in Canada unlike the United States.[42] Whatever the cogency of this argument, it is hard to discover any perceptible effect on broadcasting policy of the existence in Canada of third parties (such as the CCF-NDP) that are more or less socialist in ideology. The broadcasting acts of 1932, 1936, 1958, and 1968 have been introduced and passed by Conservative and Liberal governments, and for the most part they have had all-party support. Similarly, the committees of inquiry, from the Aird Commission onward, have accepted the existence of a Crown Corporation (the CBC) as a necessary component in the Canadian broadcasting system, but these committees have not had any ideological bias toward socialism: the reverse, if anything.

While a mixed system of public and private ownership in broadcasting has been generally accepted, the private element has increasingly had the upper hand. This may be due partly to persistence in lobbying by special interests, but it seems probable that the long-term effect of the liberal and market ethos in Canada, as well as in the United States, explains the course of this development. It has been intensified by the nature of U.S. programs that appeal to Canadians as "consumers."

This development results in a dilemma and a seeming no-win situation for the CBC. The new technologies make U.S. programs more readily accessible to nearly all Canadians. The private broadcasters attempt to survive as distributors of a largely U.S. product. The odds against the CBC as the chief originator of Canadian programs lengthen at the same time as the public philosophy is turned against public enterprise, partly in response to U.S. political currents. It is ironic that as the CBC occupies a smaller share in the total Canadian system, it comes under criticism for a lack of success in maintaining Canadian distinctiveness!

While the CBC has a smaller place in the total broadcasting picture than formerly, it continues to present a large variety of informational and cultural programs that scarcely have a counterpart in U.S. television or especially radio. Many of these programs draw very large audiences in Canadian terms. For example, a 40-minute nightly current affairs program, The Journal, on the English television network in prime time, attracts audiences of over 1.5 million each weekday (multiply by 13 for an equivalent audience in the United States). A weekly science program, The Nature of Things, regularly draws an audience of 1.25 million. Documentaries, children's TV programs, and features on the visual and performing arts round out the schedule, as they do on the French television and radio networks. Both private and CBC networks secure large audiences for news and sports, each reflecting Canadian perspectives.

Still, the CBC's popular base is being eroded, and the regulatory agency and the government are turning to other expedients, such as capital cost allowances, to encourage the private production industry. The irony is that such taxation measures are likely to be wasteful or ineffective unless combined with stronger regulation, increasing the danger of greater intrusion by government in a sphere

that most liberally minded persons think government should enter
with great caution if at all.

I conclude that regulation alone is unlikely to produce the desired results in Canada, and that aside from the dangers to a liberal
society in a too-active regulatory policy, such a policy opens the
way for further quarrels and misunderstandings between the United
States and Canada. It is easy for measures intended as safeguards
for Canadian stations or program producers to be interpreted as
moves that discriminate against American interests. I continue to
believe that the maintenance of a strong and well-financed public
agency in radio and television production is a necessity in Canada,
and that this part of the communications policy will receive the sympathetic understanding of Americans if it is explained in terms of
sovereignty and distinctive Canadian needs.

One wonders whether Canada is the first nation-state whose
continued existence is put in jeopardy by media influences arriving
from another country. If for another 10 or 20 years Canadians can
hold to the belief that communications should serve a public and a
social purpose rather than merely private ends, the crisis may resolve itself. It is doubtful if the explosion of consumerism first
manifest in the United States will continue until the century ends.
We seem to be entering a new age when economies will grow more
slowly and when resources must be husbanded rather than thought-
lessly consumed. If that is so, the United States itself may find
that a broadcasting system geared to promote the consumption of
goods is no longer appropriate. In that event, perhaps each of our
peoples will understand that the media of communication are best
employed to encourage social interchange and to speak to the full
variety of human needs and expectations.

NOTES

1. The two governing acts were, in the United States, the
Radio Act of 1912, and, in Canada, the Radiotelegraph Act of 1913.
2. F. W. Peers, The Politics of Canadian Broadcasting,
1920-1951 (Toronto, 1969), 34-38, 69-72.
3. See Sydney W. Head, Broadcasting in America, 2nd ed.
(Boston, 1972), 160-61.
4. T. P. Robinson, Radio Networks and the Federal Government (New York, 1943), 22, 24; Peers, Politics of Canadian Broadcasting, 11.
5. Erik Barnouw, A Tower in Babel (New York, 1966), 218,
259.
6. Peers, Politics of Canadian Broadcasting, 38.

7. Margaret Prang, "The Origins of Public Broadcasting in Canada," Canadian Historical Review, 46 (March 1965):1-31.

8. This summary is taken from David Ellis, Evolution of the Canadian Broadcasting System: Objectives and Realities, 1928-1968 (Ottawa, Dept. of Communications, 1979), 75-76.

9. Head, Broadcasting in America, 165.

10. Barnouw, The Sponsor (New York, 1978), 31-32.

11. Ibid., 36, 32-33.

12. Erwin G. Krasnow and Lawrence D. Longley, The Politics of Broadcast Regulation, 2nd ed. (New York, 1978), 15.

13. John Tebbel, The Media in America (New York, 1974), 366.

14. By 1939, the networks had affiliated all the 52 clear-channel stations but 2. See Christopher H. Sterling and John M. Kittross, Stay Tuned: A Concise History of American Broadcasting (Belmont, Calif., 1978), 156.

15. Head, Broadcasting in America, 461.

16. Ibid., 184.

17. Barnouw, The Image Empire (New York, 1970), 65, 80.

18. Sterling and Kittross, Stay Tuned, 335.

19. James M. Landis, "Report on Regulatory Agencies to the President-Elect," quoted in Krasnow & Longley, Politics of Broadcast Regulation, 28.

20. Minow, in Preface to ibid. (1978).

21. This story is more fully recounted in Peers, The Public Eye (Toronto, 1979), chap. 5.

22. Canada, Statutes, Broadcasting Act, 1958, 7 Elizabeth II, c.22.

23. The Broadcasting Act, 1967-68, c.25; R.S.C. 1970, c.16; S.C. 23-24 Elizabeth II, c.49, 1975.

24. An amendment to the Broadcasting Act in 1976 extended the authority of the CRTC to telecommunications, and the commission was enlarged from five full-time and ten part-time members to nine full-time and ten part-time members.

25. The CBC board continues to report directly to Parliament, but it is fully answerable to the CRTC for the observance of CRTC regulations.

26. These provisions are in Section 3 of the Act as amended in 1970; they were in Section 2 of the Act as originally passed.

27. Head, Broadcasting in America, 206.

28. Barnouw, The Image Empire, 310.

29. Quoted in Nicholas Johnson, How to Talk Back to Your Television Set (New York, 1970), 29.

30. Ibid., 139-40.

31. Quoted in ibid., 163.

32. Barnouw, The Sponsor, 147.

33. Harry J. Boyle, "Not a Model, but PBS Has Lots to Say to Canada," The Toronto Globe and Mail, January 7, 1983, p. 7. In 1974, only about 20 percent of the U.S. population turned to public television once a week; public television viewing accounted for 1.1 percent of all viewing, and only infrequently attracted audiences as large as 5 percent of the national total. Bruce McKay, "The CBC and the Public," Institute for Communication Research, Stanford University (1976), 250.

34. Stay Tuned, 457.

35. Ibid., 461.

36. In August 1980, the percentage of households subscribing to cable was 55 percent, and the percentage having access to cable was 77.5 percent. CRTC, Facts Digest (Ottawa, January 1982).

37. "Public Broadcasting in Canada: The Ideal and the Reality," lecture at McMaster University, November 1982. The CRTC chairman, John Meisel, reports that "Non-Canadian programmes account for 70 per cent of our evening-hour viewing of English-language programming on all stations," and "39 percent of French-language viewing."

38. These observations are drawn from a speech by John Meisel to the Broadcast Executives Society of Toronto, May 11, 1982: "Just an Old Sweet Song: Canadian Content on My Mind."

39. "Five Steps to Survival," speech before the York University Conference on Mass Communications and Canadian Nationhood, Toronto, April 10, 1981.

40. "Of Babies and Bathwater, or, What Goes Down the Deregulatory Drain," speech before the Telecommunications Policy Research Congress, Annapolis, Md., April 28, 1982.

41. The Constitution Act of 1982 has introduced such a guarantee, but it is still too early to say whether the courts will interpret it as an equivalent of the U.S. First Amendment.

42. See Gad Horowitz, Canadian Labour in Politics (Toronto, 1968).

COMMENT
Barry Cole

I have been asked to comment on Frank Peers' discussion from a U.S. perspective. I congratulate the author on his comprehensive comparison of the development of U.S. and Canadian broadcast regulation. Many of his conclusions are well taken; however, I must register some reservations about several of the points Peers makes on the evolution and future of U.S. broadcast regulation.

Peers' discussion gives the impression that all important developments in U.S. broadcasting policy have been the logical, natural, and largely inevitable results of coherent principles and basic American traditions, including liberalism, competitive free enterprise, and the merchandising of goods. In fact, many of the significant policy developments in American broadcasting resulted from a piecemeal, ad hoc decision-making approach and depended on timing, the presence and strong predictions of a single government official, or dubious judgment. A number of important policies were adopted only by narrow margins in FCC or appellate court votes.

One can cite many "what ifs?" when discussing the regulation of U.S. radio and television. For example: (1) What if Freida Hennock had not been an FCC commissioner during the 1948-52 freeze and had not led the fight to allocate a large number of channels for educational television use, or if Robert E. Lee had not championed UHF broadcasting during his nearly 30 years as a commissioner? (2) What if the FCC had decided on a different table of allocations in 1952, as, for example, the Dumont Plan (using only VHF in larger markets, UHF in smaller markets) or the British approach of saving UHF for color? (3) What if the interval of the Korean War and the halt of color receiver production had not enabled the FCC to reverse its decision to adopt the CBS rather than the NBC all-electronic, compatible color system? (4) What if Lyndon Johnson (who called the passage of the Public Broadcasting Act of 1967 one of his greatest domestic legislative achievements) had run and won in 1968, and he rather than Richard Nixon was in the White House during public broadcasting's infancy? (5) What if a senator with a toothache had not left the Senate floor in 1960 to go to the dentist, causing Senator Pastore to lose by one vote his effort to pass legislation that would have given the FCC power to regulate cable television through the granting of three-year licenses (Senator Pastore was so angered by the vote he vowed never to introduce a Senate cable bill until the House passed cable legislation. He remained chairman of the Senate

Communications Subcommittee for another 16 years and kept that vow. In 1983 Congress is still trying to pass its first law governing cable television.)

Peers states that the FCC has been "hobbled by its statutory authority" and restricted by the existence of the First Amendment, which Canada lacks. However, Sections 303 and 309 of the Communications Act give the commission broad powers, and the courts have given the FCC great leeway to use its "administrative discretion" as an "expert agency," supporting the FCC when it acts (e.g., prospectively banning future cross-ownership of TV and radio stations in the same market and controlling network practices) and when it refuses to act (e.g., breaking up all existing cross-ownership of TV and radio stations in the same market and adopting rules to regulate children's programming). Often the determining factor is not the limit of the law, but where the commission chooses to place the burden of proof; on those who wish to change the status quo or on those who wish to retain it. Over the years the constraints of the act and the existence of the First Amendment have been conveniently cited by the FCC when it is reluctant to regulate.* In 1983, the law (e.g., Fairness Doctrine, equal opportunities for political candidates) is actually an obstacle to "unregulation" rather than regulation. The statute is keeping the FCC regulating broadcasting to a greater extent than Chairman Fowler and the majority of his colleagues who favor "unregulation" wish.

Legal restraints are again mentioned by Peers when he discusses the FCC's relationships with the three major U.S. broadcasting networks. He points out the Communications Act of 1934, unlike British law, fails to give the FCC the power to regulate the establishment and operation of networks. It is true the commission has no such specific delegated power and, in fact, the word network does not even appear in the act (the broadcasting portions of the 1934 act were basically the same as the Radio Act of 1927, and in 1927 NBC had been in operation for only a short time, CBS was just beginning, and ABC did not even exist). But the FCC has adequate power to regulate networks if it wishes through its power to regulate both those "stations engaged in chain broadcasting" (i.e., network affiliates) and the networks' owned and operated stations. The latter are vital to the financial success of the networks (for years only the profits of ABC's owned and operated stations kept the network in the black; more recently NBC has been close to a similar situation). Beginning with its chain broadcasting rules adopted over 40 years

---

*See Reluctant Regulaters by Cole and Oettinger (Addison Wesley, 1978).

ago and continuing with its current prime-time access and syndicated and financial interest rules, the commission has demonstrated substantial powers when it decides to exercise them over the operations of networks.

Peers characterizes the Canadian broadcasting system as "spotty, feebler and less prosperous" than its U.S. counterpart. Without addressing the comparative issue, I think it important to emphasize that distribution of radio service in the United States has always been spotty. This is the reason for preserving clear channel stations for so long. Even today about one half of commercial AM stations are daylight only and over 700 towns have no FM, no television, and only a daylight AM station. Moreover, traditionally the majority of radio stations in the United States have not been that profitable, with most stations either losing money, breaking even, or earning only small (under $10,000) profits.

Peers suggests the CBC is being asked to assume greater responsibilities despite an adverse public philosophy and new competing technologies making things even more difficult. A similar phenomenon is taking place in the United States. Public broadcasting, during an era of deregulation and unregulation, is being asked to meet the needs not being met by the commercial marketplace, while at the same time the Reagan administration's Office of Management and Budget is recommending the gradual elimination of all federal funding of public broadcasting (calling it an elitist service that should be paid for by the people who watch). At the same time, new alternative delivery systems, including cable, satellite master antenna system (SMATV), subscription television (STV), multipoint distribution service (MDS), and direct broadcast satellite (DBS) are competing for programming and audience.

Peers suggests that public broadcasting in the United States resulted from great dissatisfaction with commercial broadcasting, at least on the part of "thoughtful people." He cites the creation of the Carnegie Commission and the "surprisingly" rapid subsequent passage of the Public Broadcasting Act of 1967. But the establishment of the commission and the enactment of the law were largely the results of a few people being in the right places rather than of any widespread outcry for a new system. The use of the word public was intended to give a new, "sexier" image to educational broadcasting, yet, except in its title, the law never mentioned the term or defined public broadcasting. Nor was the Carnegie Commission much help, stating that the need was for "excellence in service of diversity."

Ten years later the goals of public broadcasting were still undefined; a second Carnegie Commission called for "programs that inform, engage, enlighten and delight." In 1983, the FCC is still unable to articulate in rule making who should be allowed to use the channels it has reserved for educational or public radio and television licensees.

Peers declares that the "U.S. system has changed less fundamentally than the Canadian system." While heretofore this may have been true, the U.S. system is beginning to change rapidly and significantly. William Lilley, who helps decide where CBS should be heading in the next five or ten years, summarizes the ongoing change as follows: change from a tradition of stability to a new environment of volatility, from a scarcity to an abundance of outlets, and from a separation of broadcasting, cable, and common carrier to a substitutability. A race of tremendous economic and perhaps social importance is now taking place between entrepreneurs of a number of competing video services. The mix of new technologies creates enormously significant and complex regulatory questions that will have to be answered eventually, even if by government inaction. For example, should the teletext electronic publishing of Field Enterprises, broadcast over the vertical blanking interval (VBI) of Ted Turner's superstation in Atlanta and distributed via satellite transmission to thousands of cable systems, be regulated as a newspaper, a television signal, a common carrier transmission, a cable signal, or something in between? Each form of regulation is different, and will help determine who will own, control, or have access to the signal, who will be able to receive it, where and how much the service will cost, what content controls will be imposed, if any, and so forth.

For years, observers of Canadian broadcasting have debated the wisdom of minimum Canadian content quotas. Do people in Canada really care whether the programs they watch are the product of Canada or the United States? Should they care? In the United States a similar future debate may well revolve around the importance of localism. Preservation of local services has been the rationale for preventing or controlling the appearance of new broadcasting technologies. But the current FCC has applied no local requirements to DBS, MDS, or low-power television, SMATV is not even regulated, and broadcasting and STV are being relieved of any local programming responsibilities. In their excellent contribution to this volume, Hagelin and Janisch (Chapter 3) state that localism is fundamental to the U.S. broadcasting system. This has certainly been true, at least in theory, in the past. Whether it will be in the future is unclear.

In his final paragraph, Peers suggests that in an era of declining resources and economic downturn, the United States may find its current broadcasting system, which is based on promoting consumption of goods, inappropriate and will then turn to a system designed to "encourage diversity and social interaction." Perhaps a more realistic hope is that eventually the increasing number of video and audio outlets will fragment the audience for mass entertainment enough that outlets will increasingly turn to narrowcasting more specialized programs for small target audiences, as has occurred on radio in larger cities.

One thing is clear. The audience in the United States will be undergoing significant changes during the latter part of this century. When one examines the nation's population projections for the twenty-first century—with Hispanics replacing blacks as the largest minority population by the year 2000 and the percentage of whites dropping to less than 50 percent (perhaps as low as 38 percent) by 2080—one begins to realize that despite its French and English dichotomy, the Canadian broadcast audience of the future may be more homogenous than its U.S. counterpart. As one considers the current trends requiring users to pay for each individual telecommunications or program service they may wish to use, the danger of creating a society of information-rich and information-poor people becomes more real. The challenge for broadcasters in the United States, as well as in Canada, will be to serve diversity while at the same time to inform and unify an entire national population.

3

THE BORDER BROADCASTING DISPUTE IN CONTEXT

Theodore Hagelin and Hudson Janisch

> The effects of this bill [C-58] do not only relate to
> the over-all health of the industry but to the main-
> tenance of Canadian culture and identity with all the
> impact television can have in Canada in helping to
> maintain and establish them.
>
> > Jim Fleming,
> > Parliamentary Secretary to
> > Minister of Communications,
> > November 17, 1975
>
> A rather simple, straightforward trade dispute.
>
> > Senator Patrick Moynihan,
> > June 15, 1982

INTRODUCTION

At the outset of our thinking about the border broadcast dispute and our proposal for this conference, we came to the conclusion that it would be necessary to stand back from the immediate
issues and identify the underlying principles on which broadcast
regulation is based in our two countries. Our thesis was that the
dispute had to be related first to these differences in approach and
expectation and that it could only be understood in that broader and
deeper policy context. [1] Essential as we considered the excavation
of the underlying principles to be, we also recognized that once that

was done, the practical dollars and cents issues still had to be addressed.

As law teachers we are required by our calling to be professional optimists and thus approach this subject with the hope that our analysis will at least clear away some of the obstacles to a possible resolution of the dispute. If our efforts and those of other participants at this conference only lead to a clearer understanding of the differences between Canada and the United States on broadcasting matters, that would, in itself, be a useful accomplishment. Differences are surely to be preferred to misunderstandings, since differences may be contained while misunderstandings are always volatile and uncontrollable. As Robert Southey reminded us, nations and individuals have often "agreed to differ."

Our discussion is divided into three parts. The first part highlights chronologically the development of the border broadcast dispute between Canada and the United States. Here we consider the initiatives and interests of both countries that have brought us to the present state of disagreement, which many believe now threatens the "special relationship" between these great and friendly neighbors.

The second part considers the constraints on, and contradictions within, U.S. and Canadian domestic communication policies. While it is undoubtedly true that present U.S. policy seeks to maximize consumer choice through market competition, whereas Canadian policy seeks to maximize cultural development through regulation, we believe that it is important to consider the limitations of both policies and how these limitations affect reconciliation of Canadian-U.S. international policies.

The third section proposes a model for analysis of the border broadcasting dispute based on a breakdown of the interests at stake into distinct concerns. Specifically, our model distinguishes locally originated, syndicated, and network programming, local, spot, national, and multinational advertising, and broadcast stations, networks, and program producers. We believe that these interests are differently affected by the terms and conditions of transborder broadcasting and that separate consideration of them will facilitate dialogue.

Finally we should say a word about our methodology. We decided that we wanted to present a jointly written contribution rather than two separate ones to force ourselves to confront common issues and avoid going off in separate directions. As individuals and as Canadian and U.S. citizens, we, of course, have our personal preferences and biases, which are inevitably reflected in our discussion. We have not sought to disguise or discard our preferences. Rather we have sought to balance them without being bland and to use them to provoke further thought without being dogmatic. The result for us has been an exciting professional exchange.

DEVELOPMENTS IN THE BORDER
BROADCAST DISPUTE

Origins

Canadian curiosity for television greatly outpaced the rate at
which indigenous service was introduced. In September 1952, on
the eve of the inauguration of service in Montreal and Toronto,
there were already some 146,000 television sets in Canadian homes.
The popular attitude was well captured by the Montreal Gazette when
it complained: "[T]he coming of television has been much delayed.
For years the citizens of the United States, just over the imaginary
border, have had television in their homes."[2]

Direct access to American programming was soon to be made
even more ubiquitous with the advent of cable television. From
humble origins as a means to improve rural service in the early
1950s, cable soon came to play a unique role in Canada and has
come close to providing a technological means of rendering the
border imaginary.

> Two major developments in the mid to late 1960s
> caused cable television to become an important urban
> as well as rural phenomenon. First, the rapid con-
> struction of high-rise buildings in centres close to the
> U.S. border interfered with the previously adequate
> reception of U.S. stations: cable television was a tech-
> nological solution to this problem. Second, cable sys-
> tems located too far from the U.S. border to trap
> American signals off-air by traditional means began
> constructing distant "head-ends" (antennae facilities)
> closer to the border in order to transport these sig-
> nals to their communities by means of microwave re-
> lay stations.[3]

There followed, as Robert Babe has pointed out, an extraor-
dinarily rapid growth in the cable industry that dwarfed developments in the United States. By 1975 cable was available to 66 percent of Canadian households, with 43 percent of households actually
subscribing.[4]

The massive importation of whole American stations (not
simply individual programs), which this development was to make
possible, laid the foundation for the conflict to come.

Enter the CRTC

Through to 1963 there was a highly permissive system of regulation of cable by the Department of Transport. Thereafter there was some tightening up of regulatory requirements, but it was not until 1968 that cable companies as "broadcast receiving undertakings" were brought fully under the newly established Canadian Radio and Television Commission (CRTC) by the Broadcasting Act of that year.[5] In December 1969 the commission moved to block the second of the major technological developments in Canadian cable.

> The problem facing the Commission is not whether the technology of microwave should be used to help the development of cable television. It is to decide whether the use of additional techniques should be authorized to enlarge the coverage area of U.S. networks and U.S. stations and therefore their advertising markets in Canada.
> The rapid acceleration of such a process throughout Canada would represent the most serious threat to Canadian broadcasting since 1932 before Parliament decided to vote the first Broadcasting Act. In the opinion of the Commission, it could disrupt the Canadian broadcasting system within a few years.
> The fact that through force of circumstance many U.S. stations now cover parts of Canada, and that some of them seem to have been established mainly to reach Canadian audiences does not justify a decision of the Commission which would further accelerate this process.
> In consequence the Commission will not license broadcasting receiving undertakings (CATV) based on the use of microwave or other technical systems, for the wholesale importation of programs from distant U.S. stations and thereby the enlargement of the Canadian audience and market areas of U.S. networks or stations.[6]

The outcry against this decision was to demonstrate dramatically the extent to which access to U.S. stations had come to be perceived not merely as a pleasant spillover effect caused by geographic proximity, but as a right to which all Canadians were entitled. Consider the unalloyed sarcasm of the member of Parliament for Calgary

South—one of the cities denied a license to microwave in U.S. border stations.

> It is with considerable trepidation that an ordinary Canadian enters into the never-never world of the professional Canadian. But I am compelled to ask, does the CRTC really feel that it is serving the national interest by creating yet another division in an already overly-divided Canada: those who should be permitted access to U.S. stations because a fact of geography prevents the CRTC from denying such access to U.S. stations and those who should be denied it because a fact of geography permits the CRTC to deny such access? While the question of which are the first class citizens and which the second may be open to dispute by the professional Canadian, there is no doubt in so far as those who have been denied a right on purely geographic grounds are concerned.[7]

Within six months the CRTC was to back away from its no importation by microwave rule in response to what it delicately described as a "need to apply a consistent CATV policy across the country."[8] Significantly, this consistency was to be achieved by allowing cable companies to carry at least two non-Canadian stations. Even as it announced this compromise, the commission cautioned that it appeared that the advent of cable, especially where distant signals were involved, tended to disrupt the economic basis on which licenses had been granted. In a blunt warning it indicated that if a television station were to solicit "Canadian advertising outside of its market of licensed area so as to disrupt the economic balance established by the normal licensing practice, the Commission may refuse to authorize the distribution of its programs. . . ."[9]

This growing anxiety as to the perceived impact of cable culminated in a public hearing in April 1971. Assuming as its premise that "cable television is completely changing the basic characteristics of broadcast licensing in both Canada and the United States," the commission indicated in its background statement, The Integration of Cable Television in the Canadian Broadcasting System,[10] that drastic measures might be called for to ensure that cable make a positive contribution to the Canadian broadcasting system. It is important to note just how fundamental were the concerns cable was seen to have raised. The importation of distant signals was not seen as merely something calling for a readjustment in the existing ways of doing things but as a threat to the very existence of an independent national broadcasting system. As the commission stated at the very outset:

Canada has a limited ratio of population to territory
and the larger part of this population is concentrated—
for reasons that vary from economic opportunity to
climatic advantage—along the border shared with the
most highly developed and influential country in the
world.

Notwithstanding, Canada is still determined to
maintain a national purpose. A Canadian broadcasting
system, rooted in this cause, becomes even more vital
in a time of scientific and technological developments
which tend to blur national boundaries and dilute cultural aspirations. [11]

The commission was not at all reticent in dealing with the impact of U.S. stations on Canadian audiences and the attractiveness
of advertising on those border stations.

It is also estimated that some $12-million to $15-
million a year of Canadian money is spent to buy commercial time on U.S. television stations. The indirect
effect is more difficult to calculate, but international
advertisers would probably have to spend about double
that amount per year on Canadian television stations to
achieve the same impact if the border spill-over did
not exist. [12]

This, at a time when the commission saw some Canadian stations
as already economically marginal even without this additional competition, and some Canadian cities, which might have had several
television stations, limited to one or two. A response had to be devised not as a means to safeguard vested interests or to maintain a
technology that might have outlived its usefulness, but to cope with
"specifically Canadian problems" that were seen as being different
from those that the spread of cable had presented to the FCC.

The danger to the Canadian broadcasting system is
real and immediate. . . .

The Commission has indicated in previous policy
announcements how unlimited penetration by United
States stations on a wholesale south to north basis
would completely destroy the licensing logic of the
Canadian broadcasting system as established by the
Broadcasting Act. If a solution is not found to inte-
grate cable into the overall system, the impact, by
fracturing the economic basis of private broadcasting,

would also disrupt the Canadian cultural, educational
and informational imperatives of both the public and
private sectors of the Canadian broadcasting system.

At stake is more than a system of national communication, because broadcasting also has the vitally
important task of identifying and strengthening cultural entities, regional identities and community loy-
alties. [13]

The most striking feature of the commission's July 1971 Policy
Statement, Cable Television: Canadian Broadcasting 'A Single System,'[14] is the firmness with which it rejected any notion that cable
television operators were simply selling a sophisticated antenna service.[15] Not only must cable not undermine the economic viability of
on-air broadcasters, but it was expected, as part of a "single system," to provide tangible support for Canadian programming. This
approach was most prominently reflected in the proposal that cable
operators should pay for the programming they distributed. As the
commission put it, "[T]he basic principle involved is: one should pay
for what he uses to operate his business."[16] However, the concern
was with Canadian programming and this "basic principle" only extended to compensation for the use of such programming.[17] In any
event, while this proposal did give an indication of the commission's
basic thinking about cable, it was "not intended as policy but rather
as a basis for discussion between television and cable television
licensees,"[18] and it has never been implemented to any significant
extent. This was not to be so with respect to the other proposals
designed to restore "the logic of the local license."

To find a firm foundation for its policy the commission reached
back to an objective it said has always been fundamental to the broadcasting system adopted throughout North America. That objective
was to favor services that were as closely relevant as possible to
the particular community to be served. (As will be developed later,
the FCC's concerns for the viability of local television broadcast
markets and its protection of local stations from competition by new
applicants and technologies have been long standing in the United
States. The similarities between local markets and local service in
the United States and Canada are important to the question of "national
treatment" raised by the U.S. broadcasters.) The relationship between a local station and its community could only be achieved if the
licensee was granted an area of service deemed sufficient to provide
the required economic basis for service. Cable threatened to destroy this traditional arrangement by fragmenting audiences and
diverting advertising revenue.

As a result, the franchise which the Commission, according to the law of the land, has granted to a licensee for that area becomes gradually less and less meaningful. The obligations in terms of public service which, again according to law, the licensee has undertaken to fulfill become more and more difficult to fulfill. Thus the license gradually loses its meaning.[19]

The commission pointed out that it was obliged by the Broadcasting Act to supervise the publicly owned radio frequencies of Canada "so that the Canadian broadcasting system is not disrupted as a result of purely technological and marketing pressures which take no account of the social, cultural, economic and political objectives of the country."[20] Thus a number of steps had to be taken to restore the logic of the local license.

First, a policy would be adopted to establish the basic services to the community that cable operators must provide, including carriage of CBC and other Canadian local and regional stations, community channels, and, where requested by provincial authorities, access for educational programming.[21] Second, program deletion and replacement where identical programs were scheduled by stations already serving the community would allow those stations to regain their share of the local audience without reducing or restricting viewer choice.[22] Third, a new policy would permit "the removal by cable licensees of the commercial value contained in the signals of stations not licensed to serve Canada."[23] And fourth, the government would be requested to amend the Income Tax Act with respect to "advertising purchased by Canadian advertisers on stations not licensed by the Commission."[24]

Canada Makes Its Move: From
Deletion to Nondeductability

It was appropriate that the CRTC's commercial deletion policy should have been first implemented in Calgary, a city that played so prominent a part in the commission's strategic withdrawal on importation by microwave. In December 1972, license amendments were granted to the Calgary companies to allow for the carriage of an additional U.S. commercial signal provided they agreed to delete commercial messages from signals received from stations not licensed to serve Canada, if so requested by local broadcasters.[25] However, not until August 1973, when Rogers Cable Television in Toronto began randomly deleting commercials from the signal from WKBW-TV, Buffalo, did the commission's policy really threaten to bite. Thereafter, in the face of protests from the Buffalo stations, Rogers applied to the CRTC for an amendment to its license providing for deletion, the Buffalo stations intervened before the CRTC, and in May 1974, the commission allowed amendments specifying that only public service announcements were to be carried as replacements.[26] In April, the Buffalo stations began a wide ranging test of commercial deletion in the Federal Court of Canada, Trial Division. Neither this, nor an appeal testing the legality of the CRTC's condition of license approach, was successful.[27] Ironically, the Supreme Court of Canada's decision was handed down some nine months after the commission had decided, in consultation with other branches of the Canadian government, to suspend any further implementation of the commercial deletion policy.[28]

Commercial deletion, as one might have expected, had turned out to be a rather crude and blunt policy instrument that was expensive to implement, and, as it involved actual interference with signals, gave support to those who alleged that it amounted to little less than piracy and theft. A tax approach was seen as more appropriate and had already been recommended by both the CRTC[29] and the Davey Report on Mass Media[30] when the government first indicated in October 1974 that it was considering an amendment to the Income Tax Act to limit the deductability of the expenses of advertising on U.S. stations for advertisements directed at a Canadian audience.[31] Legislation to this effect, Bill C-58, was introduced in April 1975.[32]

Bill C-58 dealt, as well, with the tax advantages conferred on certain American periodicals (primarily Time and Reader's Digest), and this issue received most of the attention during the debates, with repeated accusations of censorship directed against the government. The broadcast issue was characterized more as a straightforward matter of dollars and cents, although, as we shall see, behind this bland accounting approach lay some very strongly held beliefs.

Hugh Faulkner, who, as secretary of state, described himself as being responsible for federal government policy and programs aimed at the betterment of cultural and artistic activity and achievement, set out the basic rationale behind Bill C-58 in a speech in May 1975 in the House of Commons.

> There are about a dozen American television stations located close to the Canadian border whose programs are seen by a great number of Canadians either directly or through cablevision. Those stations have reaped substantial advertising revenues in Canadian towns where their programs are widely seen. Indeed, the

very existence of some of those stations is based on advertising made in Canada.

According to some estimates, some $20 million are paid each year out of Canada to those American stations for advertising directed to Canadian viewers. From that yearly amount of $20 million, some $9 million comes from the television market in the Toronto area and some $7 million from Vancouver. Southern Manitoba loses about $1.5 million each year to American stations. The remainder comes from Ottawa, Montreal and a few other small markets.

Most of the American stations involved, especially those situated in Buffalo (N.Y.), in Pembina (North Dakota), in Bellingham (Washington) are actively canvassing advertising accounts with Canadian companies who wish to sell their products to Canadians. It can be safely stated, Mr. Speaker, that some stations have been created for the sole purpose of tapping the Canadian market.

The economic exploitation of the Canadian advertising market has important consequences for our broadcasting system. The licensing policy of the Canadian Radio-Television Commission is based on the ability of each local market to support with advertising revenues the Canadian stations licensed to serve it. Clearly, when revenues which would otherwise go to local Canadian stations are siphoned off to United States border stations, the CRTC's licensing policy is undermined.

We are confident that this measure will not in any way limit the choice of programming available to Canadians. However, uncontrolled siphoning off of advertising revenues adversely affects the financial viability of many Canadian stations. Affected, as well, is the ability of Canadian stations to assume greater and more costly policy obligations such as local program production.[33]

Jim Fleming, parliamentary secretary to the minister of communications, was to reveal the intensity of feeling the transborder broadcasting issue could arouse. He pointed out that under no circumstances could Canada constitute a threat to the establishment and dissemination of U.S. culture. "But, certainly, with no content rules, no Canadian obligations and no added costs, their penetration of our area can seriously threaten our identity and culture if that penetration undermines the very existence of healthy Canadian television."[34] He went on to dismiss out of hand the protestations of the U.S. border broadcasters at a proposal that would cut off the flow of advertising revenue but still continue to license Canadian cable companies to distribute their signals.

> Over the 24 or 25 years that all these Canadian dollars have poured south of the border, these stations, to my knowledge, have never been questioned about their huge windfall gains by their own regulatory body, the FCC. Now, when we try to protect our own, we hear angry cries about the morality of windfall gains such as taking United States programming which enters our airwaves while rejecting commercials out of the United States. Surely, on moral and ethical grounds such indignation from the U.S. rings very hollow indeed.
>
> For years their windfall gains have made them among the richest of the United States stations, despite the fact that they are among the smallest U.S. licensed stations serving urban areas. That windfall threatens our entire industry. If we in turn have United States programming and pay nothing for it, then under United States licensing not only are we not contravening any of their rules but also we are not costing them anything. In that case, what are we doing that is so wrong and why do they cry so loudly and angrily at this point in time?[35]

The United States Responds: From Mirror
Legislation to Linkage and Retaliation

There were two main avenues open to the U.S. border broadcasters by which to respond to these developments; first, direct approach to the Canadian policy makers, and second, involving the U.S. government. Both were pursued with considerable vigor.

As we have seen, the Buffalo stations intervened before the CRTC in November 1973, when Rogers applied for an amendment to its license to provide for deletion and thereafter actively pursued relief in the Canadian courts. In March 1976 there was an inconclusive meeting between the CRTC and the border broadcasters to discuss alternative ways of meeting objectives. As Bill C-58 had by then been introduced in the House of Commons, discussion was confined to commercial deletion.[36]

A number of border broadcaster witnesses appeared before the House of Commons Standing Committee on Broadcasting, Films and Assistance to the Arts when Bill C-58 reached it in December 1975.[37] Philip Beuth, vice-president of Capital Cities Communications, argued that the measure would simply not divert advertising revenue to Canadian stations. As he put it:

> [I]t is alleged that the fall of Canadian revenue to the Buffalo stations puts Toronto stations in real financial jeopardy. We think that allegation is grossly overstated as well. The real problem our presence in Toronto creates for Canadian stations is an audience problem. Some 45 per cent of the metro Toronto audience watches the Buffalo stations. Preventing Canadian advertisers from using the Buffalo stations will not increase the audience of the other Toronto stations. Our audience will remain. It will simply cripple television as a medium for reaching the total Toronto market-place.[38]

Border broadcasters were also very active before the Senate Banking Trade and Commerce Committee in June of the next year.[39] On that occasion, there was some complaint that aside from the meeting with the CRTC and an appearance before the House of Commons Committee, there had been no opportunity to meet with any government officials, particularly the minister of communications. Although they were to receive a somewhat more sympathetic hearing from the Senate committee than from the House committee, the border broadcasters had nothing to show from these direct approaches except some concession on the date on which Bill C-58 would take effect.

Within two months of the Calgary licensing decision, the U.S. State Department delivered a request that the Canadian government intervene to rescind or modify the decision. This request was eventually rejected by the Canadian Department of External Affairs, and a subsequent note calling for delay in any further implementation of commercial deletion was similarly turned aside.[40] Inconclusive as this preliminary skirmish had been, it did reveal two problems: first, a serious misconception of the nature of the dispute, and, second, the particularly difficult nature of the domestic decision-making structures involved.

Commercial deletion was seen as being a purely economic matter and thus was initially dealt with by the Bureau of Economic and Business Affairs rather than the Canadian Desk. It is still not clear that even with the shift to the Canadian Desk there has been a concomitant shift in appreciation of the nature of the border broadcasting dispute. When the Department of External Affairs responded in January 1974, it pointed out that the CRTC was an independent regulatory agency with a separate statutory mandate on broadcasting matters. As the Calgary decision had been made in the exercise of this mandate, the Canadian government could not agree to modify or rescind the decision.[41]

Jurisdictional uncertainty also poses problems in the United States, where many institutions are concerned with matters involving international broadcasting, each with its own composition and constituency. The Federal Communications Commission, the National Telecommunications and Information Agency, the Department of State, the Office of the U.S. Trade Representative, and House and Senate subcommittees all have within their jurisdictions matters directly affected by the border broadcasting dispute.[42]

There were not to be formal negotiations on the border dispute until January 1976. In the meantime there had been a hearing before the House of Representatives Subcommittee on Inter-American Affairs (April 1974), at which the inactivity of the State Department was roundly criticized; informal discussions in Washington between the chairman of the FCC, the deputy assistant secretary for Transportation and Telecommunications, and the chairman of the CRTC (June 1975); and a meeting in October 1975 between Henry Kissinger and Allan MacEachen, Canadian secretary of state for foreign affairs. Commercial deletion was discussed at this meeting but, pending a decision from the Supreme Court of Canada, matters were not pushed through to any conclusion.[43]

By the time of formal negotiations involving the U.S. deputy assistant secretary for Canadian Affairs, the chairman of the FCC, the director of the United States Division, Department of External Affairs, and officials from the Department of Communications, and the CRTC, Canada was not prepared to discuss Bill C-58, which was now clearly becoming far more important than commercial deletion. In October 1976, there was a similar set of negotiations, but again Canada held firm to the nonnegotiability of the tax amendment.[44] In December 1976, the Canadian cabinet recommended a two- to three-year moratorium on commercial deletion, and on January 21, 1977, the CRTC effectively suspended further deletion.[45] Thus the only item that Canada might have been prepared to compromise on receded into the background to be replaced with an essentially nonnegotiable position.

Frustrated both by this lack of progress in official talks and by the Supreme Court of Canada decision upholding the validity of CRTC actions, the border broadcasters filed a complaint with the Office of the United States trade representative under Section 301 of the U.S. Trade Act.[46]

In a move that signaled a crucial escalation in the dispute, the petitioners sought to link resolution of the border broadcast dispute to retaliation by way of restrictions on the importation of Canadian films and recordings and on U.S. modification of the bilateral Automotive Agreement.

There had been, as Andrew Stoler recalled, a previous escalation like this in 1976.

> The linkage of U.S. action on para. 602 of the Tax Reform Act of 1976 with Canadian action on C-58 originated with those Members of Congress concerned over the impact of C-58 on border broadcasters in their districts and was never publicly condoned by the Executive Branch. Para. 602 severely restricted income tax deductions by U.S. taxpayers for the costs of attending conventions outside the United States, and its enactment was said to have cost Canadian businesses hundreds of millions of dollars in lost revenues. [47]

Most significantly, the Canadian delegation, at consultations provided for under Section 301 proceedings, urged that the border broadcasting question be viewed as an issue unrelated to others and particularly that it not be linked to the Automotive Agreement. As Andrew Stoler noted: "This would be consistent with the general conduct of U.S.-Canada relations at the time. Historically, both the U.S. and Canadian Governments have made it a policy to avoid linkages in the discussion of bilateral trade issues, as linkages tend to lead to an escalation of problems in the relationship." [48]

In the end, the decision of the Section 301 Committee, while finding Bill C-58 "unreasonable" because, in effect, it placed the costs of attaining the objectives of a stronger broadcasting industry on the U.S. companies affected, backed away from any escalation. [49] All that was recommended was that a U.S. statute be enacted to mirror Bill C-58, and in September 1980, in a message to the Congress of the United States, President Carter urged the early passage of U.S. tax legislation to mirror Bill C-58. [50] The Ninety-sixth Congress, however, adjourned before considering the proposal. President Reagan sent a similar message to Congress on November 17, 1981.

The change of administrations had not altered executive policy on border broadcasting. Unlike Carter, however, Reagan's request for mirror legislation included an implied threat of linkage: "Therefore, I note that I retain the right to take further action, if appropriate, to obtain the elimination of the practice (C-58) on my own motion under the authority of Section 301 (c)(1)." [51]

Had straightforward mirror legislation been introduced, the border broadcasting dispute might have ended as an unresolved but controllable matter. It would have remained a nagging irritant in Canada-U.S. relations, but no more. Recent developments make it clear that the dispute remains a volatile one, a constant danger to broader relations, especially at a time of rising protectionist sentiment. [52]

Bill S.2051, as originally introduced early in 1982, was a precise mirror to Bill C-58. [53] However, a "strengthening amendment" was added in June by Senator Patrick Moynihan that would deny to U.S. businesses a tax deduction and tax credit for purchases of Canadian-developed videotext technology, Telidon. [54]

As the senator explained:

> It is unfortunate that this amendment is necessary to resolve the border broadcast dispute which is a relatively small trade problem. However, the Canadians have made the issue a major test of our will to protect U.S. service industries faced by unreasonable and unfair discrimination by a U.S. trading partner. Canadian officials have made it clear that the "mirror bill" as introduced will not move the Canadians from their six-year-old position of non-negotiability on the border broadcast problem. . . . The border broadcast issue is indeed a test of our trade laws. We must demonstrate to the border broadcasters who have shown admirable patience in pursuing a remedy through the 301 process, and to other service industries, that Section 301 of the Trade Act of 1974 is an effective means to remove foreign barriers to U.S. service exports. [55]

There were five reasons why this link to Telidon was thought appropriate. First, this technology had been developed by the Canadian government and was being subsidized and supported "by the same Canadian interests that endorsed the unfair trade practice against U.S. border broadcasters." Second, the amendment would terminate as soon as Canada removed its unreasonable border broadcast trade practice.

> Third, Canada views the American videotext-teletext market as essential to Telidon's success. Canada seeks access to a new, developing telecommunications market at the same time it attempts to exclude the U.S. from a Canadian telecommunications market. It is my belief that this amendment will finally persuade Canada

that resolving the border broadcast problem is in both
countries' best interests. Canada has placed a high
priority on developing its domestic telecommunications
industries. They need access to U.S. markets to reach
their full development.

Fourth, the amendment will gradually increase
the economic pressure on Canada to come to the nego-
tiating table. Today there is no established U.S.
videotext market. By 1990 the Canadians predict an
annual U.S. market of $12 billion and they hope to get
$1 billion of it. The amendment will not cause Canada
serious economic harm this year or next. If Canada
chooses to reject reasonable solutions to the border
broadcasting problem, it will also be choosing to sustain greater and greater economic consequences.

Finally, I believe there are few, if any negative
consequences for U.S. interests. There are several
other available and competing videotext technologies.
The British have developed a system called Prestel
and the French have developed one called Antiope.
Both AT&T and IBM are expected to commence systems, as well. Denying a tax deduction to the Canadian-
developed technology does not affect the ability of American businesses and American consumers to utilize videotext technology. [56]

The other warning flag may be found in Senator Barry Goldwater's Bill S.2172, which would give the FCC authority to establish
rules and regulations to prohibit foreign ownership of cable if no
reciprocal rights are granted by that foreign country to U.S. companies to provide cable therein.[57] This proposal is particularly
striking because the FCC itself had but recently investigated this
matter and rejected any such restriction. In 1976 the commission
had concluded: "It is difficult for us to perceive how the TV viewing
public would benefit in any way. . . . Rather, such a restriction
would merely promote the self interest of the domestic cable industry at the expense of additional competitive alternatives for the public." This sentiment was reiterated in 1980: "In the absence of
demonstrable harm and where benefits may arise the Commission is
inclined to allow free market forces to determine the direction of
capital flow within the industry."[58]

TENSIONS IN CANADIAN AND U.S. COMMUNICATIONS
POLICIES: COMPETING POLITICAL AND ECONOMIC
CONSIDERATIONS

Canadian and U.S. domestic communications policies differ
both in their ends and their means. Canadian policy seeks cultural
development; U.S. policy seeks consumer choice. Canadian policy
relies on program content regulation and a strong public broadcasting system to achieve its objectives. U.S. policy relies on structural, or industrial, regulation and a strong commercial broadcasting system to achieve its objectives.[59]

These differences, however, are more in the nature of varying
emphases than fundamental inconsistencies. Canadian policy does
concern itself with industrial development regulation and has relied
increasingly on private broadcast and cable investment to achieve
its cultural content objectives. U.S. policy does concern itself with
content regulation, especially in television, and has relied increasingly on public broadcasting as a safety net for community needs and
interests not satisfied by market forces in the commercial system.[60]

Because of the competing political and economic considerations
within Canada and the United States, it is inaccurate to conceive of
their respective domestic communications policies as monolithic,
mutually exclusive, or irrevocably opposed. Rather, Canadian and
U.S. broadcast policies might better be conceived of as criss-
crossing or intersecting over time. The dynamic administrative
adjustment of political, cultural, and social values, industry economics, and new technology forms the backdrop against which ac-
commodation of U.S. and Canadian international policies must be
considered and is the subject matter of this section. We have attempted to develop the tensions that exist in the aggregation of these
interests and to raise questions about the trade-offs of conflicting
claims.

Canadian Policy

With the stage now set for the dispute, we can consider some
of the tensions (if not, indeed, contradictions) presented by the
Canadian position. On the one hand, it had been found that it simply
was not possible in a democratic society to prevent the wholesale
importation of entire U.S. stations into Canada. The availability of
U.S. programming has been steadily increased over time.[61]

On the other hand, Canada was not prepared to accept the adverse economic impact of such importations on the ability of Canadian broadcasters to live up to the Broadcasting Act's requirements

that the broadcasting system "safeguard, enrich and strengthen the cultural, political, social and economic fabric of Canada" by employing programming "of high standard, using predominately Canadian creative and other resources. . . ."[62]

It might seem that Canada wished to have its U.S. stations and preserve a unique Canadian identity, too. Or, to put it another way, government sought to assuage the popular view of an imaginary boundary and to accommodate an elite that aspired, as the title of a contemporary book exhorted, to Close the 49th Parallel.[63] Yet to dismiss these moves simply as protectionism induced by self-serving private broadcasters or hypocritical "professional Canadians" would miss (or at least greatly underestimate) the profound nature of the aspiration for a viable and distinctive Canadian broadcasting system in the face of threatening technological developments and economic forces.

This fundamental Canadian ambivalence between pursuit of unique cultural identity and development of a viable mass media infrastructure through which this identity could be communicated is reflected in other aspects of Canadian broadcast policy.

The Uncertain Nature of the Canadian Mixed Broadcasting System

As other participants point out, Canada has moved away in recent years from proposals for a purely public broadcasting system in favor of a complex (and possibly internally self-contradictory) mixed private and public system. This uneasy compromise between commercialism and public service reflects a somewhat schizophrenic approach to broadcasting. As David Ellis observes,

> This tension between national purposes and vested interest has been the major problem of broadcasting policy since the early days of the system. The founding father of the system, R. B. Bennett, had a strong attachment to both private enterprise and public broadcasting—an ambivalence once described by Graham Spry as a 'conflict within his soul.' It is a conflict which has been shared by many other Canadian political leaders since Bennett.[64]

This ambivalence has deprived the CBC of its ability to provide a strong national television service (such as it does in radio) that is capable without regulatory protection of remaining uniquely Canadian right next door to the world's most successful producer of popular television programming. Moreover, had Canada chosen to

follow the BBC model, this would have provided a clearly distin-
guishable alternative to the American approach in which attention
could have been focused directly on the protection of cultural identity and not indirectly by protection of commercial revenue.

The Extent of Demands Placed
on Canadian Broadcasters

This ambivalence has also led to the imposition of an extensive
system of regulation designed to accomplish purposes that run sharply counter to the immediate economic interests of the broadcasters.[65]
It has proven to be particularly difficult for American broadcasters
and policy-makers to appreciate the extent of the regulatory demands
placed on the Canadian private broadcasters that appear to be just
like their U.S. commercial counterparts. Such apparent similarities can easily lead to misunderstanding. As Oscar Wilde noted,
the only thing that keeps the English and the Americans apart is the
"barrier of a common language." The Canadian private broadcasters are chosen instruments for the implementation of national policy
as set out in the Broadcasting Act.

At first glance, the burden does not appear particularly onerous.
The television regulations,[66] which have been in force since October
1970, require Canadian television broadcasters to provide a minimum annual total of 60 percent Canadian content between the hours
of 6:00 A.M. and midnight. Private television broadcasters are
also required to show at least 50 percent Canadian content between
6:00 P.M. and midnight, while CBC stations must provide a minimum of 60 percent during this time period. (In contrast, U.S. commercial broadcasters are required to devote less than 10 percent of
their broadcast time to local service programming.)

However, when set in its economic context, the significance
of this requirement becomes more apparent.

The economics of television program production is governed
by the fact that costs are constant regardless of the size of the audience. The potential size of the U.S. audience is ten times as large
as the potential Canadian audience. U.S. producers can afford to
spend $200,000 on a half-hour program in the hope that they might
sell it profitably to one of the networks. Foreign rights to this program might be purchased by a Canadian broadcaster for as little as
$8,000 and bring in $40,000 worth of advertising. Should Canadian
broadcasters seek to compete, it would cost them $100,000 to pro-
duce a program that would, in all likelihood, only generate $25,000
in revenue.[67]

When Canadian content requirements (particularly for prime
time) and diversion of advertising revenue to stations not subject to

such requirements converge, conflict is inevitable. The resulting
sense of frustration, especially for the new generation of private
Canadian television broadcasters, was well captured by Moses
Znaimer, president of Toronto's City TV, in evidence before the
Senate Committee on Banking, Trade and Commerce when it was
looking at Bill C-58. It had been suggested that some supporters of
that legislation were merely sore losers in the commercial realm
in competition with the highly successful U.S. border stations.

> Any investigation by Canadians as to how they can com-
> pete through improved services runs up against the wall
> that there are not sufficient dollars in Canada. When
> you go looking for those dollars you find that a good
> healthy chunk of them—the cream of the top of the sys-
> tem—is taken out by American broadcasters. I would
> not mind, Senator, if the rules were the same on both
> sides of the border. But I am obliged by this govern-
> ment through the CRTC to put out 60 per cent Canadian
> content. But because I don't have the resources, the
> shows that I put on to make up this 60 per cent are not
> as attractive as the hours of police adventure and situa-
> tion comedies made in the United States which cost a
> quarter of a million or $300,000 an hour. So here is
> one element of government imposing a ball and chain
> on my foot while another element with some of you
> senators, is saying, "Why can't you compete directly?"
> I would like to get off the hook. That is really my point.
> If you like free competition, I don't think I should be
> forced to provide 60 per cent Canadian content. I have
> an obligation to the national system which I have ac-
> cepted because that is one of the rules of the game,
> but I think the guy who is competing should have some
> obligations as well. [68]

The private broadcasters are not necessarily really being
squeezed between the rock of Canadian content and the hard place of
U.S. competition. There are those who suggest that the CRTC has
been lax in enforcing its rules—that it has spoken loudly and carried
a small stick. [69] Others wonder whether this type of regulation,
which runs so diametrically contrary to economic self-interest, can
ever accomplish its public policy goals. [70] Be that as it may, what
is important for the more immediate purposes of the border broadcasting dispute is that there has been a recent escalation in regulatory expectation with respect to Canadian content, which will lead
to ever greater reliance on Bill C-58 to protect the revenue base
for relatively expensive Canadian programming.

In August 1979, CTV, the major English-language network, had its license renewed for a three-year period subject to a condition that "26 hours of original new Canadian drama be presented during the 1981-82 season."[71] The legality of this use of a particular condition of license rather than the general regulations, as well as the fairness of this somewhat unexpected resort to the condition power, was carried to the Supreme Court of Canada.[72] This, in itself, was relatively unusual, for, as compared with the United States, relatively few broadcast issues have ever reached the Canadian courts. It is not at all clear whether this reflects a general Canadian disincliniation to challenge authority or whether regulation in general, and the content regulations in particular, has never had substantial enough economic bite to warrant resort to the courts. That aside, the CTV case does represent an important escalation in regulatory expectation.

The pervasiveness of concern with "Can. con." may also be seen in the recent imposition of an ambitious made-in-Canada pay-TV program quota, tied directly to revenues, despite the discretionary, individual-choice nature of that service.[73] The seriousness of purpose with which Canadian video entertainment choice is now approached can lead to extraordinary results, such as the current row over the acceptability as Canadian content of adult programming made in association with Playboy Enterprises.[74]

In its January 31, 1983, Policy Statement on Canadian Content in Television the CRTC strongly reaffirmed its commitment to Canadian content. Again, it is important to appreciate the level of current anxiety and the degree to which the importation issue is seen to run to the very foundations of any independent national identity.

> Canadian television programming must attract, engage and entertain. It must also inform, educate and enrich our cultural experience. For if Canadians do not use what is one of the world's most extensive and sophisticated communications systems to speak to themselves— if it serves only for the importation of foreign programs— there is a real and legitimate concern that the country will ultimately lose the means of expressing its identity. Developing a strong Canadian program production capability is no longer a matter of desirability but of necessity.[75]

Despite existing Canadian content regulations, foreign programs accounted for 77 percent of the total viewing of English-language television programs over the entire day and 85 percent between 7:30 P.M. and 10:30 P.M.[76] Proposals were put forward to devise a new points-based definition of Canadian content and minimum content requirements for the "mid-evening viewing hours." Most importantly, it was proposed that wider use be made of the condition of license regulatory technique as upheld by the Supreme Court of Canada in the CTV case. These individually tailored requirements would take into account the licensee's present and projected financial capacity. "Where a condition of license is imposed, a minimum percentage of revenues or total program budget to be spent on the programming in question may be specified. Conditions may also be applied, where appropriate, with respect to the number of hours devoted to certain categories and to the scheduling of programs."[77]

While this does indicate a move to tighten Canadian content requirements that will have important ramifications "on the border," there was a very strong minority statement that dismissed the national identity passage quoted above as "rhetorical excess": "We believe that it is insulting to suggest that Canadian identity is such a fragile thing that it will be either saved or doomed by regulatory fiat."[78] In addition, the minority was opposed to the use of conditions of license. "Discretion to be exercised according to unspecific criteria by the regulator serves only to inhibit the planning and investment decisions required to sustain a stable Canadian programming industry."[79] Nor had the majority sufficiently recognized "the new broadcasting reality: the growing, even overwhelming, abundance of viewer choice from both licensed and unlicensed sources. The Commission is proposing regulations for a broadcasting world which no longer exists. . . . Fortunately, viewer preferences cannot, in this world of programming abundance, be dictated by either broadcaster or regulators."[80]

While this sharp difference within the CRTC may have a longer-run significance for the border dispute, in the shorter run the move by the majority to further tighten up Canadian content regulation will reinforce the very pressures that caused the dispute in the first place.

The Cost of Culture

When seen in the total context of U.S.-Canada trade ($70 billion in 1979), the amount involved in the border broadcast dispute appears trivial. Yet, even aside from any issue of principle that might be said to be involved, this advertising revenue was thought to be critical to the development and diversification of Canadian television broadcasting.

It is estimated that by 1974 some $20 million was being spent by Canadian advertisers on the U.S. border stations.[81] This amounted to about 10 percent of the total Canadian advertising expenditures on television. The amount of these expenditures was estimated to have declined from $21.5 million in 1975 to $10.5 million in 1977 and to $6.5 million in 1978.[82] Dramatic as this decline in expenditures in the face of Bill C-58 has been, it is more difficult to estimate the extent of the attainment of the avowed objective of the amendment to the Income Tax Act—Canadian programming.

In debate it had been strongly argued that the new stations licensed in the mid-1970s would not be able to survive without repatriation of the advertising revenue being diverted to the border stations. Their survival, it was further argued, would greatly increase the range and variety of Canadian programming. In their study for the Department of Communications, The Impact of the 1976 Income Tax Amendment on U.S. and Canadian TV Broadcasters, Arthur Donner and Fred Lazar concluded that this strategy had worked.

> Although as a proportion of total revenues the repatriated dollars may seem small, in terms of operating income and after tax profits, the flow of repatriated advertising revenue is rather significant. Moreover, when the repatriated dollars are considered against the performance of the five newly licensed stations in Canada, one concludes that the turnaround in profit performance of these stations must, to a considerable extent, have been the result of the repatriation triggered by Bill C-58.
>
> The creation of five new television stations in Canada together with the 60% Canadian content rule guarantees an increased volume of Canadian programming. Even if ratings are rather dismal at first, the increased fragmentation brought about by these new stations will also ensure an increase, albeit a marginal one, in the viewing of Canadian programs by Canadian viewers.[83]

The viability of these new Canadian stations may be seen as having been bought specifically at the expense of the U.S. border stations. Thus, while the total amount involved in the dispute might appear comparatively small, its significance is important enough in the context of broadcasting for the Canadian authorities to stand firm, and its impact is great enough on a small number of border broadcasters (who have demonstrated no lack of political support or media access) to ensure that the dispute will never simply reflect its financial worth.

Moreover, to the extent that Canada elevates the dispute beyond its dollar significance on the basis of cultural principles, the
United States can do likewise on the basis of commercial principles.
An example of this elevation is contained in Senator John C. Danforth's testimony before the U.S. Senate on behalf of mirror legislation:

> Viewed in trade policy terms, the border broadcasting
> case is simple: A restrictive foreign trade practice
> has impacted adversely on the export of a U.S. service.
> That foreign trade practice is a clear distortion of the
> principle of free trade. . . . The border broadcast
> case, as the first Section 301 service sector case to
> proceed to a Presidential recommendation of a recipro-
> cal response, has assumed symbolic importance for
> our service industry exporters. [84]

As we have seen, viewed from a Canadian perspective this is
a startling misconception of what is involved in the dispute. As a
leaked draft of the new broadcasting policy complained, "The U.S.
Administration generally is not sensitive to Canadian cultural concerns and often appears to have great difficulty in understanding the
Canadian position on most broadcasting issues."[85] There appears
to be little hope for constructive dialogue until the parties are on the
same wavelength—a possibility if Canadians acknowledge their ambivalence toward broadcasting despite all the cultural rhetoric and
the United States acknowledges that what is involved is not just a
trade practice.

Differing Concepts of Freedom of Speech

As Katherine Swinton has noted, "it is difficult for non-
Americans to realize the depth of attachment to the symbolic value
of the free speech guarantee in the U.S. Constitution. Nationals of
states more accustomed to government regulation or unused to an
active system of judicial review to protect fundamental freedoms
may not understand how distasteful government regulation of broadcasting content is in the United States."[86]
A distinction is maintained in the United States between electronic and other media, based, in part, on limited spectrum rationale
and in part on the "intrusive" nature of broadcasting. This distinction is used to justify some regulation of broadcast service.[87] Nevertheless, content regulation, especially of the type and amount relied
on in Canada, might strike an American as being inconsistent with
the fundamental value of free speech. Even more striking would be

the ease with which any attack has been brushed aside, as in the
Supreme Court of Canada decision in the CTV appeal, where the
whole issue of free speech was curtly dealt with in one paragraph. [88]

Canadians presently have an opportunity to reassess their approach in light of the new constitutional guarantee of "freedom of
expression." Provincial film censorship is already before the Ontario courts, [89] not surprisingly in view of the attitude of the head of
the provincial Board of Censors. She recently announced that the
film medium "with disturbing consistency denigrates, ridicules and
attacks those values promoted in most families." These values include "a permanent commitment between a man and a woman in mar-
riage, the honoring of parents as well as respect for authority and
religion." She supported the banning of Pretty Baby and The Tin
Drum as examples of the "thin edge of the wedge—artistic presentations of young people's sexuality that open the door to less artistic
and more exploitative treatments."[90]

There will, no doubt, be concern that Canadian content requirements survive constitutional scrutiny as positive, general
statements that do not refer to particular programs. This may well
be possible because, having set out freedom of expression in absolute terms as a fundamental freedom, the charter provides that its
guarantees may be subject to "reasonable limits prescribed by law
as can be demonstrably justified in a free and democratic society."

A crucial and immediate question will be whether the condition
of license regulatory technique as upheld in the CTV case (prior to
the new constitutional guarantees) and so much emphasized in the
very recent policy statement on Canadian content (by the majority,
at least) will meet this test. So too should there be concern at the
prospect of scheduling and specific program type regulation. There
should be concern that Canada not allow its cultural development to
come at the expense of pervasive content censorship.

Canadians, however, should not be the only ones to reconsider
their position on freedom of speech, for rigid adherence to the free
flow doctrine is receiving little support internationally, and it may
well prove necessary for the United States to move away from its
absolutist position.[91] Perhaps the reason why Canada has been able
to make a significant contribution to the debate on international standards is because it does not start from too inflexible a notion of what
the ground rules should be in an international marketplace of ideas.

The Positive Contribution of Border Broadcasters
and the Role for Cable in the Proposed New
Canadian Broadcasting Strategy

There has been too little recognition of the role of the U.S.
border broadcasters in helping to develop the Canadian cable industry. As Paul W. Shaw has suggested:

[T]he ability to transmit U.S. network programs to
Canadian homes has been the sole, solid basis for the
tremendous growth development of Canada's cable television systems. United States signals are recognized
as the key attraction which most Canadian cable companies offer to their subscribers; Canadian viewers
prefer U.S. stations to their own when they are available. By using U.S. network programs as a sales
tool, the Canadians have been able to finance their
cable ventures at a relatively low cost because they
are not required to compensate the U.S. stations for
carrying their programs.[92]

Even if the attribution of "sole, solid basis" is exaggerated,
this is surely a perception that has to be kept in mind. It would be
especially ironic if the early maturity of the Canadian cable industry, made possible by the "contribution" of the U.S. border broadcasters, also gave Canadian companies the experience and capital
to later move into U.S. cable markets, which, in turn, has provoked
the Goldwater response. When the FCC's prohibition of distant signal importation by U.S. cable systems, at the insistence of U.S.
broadcasters, retarded the growth of U.S. cable firms and put them
at a disadvantage in competition with Canadian cable firms, the paradox was complete.

The cable industry in Canada has usually been cast in a negative light as the fragmenter of markets and destroyer of the logic of
local licenses. It is thus interesting to read in the latest Canadian
government policy statement that cable is now to be seen as the
means by which diversity and choice is to be brought to Canadian
homes, and, through an 8 percent subscriber tax, act as a new
source of support for local programming. In broad terms, the new
approach seems to envisage freer access and a greater diversity of
sources of programming, and, as a quid pro quo, a substantial contribution to a fund for indigenous programming. In short, if you
can't beat them, tax them!

The New National Broadcasting Policy of March 1, 1983, en-
visages that programming diversity will no longer be attained simply
by grabbing signals off the airwaves. "Preferably, the foreign signals would be repackaged to include Canadian material. If such an
approach proves unfeasible, cable licensees will be permitted to
distribute these signals—except for foreign pay television signals—
subject to regulatory approval, the conclusion of contractual agreements, and the pertinent international arrangements."[93] This will,
of course, place considerable pressure on Canadian and U.S. authorities to do something about resolving the present border dispute before

proceeding to deal with all the new services offered by burgeoning technology.

Draft versions of the new policy, which were widely leaked during 1982, had contained a candid discussion of the inevitability of conflict when the "gradualist, culturally sensitive approach" of the CRTC met the United States' "laissez-faire policies of de-regulation and the concept of 'free flow' of goods and services." At the same time, these drafts were positive about opportunities for Canadian access to U.S. markets in the new atmosphere of "contractual agreements."

> By opening the Canadian system to additional foreign suppliers, closer relationships can be expected to develop with export of Canadian material and joint production exchanges with many countries. Moreover, the rapid expansion of the demand for programming in other countries as new programming services develop, particularly in the USA, will provide new markets for the distribution of quality Canadian product. Based on 1979 figures, almost 1.5 million U.S. cable subscribers (or over 9% of total subscribers) already receive one or more Canadian off-air television signals and two popular CBC current affairs radio programs currently being distributed by the National Public Radio satellite network in the USA have been well received by the listeners. Accordingly, there is every reason to expect that with proper marketing efforts quality Canadian broadcast material will find its way into the many new U.S. markets being created by the proliferation of pay-and-advertising supported satellite/ cable TV systems and specialized networks. Because of the size of the U.S. market, the financial returns could well be significant—if sales of Canadian TV program material were to capture only one percent of the U.S. market, they would realize some $30 million annually. [94]

U.S. Policy

U.S. policy generally seeks to maximize the free flow of information and ideas and the free competition of goods and services. These objectives sometimes coincide and sometimes conflict. As applied to the border broadcasting dispute, these policies at first appear to coincide and argue for unfettered importation of U.S.

programming into Canada and for unfettered competition of border broadcasters for Canadian advertising revenue. Between these two concerns, competition and trade practice have received primary emphasis, reflecting the dominant role played by the border broadcasters, and specifically the Buffalo broadcasters, in the dispute. This section will first consider the arguments advanced by the border broadcast stations in their campaign to repeal Bill C-58 and then the U.S. policies, explicit and implicit, that underlie the border broadcasters' claims.

Intermarket Competition

The border broadcasters' position is:

Since Canadian viewers insist on receiving U.S. programming services, U.S. stations have a right to seek market place compensation for their programming. The U.S. has offered a series of compromises, including a proposal to contribute a portion of Canadian revenues to a Canadian program production fund. As long as Canada benefits from U.S. television signals, U.S. television stations should be able to sell advertising services in Canada free of discriminatory trade barriers.

In their petition under Section 301 of the United States Trade Act the border broadcasters charged that "Bill C-58 was discriminatory, unreasonable, unjustifiable and a burden or restriction on U.S. commerce within the meaning of Section 301." Section 301 was significantly amended in 1979 to redefine "commerce" so that the term would include services and so that broadcasting would be considered a form of commerce under the act.[95]

In arguing that Bill C-58 was "discriminatory," the border broadcasters relied on the fact that Bill C-58 differentiated between domestic Canadian broadcasters and non-Canadian broadcasters. The discrimination argument was based on the concept of "national treatment"; e.g., that Canada could not treat U.S. firms differently from domestic firms. "Most favored nation status," the alternative standard of international trade, would require only that Canada not treat U.S. firms differently from other foreign firms. In support of their contention that Bill C-58 was "unreasonable," the border broadcasters argued that (1) Canada should pay for the services it receives; (2) Canada unreasonably restricted trade in services; (3) the amount of money repatriated due to Bill C-58 would not be adequate to establish a domestic programming industry in Canada; and (4) it was unreasonable for Canada to act unilaterally through Bill

C-58 to solve a bilateral telecommunications problem. Finally, the border broadcasters argued that Bill C-58 was "unjustifiable" because it violated Canada's international obligations under the General Agreement on Tariffs and Trade (GATT).[96]

The border broadcasters' Section 301 petition rests on a number of questionable assumptions. First, accordance of "national treatment" typically depends on a bilateral Treaty of Friendship, Commerce, and Navigation, and Canada and the United States have not entered such a treaty. Moreover, it is arguable that even if an FCN treaty did exist between Canada and the United States, Bill C-58 would not violate the "national treatment" principle. Neither Canada nor the United States allows intermarket competition between broadcast stations domestically. It was precisely concern for local market fragmentation and the loss of local service that caused U.S. policy makers to restrain cable television development for a decade.[97] Canadian policy as embodied in Bill C-58 does not appear to differentiate between Canadian and U.S. firms. Surely Canada could amend its tax code to deter unauthorized domestic intermarket competition by Canadian stations. If so, restrictions on U.S. stations would be in conformity with "national treatment." It follows, of course, that the United States could also impose restrictions on Canadian broadcasters if necessary to protect U.S. broadcast markets.

The lack of intermarket competition in broadcasting makes it a unique service compared to such industries as insurance, management, and financial services. The uniqueness of broadcast services causes one to wonder whether it is a good first test case on which to stake the U.S. service industries' future international trade opportunities.

Second, the border broadcasters' reliance on the General Agreement on Tariffs and Trade is misplaced. Article I of the GATT obligates both countries to "most favored nation treatment," or nondiscrimination as between foreigners entitled to MFN treatment; Bill C-58, which applies equally to all foreign firms, would not be considered discriminatory under MFN principles. Article III of GATT does obligate both countries to provide "national treatment," but only to goods imported from the other.[98]

The most substantial of the border broadcasters' claims, and the one upheld by the Section 301 Committee, was that C-58 was unreasonable because, in effect, it "placed the cost of attaining its objectives of a stronger Canadian broadcast industry on U.S. companies. Thus, such an action by the Canadian Government unreasonably and unnecessarily burdened and restricted U.S. commerce." This claim is essentially a property right argument; as long as Canada makes use of the border broadcasters' signals, it must allow them compensation through the sale of advertising to Canadian firms. In further support of their argument, the border broadcasters point to the 1952 agreement between the United States and Canada, which allocated broadcast frequencies and transmitter power as a de facto authorization of their service in Canadian markets. They urge that to the extent the 1952 agreement accommodated the reception of U.S. signals in Canada, and U.S. signals have been accepted ever since, they have ripened a right to continue serving Canadian markets. The border broadcasters also point to the many cable franchises approved by the CRTC that contain large amounts of U.S. program product as further evidence of official sanction of their Canadian service. The U.S. broadcasters argue that whether their interest is designated a property right ripened by prescription over time or an informal license ripened by past service, their claim must be respected.

Beyond the questions of intermarket competition discussed above, this property right argument raises issues of program types covered by the claim and of implications for development of new technologies and distribution systems. We will return to a discussion of both of these issues in the third section of this chapter. For now it is sufficient to note that the property claim of the border broadcasters might be much stronger with respect to locally originated programming than syndicated and network programming, and that it might be possible to support the claims of the border broadcasters for compensation for past service as the technological gateways for distribution of U.S. programming in Canada without endorsing a claim of right to provide future service when many more gateways are open. The property rights claimed by the border broadcasters cannot be protected at the expense of perpetuating less technologically and economically efficient distribution systems.

Local Markets and Local Service

An appreciation of the relationship between regulatory public policy objectives and the limitation on competitive entry into local broadcast markets is the key to the border broadcasting dispute. It is surprising to find that the border broadcasters as the beneficiaries and the FCC as the promulgator of such domestic policies fail to appreciate the concerns raised by Canada about this relationship.

Both Canada and the United States seek to advance public policy objectives in television broadcasting through cross-subsidization of programming services and regulation of program content. Stations are permitted to earn additional profits in the distribution of the most commercially profitable programming in exchange for airing varying amounts and types of "merit programming," or programming relatively less profitable that by definition would not otherwise be presented. In the United States the merit programming is generally referred to as "local service programming," programs intended to treat the needs and interests of the local community of license; the subsidized programming comes largely from national network and off-network sources.[99]

This cross-subsidization of merit programming by commercially more profitable and more popular network programming is achieved through establishment of distinct broadcast markets and assignment of a limited number of station licenses within each local market. Continuation of the cross-subsidization and advancement of the public policy objectives depends on limiting competitive entry into local markets, since competition tends to force a station's advertising prices closer to its program costs, thereby reducing the profits available for cross-subsidization of merit program services. This limitation of competition in pursuit of public service objectives increases the price that must be charged advertisers to cover the less profitable, higher cost merit programming.[100] Where these increased costs cannot be fully passed on to advertisers they will be borne indirectly by a combination of station owners, program producers, cable operators, and consumers.

Regulatory choices of public policy have a ripple effect and entail real financial costs and benefits to a wide range of industry actors related vertically and horizontally to the immediate addresses of the policy. The interaction of political and economic interests is complicated in the international arena because the public policy objectives are of primarily domestic import while the financial costs and benefits are distributed internationally.

U.S. Domestic Deregulation

Broadcast deregulation in the United States, while much discussed, has thus far been implemented principally in the radio industry, where the number of stations has grown so large that competition for advertising and audiences can generally be relied on to reflect consumer preferences better than administrative decision making.[101] Although deregulation of television has been proposed, and some small steps regarding license terms and advertising limits have been taken, television is still subject to considerable content regulation.[102] Moreover, both radio and television continue to be responsible for the performance of duties under the fairness doctrine and the equal opportunities doctrine, which can only be lifted by congressional action.[103]

It is very doubtful that congressional abolition of the fairness and equal opportunities doctrines will be forthcoming in the near future, especially in television. First, abolition poses the risk to the political party out of power that it might be treated unfairly by the party in power: neither the Democrats nor the Republicans have in the past appeared willing to trust each other to provide politically impartial treatment in the absence of content regulation. Indeed, it might be argued that statutorily guaranteed political neutrality and a fair share of local service to the home constituents are the essential first steps in reaching legislative accord on broadcast policy in the United States.

Second, abolition of these content regulations poses First Amendment risks for broadcast stations. Although the fairness and equal opportunities doctrines are often criticized as chilling broadcasters' free expression, these doctrines also protect broadcasters from partisan political pressures. As long as broadcasters are dependent on government licenses for the privilege of operating, they will be vulnerable to political pressures and implied threats of license renewal problems.

Finally, the doctrines, especially the equal opportunities doctrine, have a wealth-equalizing effect. They serve to ensure broadcast coverage of ideas and candidates regardless of financial support. There is great concern in the United States today about the influence of wealth on the political process and the role of television in election campaigns. The abolition of the fairness and equal opportunities doctrines would conflict with these growing public concerns.

Public interest in the quality of television programming in the United States and its impact on the society also does not appear to have diminished in proportion to the availability of new channels and services. Obscene, indecent, defamatory, and inflammatory programming always arouse widespread concern and pressure for control within the United States.[104] Ironically, some of the staunchest free market proponents of deregulation are also the most demanding of content controls to protect moral and ethical values.

Deregulation of commercial broadcasting in the United States has rested to an important extent on the existence of public radio and television networks. It has been argued about both media that when market forces fail to satisfy important community needs and interests, public stations will stand ready to fill these gaps. The federal government's withdrawal from direct content regulation of broadcasting has in this sense been justified by its competitive entry into the industry. Government as a competitor has replaced government as a regulator.

Probably the most fundamental of the unresolved questions of U.S. deregulation reform is how the scarce frequency spectrum resources are to be awarded among competing applicants in the absence of the imposition of public interest obligations on licensees. At present, the renewal of licenses depends on some showing of local public service through programming. In the absence of some programming responsibility, how is one applicant to be preferred over another in the granting of the free broadcast license?

The FCC has yet to resolve this problem with respect to the deregulated radio licensees who have no specific public service responsibilities during the term of their license but who might be called to account for their public service performance if challenged in a comparative license hearing at renewal time.

The market solution to allocating licenses, of course, is to sell, lease, auction, or otherwise offer for use spectrum space to the highest bidder. Again ironically, many people who support reliance on a market model to govern the operation of the broadcast industry after licenses are granted are unwilling to accept a market model to govern competition among firms for licenses. Nonetheless, proposals have been made in the United States for some type of spectrum charge, the revenue from which would be available to underwrite public broadcasting operations.[105] Government as a regulator would be further replaced by government as a competitor. It can be argued that the influence of government on the U.S. broadcast media is enduring and that only the form of its involvement changes.

Finally, deregulation in the United States has caused a mounting tension between political claims of states' rights and economic claims of free competition. Telephone and cable structural deregulation have been accompanied by significant expansion of federal jurisdiction and preemption of state regulatory authority.[106] This conflict between the centralization of regulatory authority in pursuit of decentralized economic activity inherently limits deregulation reforms.

U.S. Free Flow Policy

The United States is the strongest supporter of the free flow of information in the world. It is also the world's largest exporter of television programming. The U.S. commitment to freedom of expression, however, should not be demeaned by its economic interests. The depth and breadth of U.S. protection of free expression domestically, from the publication of stolen Pentagon documents and the parade of swastikas in Skokie to the revelation of bare breasts and bomb secrets, may be as alien to Canadians as Canada's cultural imperatives are to Americans.[107] The First Amendment guarantee of free speech and press, while not absolute, is surely the least qualified and foremost of the fundamental freedoms in the

United States. As Judge Learned Hand has said, "To many this [free expression] is, and always will be, folly; but we staked upon it our all."[108]

Many officials in the United States are also deeply concerned about the threats to free expression in other parts of the world and about losing ground in a perceived battle between open and closed communications, and consequently political, systems. Many urge that the United States has a unique international responsibility to lead the cause of free speech and press throughout the world. However, U.S. advancement of the free flow principle must take into account foreign and domestic realities. First, the United States, as the largest contributor to the international flow of information and the largest exporter of television programming, is easily portrayed as serving domestic political and financial interests rather than as serving the cause of human rights.[109]

Second, the United States must be sensitive to the legitimate privacy and political concerns of other peoples. As in other areas of international human rights, the United States must inevitably distinguish spurious claims of political integrity designed to deprive people of information in order to perpetuate ruling elites and to suppress human rights from claims genuinely advanced for gradual, planned development of modern and culturally distinctive communications systems, some in societies only recently receiving telephone or electric service.[110] There is some inconsistency in the Reagan administration's insistence on a more relativistic human rights policy for undemocratic Central American countries and its insistence on an absolute freedom of foreign expression within Canada, a most democratic country.

Third, U.S. advancement of an uncompromised free flow of information internationally is at odds with domestic television regulation, which, as noted above, continues to be pervasive despite deregulation proposals.

U.S. Domestic and International Trade Policy

The U.S. retaliatory initiatives (nondeductibility of conference expenses incurred in Canada, limitations on investment in U.S. cable systems by Canadian companies, and restrictions on the import of Telidon videotext) are highly anticompetitive and would retard market forces in contradiction of current domestic deregulation reforms, which affirm and advance the role of competition in industrial development. One would think that these initiatives would pose particularly troublesome policy questions for a market-oriented administration. Whether the restrictions on trade and investment in telecommunications systems and services are initiated to advance domestic public policies or to retaliate against perceived foreign protective tariffs, the result is the same—decrease in consumer choices and increases in consumer prices.

These initiatives go beyond mirror legislation and seek a linkage between the border broadcasting dispute and other areas of trade in disregard of past practice and long-range self-interest. Modern telecommunications technology entails ever greater specialization of functions that defy established industry lines and national borders. The great reorganization of AT&T in the United States into vertically divisible operations to accommodate new technological possibilities is an example of the specialization imperative. [111] Both Canada and the United States have a stake in limiting the border broadcasting dispute and not allowing it to spread into other areas, causing further disruption and diseconomics.

A STRUCTURAL ANALYSIS OF THE BORDER BROADCAST DISPUTE

In this section, we consider the economic implications of the dispute on industry actors and how these actors relate to issues posed by border broadcasting. In the process, we draw important distinctions between available sources of programming and advertising. We suggest that these distinctions provide new opportunities for compromise between the two countries. Our analysis focuses on the Buffalo and Toronto markets because they have been of principal concern in the controversy.

Sources of Dispute: Different Conceptions of Culture and Competition

Under the U.S. market model of regulation, commercial broadcasters and networks are conceived of as sellers of an audience (the product) to advertisers (the consumers) through entertainment programming (the delivery vehicle). Under Canadian content regulation, commercial broadcasters and networks are conceived of as the delivery vehicles for Canadian cultural programming (the product) to audiences (the consumers) paid for through the sale of advertising. These different conceptions of broadcast service, however, have inherent limitations. Although the U.S. model places the interests of the advertiser first, the interests of the audience cannot be ignored by the stations or networks, since to do so would reduce audience size and revenues. Likewise, although the Canadian model places the cultural interests of the audience first, the stations and networks cannot ignore the interests of the advertisers, since to do so would reduce support for additional Canadian program service.

The Canadian program content requirements, in essence, mandate demand for Canadian program product without regard to its available supply and have disadvantaged Toronto broadcast stations in their competition with Buffalo stations. The higher costs of Canadian programming have forced the Toronto stations' price of advertising higher than the rates of the Buffalo stations, which are not subject, of course, to Canadian content requirements. This disadvantage is especially pronounced in network programming. As the Toronto stations raised their rates to cover the increased costs of Canadian content programming, more Canadian advertising revenue was diverted to the Buffalo stations and unavailable for support of Canadian program production. The alternative to raising advertising prices on the Toronto stations was to allow a drop in their profit margins. To the extent that profit reductions forced Toronto stations off the air, fewer outlets were available to stimulate development of Canadian program production in the short run and to distribute increased supply in the long run.

The competitive imbalance between the Buffalo and Toronto stations is much less in programming originally produced by these stations. The great economies of scale in network and syndicated programming are absent in local programming.

Sources of U.S. Programming

The Buffalo broadcast stations distribute three types of programming. First, they are responsible under U.S. law to serve the needs and interests of the Buffalo community through the original production of programs responsive to local concerns. [112] The cost of this locally originated programming is borne directly by the Buffalo stations and must be recovered from advertising revenues realized through direct "spot" sales of time on Buffalo stations to advertisers seeking to reach the local market.

Secondly, the Buffalo stations purchase off-network programming from syndication companies for local distribution. Off-network programming has an audience appeal beyond the local market and, therefore, requires negotiation of exclusive rights to markets between the broadcast stations and the syndication companies. The broadcast stations realize profits on the spread between the acquisition costs paid to the syndicator and the revenues from sales of time during and adjacent to the syndicated program's broadcast.

Finally, the Buffalo stations are network affiliates and distribute network programming in their market of license. Although the direct sales revenues of the Buffalo stations have declined over time, they continue to be larger than revenues realized from network program carriage. The stations are compensated by the networks in two ways for "clearing time" for network exhibition. First, the affiliates receive a cash payment, which generally reflects the size and hence the value of the affiliate's market, but that is far less than the price paid by advertisers buying time directly from the station, reflecting the fact that the costs and risks of the programming are borne by the network and not the station. Second, the affiliate is compensated in kind through the reservation of advertising time adjacent to network programs, which is available for direct sale by the affiliate to local and regional advertisers. [113]

These three types of programming may warrant different treatment. Locally produced programming that covers matters of public interest in Buffalo and, incidentally, Toronto, seems to deserve U.S. and Canadian advertising support, if enough intermarket advertising demand exists. Where a U.S. border broadcast station serves the needs and interests of a local Canadian market directly or indirectly, it seems just to allow recovery of these program costs through sale of advertising time to Canadian advertisers.

North-south locally originated service by U.S. border broadcasters advances the cultural objectives of Canada and the public interest objectives of the United States. The citizens of Buffalo and Toronto have a great deal in common, and Canadian concern for strong east-west domestic links and overdomination by its neighbor to the south cannot ignore the important regional north-south community connections. The U.S. objective of local public service is likewise fulfilled through local program origination. In addition, as will be discussed more fully later, locally produced programming does not pose the same competitive unfairness that Canada has alleged with network and off-network programming. The Buffalo stations enjoy no natural advantages in competing for Toronto advertising in conjunction with locally produced programming. Indeed, the Toronto market is bigger and wealthier than the Buffalo market and therefore has a stronger base over which to spread program production costs. In addition, Toronto stations have a much greater percentage of national advertisers than the Buffalo stations.

There is a limit, however, to the amount of such cross-border service a U.S. station can provide and hence Canadian advertising it can realize. The U.S. station is licensed exclusively to serve a U.S. market. Obviously, a license could not be issued by one country authorizing service in another. Therefore, when there is a difference between the needs and interests of the local U.S. market and the needs and interests of the local Canadian market, service by the border broadcast station aimed at the Canadian market would disserve its U.S. local market responsibility. KVOS, Bellingham, Washington, which has claimed exemplary and extensive service to the Vancouver market, might pose a tough license renewal question for the FCC, if challenged by an applicant promising to serve the Bellingham market only. On the other hand, KVOS's Vancouver revenues may allow it to provide services to the Bellingham market that could not be provided if the station served Bellingham exclusively. To the extent that regional service reinforces local service, both Canada and the United States should encourage its development and support joint production ventures.

Off-network programming is acquired from syndication companies for exclusive distribution within a specified market.[114] The Buffalo broadcasters have asserted that they have a right to earn a return in the Toronto market on their investment in syndicated off-network programming because they purchase, in essence, Toronto distribution rights when they acquire such programming. The Buffalo broadcasters do not claim to have legally enforceable exclusive distribution rights in the Toronto market for off-network programming. Rather, they assert that the syndication companies, knowing that the Buffalo stations have a significant Toronto viewership, take this increased audience and potential advertising revenue into account in setting prices for distribution rights in the Buffalo market. Unlike the Bellingham-Vancouver market, syndicated programming is sold separately in the Buffalo and Toronto markets. If the Buffalo stations do pay a syndication premium, therefore, it is not for exclusive rights, but for first-run rights, and the service they provide is alternative program time availability. The critical question is the amount of the premium paid by the Buffalo stations due to the Toronto market. If the Buffalo broadcasters are not required to purchase the Toronto market together with the Buffalo market, or the Toronto market is separately licensed by the syndication company, the Buffalo stations would have no complaints, any more than they could complain about separate syndication rights in Rochester or Syracuse.

The Buffalo broadcasters have also urged that they have a right to realize revenues from the distribution of U.S. network programming in the Toronto market through the sale of advertising to Canadian firms. They argue that as network affiliates they own the distribution rights in this intermarket area and that when network programming has contributed to the development of cable and broadcast facilities in Canada they should be compensated for this contribution. Interference with this right to distribute network programming through commercial deletions or withdrawal of tax deductions is claimed to be an infringement of the Buffalo broadcasters' copy-rights and a deprivation of their property rights.

However, the Buffalo stations also claim, somewhat inconsistently, that they are not paid a premium by the networks for delivery of the Toronto market because national advertisers will not pay additional money for this small, incremental increase in audience above the national U.S. market. Apparently, when Buffalo stations receive no additional cash compensation for delivery of the Toronto audience, they are indifferent about network distribution rights. This may not be the case, however, because of the in-kind payments made by the networks to the affiliates in the form of advertising time available adjacent to the network programming and available for direct sale by the affiliate. Regional advertisers purchasing time directly from the affiliates, unlike national advertisers purchasing time from the networks, would be more likely to pay a premium for the Toronto audience.

When advertisers are unwilling to spend additional sums to reach the Toronto audience or networks are unwilling to value these additional program exposures, U.S. program producers are under-compensated. U.S. program product is attracting viewers that are not being fully valued by the advertisers or the broadcast networks. This failure fully to value Canadian audiences will become more important as competition among program services increases. As with syndicated programming, the Buffalo stations could not complain if the networks arranged alternative distribution systems for Canadian markets. The Buffalo stations have admitted as much in accepting simulcasting of network programming by Toronto broadcast stations.

In summary, it seems that the claim of the Buffalo stations to realize revenues from the Toronto market is strongest for locally produced programming when it is of interest in the Toronto market and does not entail sacrifice of service in the Buffalo market, and is weakest for syndicated and network programming. When direct distribution by networks and syndicators allows for more accurate pricing of program product and advertising time it should be preferred over the less economically efficient indirect distribution.

Sources of Advertising Support

Just as the type of programming must be separately considered so must the sources of advertising support. Advertisers will be unevenly affected by the flow of programming from Buffalo into Toronto depending on whether they seek to reach predominantly local, regional, national, or multinational audiences. In essence, the export of Buffalo programming into the Toronto market has caused a merger of these advertising markets and created new cost-benefit possibilities for all Canadian and U.S. advertisers.

Regional advertisers interested in reaching both the Buffalo and Toronto markets are benefited most by the Buffalo competition and increase in supply of advertising time. These advertisers can buy both markets for one price and do not have to value separately the Buffalo and Toronto audiences. The price at which the Buffalo stations will sell time to regional advertisers will be a function of the supply of and demand for time in both markets. The greater the scarcity of time on the Toronto stations the higher the Buffalo station price can be set; the greater the surplus of time available on the Buffalo stations the lower the price will be set. The Buffalo stations will not price their time for regional advertisers below the price at which they could sell time to purely local advertisers, nor above the price at which regional advertisers can purchase time on Toronto stations. However, when Buffalo station programming is more popular than Toronto station programming, the Buffalo stations will be able to charge a higher price or pass profits on to the advertisers in the form of price discounts.

Local advertisers interested in reaching only the Buffalo or Toronto audience will be affected differently. Local Toronto advertisers may benefit when purchase of time by Canadian regional advertisers on Buffalo stations reduces demand for and price of time on Toronto stations. The greater the availability of time on the Toronto stations the less the cost to local Toronto advertisers of reaching the Toronto audience. However, over 80 percent of the Toronto stations' advertising revenue comes from national advertisers, which more than offsets the price reductions due to regional advertisers switching to Buffalo stations, and may account for such switches. The same savings may not exist for local Buffalo advertisers interested in reaching only the Buffalo audience. When there is increased demand for time on the Buffalo stations from Canadian regional advertisers, the price of time will rise and local Buffalo advertisers will be increasingly unable or unwilling to pay this increased price for a Toronto audience they do not seek to reach. The most suitable programming for local Buffalo advertisers is locally originated programming. However, when locally originated programming attracts Toronto viewers, local Buffalo advertisers will have to compete with regional advertisers for time, and the cost of reaching the Buffalo audience will be increased. If the programming does not attract Toronto viewers the price of the time still might increase because of displacement of local advertising by regional advertising in other time slots and the resulting concentration of local advertising demand at the few points in the day when purely local Buffalo programming is available.

National advertisers appear to be the least affected by inter-market competition. National U.S. advertisers interested in reaching the Buffalo market as part of a national U.S. exposure may be indifferent, as the Buffalo stations claim, to the Toronto audience. And national Canadian advertisers, the largest of which is the Canadian government, may be indifferent to the Buffalo audience. National advertisers generally will not realize the benefits of intermarket competition until there is enough of an increase in the number of outlets to create new networks and greater availability of national time.

Multinational advertisers also seem indifferent about inter-market competition between Buffalo and Toronto broadcast stations. Multinational advertisers interested in reaching both Buffalo and Toronto audiences as part of U.S. and Canadian national market exposure would in the short run be unaffected by whether these national audiences are sold together or separately. As with national network advertisers, the multinational advertisers are not affected by increased local intermarket competition until this competition is sufficiently widespread so that additional multinational outlets become available. When multinational advertisers, for example, oil companies, do have a choice of reaching the Canadian market through Canadian or U.S. networks, their choice will depend on the cost per viewer exposure of a separate or single purchase. When U.S. networks do not separately value Canadian audiences and the purchase of U.S. network exposure automatically includes Canadian audience exposure, the multinational advertisers will always choose the single, U.S. network purchase. There can be no true competition between U.S. and Canadian networks for multinational advertisers because Canadian networks cannot deliver significant U.S. audiences. The purchase of U.S. network time gives the multinational advertiser the national Canadian audience for free, whereas the purchase of Canadian network time, no matter how high the price, could not give the multinational advertiser the U.S. national market. Even at a zero price for Canadian network time, multinational advertisers would be indifferent about whether they bought U.S. or Canadian time. Canadian networks must rely on Canadian national advertisers who do not care about U.S. audiences and are interested solely in Canadian audiences.

This competitive advantage of U.S. networks in competition for multinational advertising can be viewed in two different ways. On the one hand, this advantage may be viewed as a result of the lower marginal costs of the U.S. networks. Once the U.S. networks have acquired national exhibition rights for programming and established sales divisions, their costs are not increased by additional sales of advertising time to firms interested in reaching Canadian audiences. These low marginal costs are inherent in the greater U.S. audience base, over which the networks' program and sales costs can be spread. On the other hand, this advantage may be viewed as the result of inefficient and anticompetitive U.S. network pricing. The U.S. networks' failure to value the Canadian audience separately and thereby offer it as a bonus to all network advertisers comes at the expense of financial interests vertically related to the networks in the distribution chain. The costs of this lost program or advertising exposure will be borne by other firms in the industry and ultimately by copyright holders, who will not be fully compensated for the total number of exposures of their copyrighted programs. Indeed, the increase in direct studio and syndication sales in Canada and the reservation of Canadian exhibition rights in network contracts is a market reaction to this undercompensation.

U.S. policy should acknowledge the inefficiencies of the present distribution system and explore new means of distributing U.S. programming in Canada with careful attention to distinctions between available advertising bases. Likewise, Canadian policy should acknowledge the obstacles and opportunities posed by regional and multinational advertising. While regional advertising revenue might be repatriated at some cost to local Canadian advertisers, multinational advertising revenue cannot be repatriated without commercial deletion. Canada's choice, then, is to accept U.S.-placed multinational advertising and obtain U.S. network service free or to delete U.S.-placed multinational advertising and pay royalties to copyright holders, financed either through the sale of stripped time to multinational and national advertisers forced to buy the Canadian market separately or through a viewer fee of some sort.

The Tiering of U.S. Programming
on Canadian Cable Systems

The latest Canadian proposal for dealing with the border broadcasting dispute appears to involve a tiering of cable services between Canadian and U.S. programs and a flat tax on all cable subscriber revenues. Under the tiering proposal, U.S. programming would, in effect, become compulsory pay cable programming, and subscribers desiring U.S. programs would be required to pay an additional charge beyond that levied for the basic service package, consisting solely of Canadian content programming. These additional charges for U.S. programming would presumably be paid as royalties to U.S. copyright holders, and commercial advertising in conjunction with this programming would be deleted. The flat rate tax on cable subscriber revenues, somewhere around 8 percent, would be used to subsidize Canadian program production.

The tiering proposal provides Canada a number of benefits. It does not eliminate U.S. programming; quite the contrary, for the first time it expressly embraces U.S. programming as part of diversified Canadian broadcast services. Tiering does, however, improve the competitive position of Canadian programming by making it less costly to the cable subscriber than U.S. programming. The stripping of U.S. commercial messages also benefits Canadian broadcast stations by forcing advertisers desiring to reach Canadian audiences to use Canadian outlets and buy Canadian market exposures separately. Finally, the tiering proposal provides Canada with a response to the piracy charges often leveled against Canada by the Buffalo broadcast stations. Unlike the commercial deletion policy, under which program producers received no compensation for Canadian program exposures, the tiering policy provides for the collection of royalties with which to compensate U.S. copyright holders.

By passing these royalties on to the studio program producers in the United States, the compulsory compensation scheme, while honorable on Canada's behalf, appears to undercut its essential purpose—to improve the financial position of the Canadian program production industry relative to the United States. The marginal increase in viewers of Canadian programs due to the Canadian-U.S. price differential would be achieved at the expense of increased revenues to U.S. studio program producers. These royalty payments would be used to make U.S. programming still better and more competitive in Canadian markets.

The proposal is unclear about whether the royalties would be paid to the studio production companies directly or to the networks. If commercial advertising is deleted from the programming, payment to the networks would not make sense. More likely, studio producers would reserve Canadian exhibition rights in their network sale contracts. This might require the networks likewise to limit the distribution rights of their affiliates.

The tiering plan, however, has critical technological and economic limitations. It depends first and foremost on Canadian control over the entry of U.S. programming into Canada. Tiering envisions this control as coming through the CRTC's regulation of cable programming and conditions of license. If the price of the compulsory pay U.S. program package is set too high, viewers will bypass the cable system through the reinstallation of antennas providing for direct over-the-air reception from U.S. border stations. This would undermine the goal of making Canadian programming more competitive with U.S. programming, since, for direct reception viewers, the U.S. programming would now be free whereas the Canadian programming on the cable would cost the price of the basic cable service package. Having installed an antenna for U.S. programming, some viewers may decide to avoid the cost of cable for Canadian programming as well and disconnect from the cable system altogether.

In addition, any separate charge for U.S. programming is likely to be unpopular with Canadians. They have long been accustomed to "free" U.S. network programming, first over the air and then as part of the basic cable package. Forcing people to pay for what they once received free is extremely difficult. Nor is it likely that the Canadian public will be satisfied with the explanation that the payments are for royalties to U.S. firms, which may not have demanded royalty payments, or for the freedom from commercial interruptions. To offset the royalty payments, advertising time would probably be sold in the stripped time slots. Under these circumstances, Canadians would be paying for programming and also be subject to commercial advertising. Nor could this cable advertising revenue be used to reduce the compulsory pay cable charge for U.S. programming, since to do so would restore parity in Canadian and U.S. program prices.

Direct Network Distribution

Another possible distribution system would be direct network feeds from U.S. studios to Canadian cable systems' head ends via Canadian satellites. (Although direct distribution is also possible for original studio and syndicated programming, this section will consider only direct network distribution.) Under this scheme, the U.S. networks would bypass their border affiliates, and network programming, without commercial deletion, would be distributed directly to Canadian markets. The direct distribution scheme has advantages and disadvantages for Canada.

The first advantage would be Canada's security against bypass of its gateway control over the entry of U.S. network programming via over-the-air reception. Since the networks would have direct access to Canadian markets, they would not need to rely on distribution of their programming by border affiliates; nor would they have an incentive to bypass the Canadian cable systems through the U.S. direct broadcast satellite (DBS) transmission. DBS transmission would not provide a greater audience and might be much more expensive than Canadian cable distribution.

If the border broadcasters were to jam their network signals going into Canada, Canadian control of the most significant source of U.S. programming would be complete. The networks would, in turn, achieve what is, after all, their essential purpose—the organization of audiences for advertisers. Canada has the power to

provide incentives for border broadcasters to cooperate in the direct
network distribution system through selective application of Bill
C-58 to locally originated programming.

Under the direct network distribution scheme, multinational
advertisers would probably continue to buy time from U.S. networks;
hence Canada would not realize the revenues it otherwise would if it
stripped all U.S. commercials and required separate U.S. and Canadian buys. The advantage to Canada, however, would be that it
would not have to pay royalties to copyright holders, thereby avoid-
ing the necessity of charging its citizens for services that were formerly free.

Furthermore, Canada would not have to worry about the drain
of advertising revenue from regional Toronto advertisers to Buffalo
broadcast stations. It would be far too expensive for a Toronto regional advertiser to buy national network time to reach the Toronto
audience. Since the Buffalo stations would no longer distribute the
highly popular network programming in the Toronto market, Toronto
advertisers would be far more inclined to buy time on Toronto stations to reach Toronto audiences. This might even allow for repeal
of Bill C-58 and a lessening of pressures in the United States for
retaliatory legislation. Additional revenue could be realized for
support of Canadian program production if cable systems sold directly the program "adjacencies" that the networks leave open for their
affiliates. As applied to Canadian cable systems, these in-kind
transfers would operate in a sense as an access charge paid by the
networks to reach subscribers to the cable system.

The direct distribution scheme also benefits the U.S. networks.
The Canadian national market of 25 million persons, which was previously thrown away or grossly undervalued, would be organized.
The U.S. networks could offer separate Canadian and U.S. national
audiences to advertisers. This Canadian national audience would
become increasingly attractive as new program services further
fragment existing markets. Direct distribution does not violate U.S.
free flow policy. The free flow principle is content-oriented and
concerned with the free exchange of information, not the manner or
means whereby this exchange occurs. The U.S. free flow policy can
be implemented through a number of different distribution systems.
One would expect free flow policy to embrace new technologies and
distribution systems in order to enhance the flow of information
rather than staking its objectives on a single distribution system
existing at any particular time.

An important element of the border broadcasting problem has
always been the demographic difference between the United States
and Canada. As noted earlier, the U.S. market is roughly ten times
the size of the Canadian market, and the great majority of Canadians

live along the Canada-U.S. border within direct reception of U.S. border broadcast signals. It has been widely assumed that these differences in population size and geographic distribution are immutable factors favoring the United States, and that the greater audience base and per capita advertising expenditures in the United States have resulted in more expensive, technically higher quality programming that enjoys an overwhelming competitive advantage over Canadian programming.

Satellite technology will obliterate these demographic distinctions. The key figure in determining the amount of program production costs is not the absolute size of the population reachable, but the percentage of the population probably obtainable. This, in turn, is a function of the number of channels or outlets in the market competing for available viewers. The initiation in the near future of a host of new national satellite services in the United States, as part of the FCC's deregulation reforms, will greatly alter the channel-per-capita calculation between the United States and Canada. [115] This change in the channel-per-capita figures, coupled with the equalization of program access through direct broadcast and fixed service satellites, will create competition for smaller, specialty audience markets that transcend national borders. The Canadian market will become increasingly important to the U.S. networks, and Canadian programming will become more competitive (at least in production costs) with U.S. programming.

Satellite technology and interactive telecommunications systems will make it ever more difficult for either Canada or the United States to control unilaterally transborder television programming. In the coming era of fiber optic cable and computer connections through integrated systems digital networks, consumer choices will greatly increase, as will the need for government cooperation and coordination. Only a deliberate retardation of telecommunications technology development, which clearly neither the United States nor Canada would contemplate, will stop the burgeoning demand for television entertainment program services. The question is not whether but only how this demand will be satisfied.

CONCLUSION

Our analysis in the first part of the chapter has led us to conclude that although there are fundamental differences between Canadian and U.S. communications policies, there are also important similarities that have been obscured by cultural and commercial absolutism on both sides of the border. The review of the development of the border broadcast dispute suggests that both the United

States and Canada have reacted to short-term private pressures in disregard of their long-term common interests and have allowed events to escalate rather than acting to control and contain the disagreement. Fortunately, there is still time for reason to prevail and for the damages caused by the dispute to be mitigated. This may not be possible after the new generation of technologies, especially satellites, is introduced or after new protectionist practices are adopted.

Initial decisions on the implementation of new communications technologies have enduring importance, sometimes long surviving their initial rationale. Increasingly complex economic, institutional, and technical arrangements build and depend on these initial decisions, which, in turn, limit future policy options and institutional arrangements. The same durability is evident in protectionist measures as domestic firms reorganize their operations to account for new cost-benefit possibilities resulting from the altered trade rules. Changes become increasingly difficult as industry interests become increasingly vested.

Although our discussion has concentrated on the Canadian-U.S. communications relationship, we cannot ignore the temper of the times. It would be naive to believe that what is happening in this one area will not influence and be influenced by other developments. However, it would be unwise to rush headlong from the myopic and solipsistic to too general a concern about trade relations. A balance will have to be sought between the two extremes that will allow us to maintain a sense of particular concern and to engage in issue-specific analysis without overlooking the significance of broader developments, be they at the macro level of energy policy and foreign investment or the micro level of stumpage rates, trucking licenses, New York City subway cars, and fishing rights, as well, of course, as investment in cable companies, advertising revenue, and the flow of information across national boundaries.

In the second section, we considered conflicts within and constraints on Canadian and U.S. domestic communications policies to determine whether common bases existed on which to build toward reconciliation of their respective international broadcast policies. We found a number of areas of common concern related generally to continued attention in the United States to television program content and public service (despite the deregulation movement) and in Canada to continued attention to private broadcast station and cable system profitability (despite rigorous anticommercial and cultural objectives). The most important area of common concern we identified (indeed, we suggest the critical common denominator of both Canadian and U.S. broadcast systems) is localism, or regulation that defines the broadcasters' service responsibilities primarily with reference to the city or metropolitan area of license.

The commercial broadcast systems in both Canada and the United States are based on local service and local broadcast advertising markets. The fragmentation of major Canadian local markets by smaller market U.S. broadcasters is an important element of the border broadcase dispute, and we find it ironic that U.S. broadcasters who have so long led the fight for localism domestically and against new services and technologies fail to appreciate the threats to localism in Canada.

Localism in Canadian and U.S. policy is important to our analysis at two points. First, when localism has necessitated prohibitions on intermarket competition, both Canada and the United States have adopted domestic measures designed to deter distant market penetration that threatened local market service. Adoption of such measures by either country to deter penetration of their local markets by foreign stations would, therefore, not treat the foreign firms differently than each country has treated its domestic stations. "National treatment" is critical to the U.S. broadcasters' Section 301 claim, and localism is central to this issue.

Second, the principle of localism makes broadcast services very different from management, financial, insurance, and other professional and lay services. The lack of intermarket competition in broadcast services, compared to the relatively unlimited intermarket competition in these other services, has caused us to question whether the border broadcast dispute is a good first test case on which the United States and Canada should determine future policies on international trade in services. At a minimum, before the border broadcasters' Section 301 petition becomes the symbolic cause célèbre for all service industries, the distinction between broadcasting and other services must be explicitly recognized, lest the welfare of the other service industries be disserved due to their representation by dissimilar interests.

Finally, in the third section we analyze the border broadcast dispute from a structural perspective and distinguish sources of programming, sources of advertising, and alternative transborder delivery systems. Localism is also important to our structural analysis and proposals.

We identify as the principal structural problem in the dispute the exportation of U.S. network programming by border broadcast station affiliates into Canadian markets. Even Toronto, Canada's largest and most affluent broadcast market, is vulnerable to the threat of affiliate-distributed network programming. Since U.S. network program costs can be divided over a population base ten times as large as Canada, Toronto stations are at a serious competitive disadvantage in competing for local advertising revenue with locally produced programming against affiliate-distributed network programming. The Canadian content requirements have exacerbated this competitive disadvantage, and the result has been a significant loss of advertising revenue to U.S. border broadcast stations.

We offer two proposals to deal with this problem that we believe are supportable on grounds of economic and technical efficiency. First, we suggest that restrictions, such as C-58, not apply to programming produced by U.S. border broadcast stations. The full costs of locally originated programming are borne by the border broadcast stations and can only be spread over the local population base. Therefore, the border broadcasters in the smaller U.S. markets enjoy no natural competitive advantage over the private broadcast stations in the larger Canadian markets. In addition, we suggest that programming locally produced on either side of the border that serves the needs and interests of U.S. and Canadian audiences is consistent with the basic policy objectives of both the United States and Canada and should, therefore, be encouraged. We suggest also that special incentives be considered to stimulate joint U.S.-Canadian local production in service of north-south regional needs and interests.

Second, we propose that network programming be distributed directly to Canada via Canadian satellite links to Canadian cable system head ends. We suggest that direct distribution is more technologically efficient than indirect affiliate distribution and has advantages for both Canada and the United States. Direct network distribution would provide Canada gateway control of the most important source of U.S. programming and would eliminate the problem of network affiliates' capture of regional advertising through distribution of network programming. It would simply be too expensive for a Canadian regional advertiser to buy time on a U.S. national network to reach a local, or regional, Canadian audience. Gateway control of U.S. network programming would also provide Canada with additional options on national and multinational advertising. Direct network distribution does not appear to entail significant losses of revenue to border broadcast affiliates. The Buffalo affiliates have frequently asserted that the networks do not presently compensate them for their Toronto audience.

Finally, we suggest that direct distribution has advantages for U.S. program producers and networks. When the U.S. networks do not fully value program exposures in Canada, U.S. program producers are undercompensated. Direct distribution would account for Canadian exhibitions and correct this undercompensation. The U.S. networks would be able to organize the Canadian market through direct distribution and to offer national and multinational advertisers either or both the U.S. and Canadian markets at prices reflecting their true values. We suggest that the Canadian market will become increasingly important to the U.S. networks as new national services are established in the United States under deregulation. Likewise, we suggest that Canadian programming will become increasingly competitive as the national channel-per-population calculation changes and new U.S. services create additional demand for available program product supply.

We certainly do not expect our proposals to be broadly embraced by all affected parties. They are, after all, compromises and therefore cannot fully satisfy every interest. We do hope, however, that they will provide a starting point for further discussion and break the present stalemate in negotiations.

For better or for worse, Canada and the United States will forever share a common border and a common future. The question before these two great nations is whether they will stand together or apart at the threshold of the new information era.

NOTES

We are deeply grateful to Richard Austin (LL.B. University of Toronto, 1983) for his very competent research assistance in the preparation of this paper. His diligence, patience, and good humor greatly facilitated our task.

1. A valuable initial perspective may be found in the history of developments in the two countries. Consider Erik Barnouw, A Tower in Babel, A History of Broadcasting in the United States, Vol. 1—to 1933, New York, Oxford University Press, 1966; The Golden Web, A History of Broadcasting in the United States, Vol. II— 1933 to 1953, New York, Oxford University Press, 1968; The Image Empire, A History of Broadcasting in the United States, Vol. III— from 1953, New York, Oxford University Press, 1970; and Frank W. Peers, The Politics of Canadian Broadcasting 1920-1951, Toronto, University of Toronto Press, 1969; The Public Eye: Television and the Politics of Canadian Broadcasting 1952-1968, Toronto, University of Toronto Press, 1979.

A useful shorter history from a policy perspective may be found in David Ellis, Evolution of the Canadian Broadcasting System: Objectives and Realities, 1928-1968, Ottawa, Minister of Supply and Services Canada, 1979. For an insightful view of the political dynamics of the American system, see Erwin G. Krasnow, Lawrence D. Longley, and Herbert A. Terry, The Politics of Broadcast Regulation, 3rd ed., New York, St. Martin's Press, 1982.

2. Quoted in Peers, The Public Eye, above, note 1, at p. 29. Emphasis added.

3. Robert E. Babe, Canadian Television Broadcasting Structure, Performance and Regulation, Ottawa, Minister of Supply and Services Canada, 1979, pp. 123-24. This was a study prepared for the Economic Council of Canada. And see Babe, Cable Television and Telecommunications in Canada: An Economic Analysis, East Lansing, Mich., MSU International Business and Economic Studies, 1975.

4. Babe, Canadian Television Broadcasting Structures, above, note 3, at p. 124.

For an overview of the growth of cable TV and the regulatory response, see the following studies by the Canadian Radio-Television Commission (CRTC): Cable Television in Canada, 1971; Cable Television and Its Regulation: A Critical Analysis, 1973; and Policies Respecting Broadcasting Receiving Undertakings (Cable TV), 1975.

5. Broadcasting Act, R.S.C. 1970, c. B-11.

6. CRTC Public Announcement, The Improvement and Development of Canadian Broadcasting and the Extension of U.S. Television Coverage in Canada by CATV, Ottawa, Dec. 3, 1969, p. 1. An earlier policy statement, Community Antenna Television, Ottawa, May 13, 1969, had not made any mention of carriage of U.S. stations and had indicated that no alteration of programming would be permitted but that cable must complement and not compete with off-air broadcasters.

7. P. M. Mahoney, M.P., Commons Debates, January 13, 1970, p. 2350. Significantly, the minister responsible for the CRTC, after initially indicating that the government might take direct responsibility for this stand (ibid., December 4, 1969, p. 1587) a week later indicated that because this was a rejection of a license application, the government could not intervene (ibid., December 10, 1968, pp. 1822-23). This "hands off" position was to be reiterated (ibid., December 10, 1968, pp. 2092-93; January 12, 1970, p. 2222).

This whole issue of the role of independent regulatory agencies such as the CRTC in the Canadian parliamentary system of government, and the legitimacy of agency policy initiatives, remains unresolved. Consider H. N. Janisch, "Policy Making in Regulation: Towards a New Definition of the Status of Independent Regulatory Agencies in Canada," 17 Osgoode Hall L.J. 46-106 (1979). It should be noted that the latest government policy document, Towards a New National Broadcasting Policy, Ottawa, Minister of Supply and Services Canada, 1983, asserts that the "fundamental policy-making role" belongs directly to government and should be effected by way of binding policy directions issued by the cabinet. This is, of course, also an American problem, with the latest in a long line of proposals to curb "the headless fourth branch of government" being the American Bar Association, Commission on Law and the Economy, Federal Regulation: Roads to Reform, Chicago, ABA, 1979, especially chap. V, "The Need for a Balancing Process," pp. 68-91.

For instances where this issue was dragged into the international arena, see below, note 41, and into the national arena, notes 20 and 74.

8. CRTC Public Announcement, Guidelines for Applicants Regarding Licences to Carry on CATV Undertakings, Ottawa, April 10, 1970, p. 2.

9. Ibid., p. 4.

10. CRTC Public Announcement, The Integration of Cable Television in the Canadian Broadcasting System, Ottawa, February 26, 1971.

11. Ibid., p. 2.

12. Ibid., p. 5.

13. Ibid., p. 6.

14. CRTC Policy Statement, Cable Television: Canadian Broadcasting 'A Single System,' Ottawa, July 16, 1971. The title comes from the Broadcasting Act (above, note 5) declaration that all broadcast undertakings "constitute a single system . . . the Canadian broadcasting system. . . ."

15. Ibid., p. 20.

16. Ibid., p. 21. Emphasis in the original.

17. Ibid., p. 23. This inconsistency between the way in which American and Canadian programming would be treated was seen as most disturbing by one commentator, Peter W. Johansen, "The Canadian Radio Television Commission and the Canadianization of Broadcasting," 28 Fed. Comm. Bar J. 183 (1973), but as quite natural by another, Wanda Noel, "Should Cable Systems Pay Copyright Royalties," 12 Ottawa L. Rev. 195 (1980).

18. Ibid.

19. Ibid., p. 10.

20. Ibid. It is interesting to note that the commission sought to deflect any criticism as to its institutional competence to make communication policy (above, note 7) by baldly stating at the very outset of the policy document, "The basis of a Canadian cable television policy has already been established by Parliament in the Broadcasting Act three years ago. It is not to be established by the CRTC." Ibid., p. 2. One is reminded, notwithstanding this disclaimer, of Peter Woll's perceptive insight, "Policy implementation is always in the hands of administrative agencies, and it is through implementation that policy is really shaped." Administrative Bureaucracy, 2nd ed., New York, W. W. Norton, 1977, p. 7.

21. Ibid., pp. 14-15.
22. Ibid., pp. 27-28.
23. Ibid., p. 28. The commission made it very clear that only expense and not any concern of principle dictated this course, rather than a requirement that there be commercial deletion.
24. Ibid., p. 29.
25. Decision CRTC 72-364, December 21, 1972.
26. For an excellent account of these developments, see Katherine Swinton, "Advertising and Canadian Cable Television—A Problem in International Communications Law," 15 Osgoode Hall L.J. 543 at 569-77 (1977).
27. Capital Cities Communications Inc. v. Canadian Radio-Television Commission, [1978] 2 S.C.R. 141.
28. See CRTC Public Announcement, Commercial Deletion, Ottawa, January 21, 1977.
29. Above, note 24.
30. As the report bluntly put it, "Extend the provisions of Section 12A to cover the placement of advertising on American-owned broadcasting stations. This will curb the pirating of commercial dollars by stations just across the border which accept Canadian money but don't play by Canadian rules." The Uncertain Mirror, Report of the Special Senate Committee on Mass Media, Volume I, Ottawa, Queen's Printer for Canada, 1970, p. 256. The Special Senate Committee was presided over by Senator Keith Davey.
31. Commons Debates, October 8, 1974, p. 204.
32. Bill C-58, An Act to Amend the Income Tax Act, First reading, April 18, 1975.
33. Commons Debates, May 8, 1975, p. 5596.
34. Ibid., November 17, 1975, p. 9117.
35. Ibid., p. 9118.
36. For an account of this meeting, see a letter from Harry J. Boyle and Michael Shoemaker of the CRTC to Senator Keith Davey in Proceedings of the Senate Banking, Trade and Commerce Committee, 91:53-54, June 10, 1976. Further details are contained in appendixes to these proceedings, ibid., 93:23-28.
37. See Proceedings of the House of Commons Standing Committee on Broadcasting, Films and Assistance to the Arts, December 1, 1975, 29:10-12.
38. Ibid., 29:11.
39. See Proceedings of the Senate Banking, Trade and Commerce Committee, 91:6-8, June 9, 1976. As Leslie Arries, president of WBEN Inc., put it: "I have been working on behalf of my company for almost three years to discuss this problem, the total border broadcast problem, with the Canadian government or agencies of the Canadian government. It was not until we made an

appearance before the House of Commons Committee, a short time ago, that we had a chance to bring our case to anybody officially in Canada." He did, however, concede that there had been a meeting with a representative of the CRTC (above, note 36) but he was particularly upset that he had not been able to meet directly with Jeanne Sauve, minister of communications.

40. Swinton, "Advertising and Canadian Cable Television," above, note 26 at 579.

41. This cavalier disclaimer of responsibility was not well received by the U.S. authorities. "The feelings of the State Department are best summed up by one official who said of this reply, 'Nuts! How would it look if our State Department said it couldn't talk to the FCC about a problem?'" Bryce H. Pettey and Edward Allebes, "Resurgence of Canadian Nationalism and Its Effect on American-Canadian Communications Relations," 9 J. Int. L. & Econ., 149 at 167 (1974).

42. In an effort to develop a coherent approach to international telecommunications, Ambassador Diana Lady Dougan has recently been appointed to a new coordinating office. She spoke briefly at the 11th Annual Telecommunications Policy Research Conference, Annapolis, Md., April 27, 1983.

43. Swinton, above, note 26 at 580.

44. Ibid., pp. 581-82. And see Caroline D. Asher, "Purging Madison Avenue from Canadian Television II," 9 L. & Pol'y Int'l Bus. at 1023-26 (1977).

45. Above, note 28.

46. For a good overview, see Andrew L. Stoler, "The Border Broadcast Dispute: A Unique Case Under Section 301," 6 Int'l Trade L.J. 39 (1981).

47. Ibid., p. 48, note 41.

48. Ibid., p. 50, note 50.

49. Ibid., pp. 51-53.

50. Presidential Message to the Congress of the United States of Sept. 11, 1980.

51. Presidential Message to the Congress of the United States of Nov. 17, 1981.

52. See, particularly, a speech by Philip B. Lind of Rogers Cablesystems Inc., "Canada-U.S. Border Dispute Over Television Advertising," Canadian-American Committee Meeting, Ottawa, October 1, 1982.

53. A Bill to Amend the Internal Revenue Code of 1954 to Deny the Deduction for Amounts Paid or Incurred for Certain Advertisements Carried by Certain Foreign Broadcast Undertakings, S.2051, 97th Cong. 2d Sess., February 2, 1982.

54. This was done by adding a new section, 280 E, to create an "Expanded Mirror Bill."

For the Canadian reaction see John King, "U.S. Bill Limits Cable Holdings," The Toronto Globe and Mail, July 24, 1982; Eric Evans, "U.S. Cable Companies Are Out to Stop Ours," Financial Post, Toronto, August 7, 1982.

55. Letter from Senator Moynihan, June 15, 1982.

56. Ibid., p. 2.

57. A Bill to Amend the Communications Act of 1934, S.2172, 97th Cong. 2d Sess., March 4, 1982.

58. Quoted by Lind, above, note 52, p. 5.

59. These differences in approach and emphasis are reflected in the views of the current heads of the regulatory agencies—John Meisel of the CRTC and Mark Fowler of the FCC. Compare John Meisel, "Of Babes and Bathwater, or, What Goes Down the Deregulatory Drain," 3 Can. Regulatory Reporter 5-27 (1982) and "Doing the Digital Waltz: The Canadian Response to International Developments in Telecommunications," 11th Annual Telecommunications Policy Research Conference, Annapolis, Md., April 26, 1983, to Mark S. Fowler and Daniel L. Brenner, "A Marketplace Approach to Broadcast Regulation," 60 Tex. L. Rev. 207 (1982).

60. Thus for all their market fervor, Fowler and Brenner end up strongly favoring public broadcasting. Above, note 59, at 251-55.

61. For a candid assessment of the success of past policies, see Canadian Broadcasting and Telecommunications: Past Experiences, Future Options, A Report Prepared for the Canadian Radio-Television and Telecommunications Commission, Ottawa, Minister of Supply and Services Canada, 1980.

62. Broadcasting Act above, note 5, s. 3.

63. Ian Lumsden (ed.), Close the 49th Parallel etc., The Americanization of Canada, Toronto, University of Toronto Press, 1970.

64. David Ellis, above, note 1, at 76.

65. Much of this regulation has been of a pious, aspirational nature and there has been all too little down-to-earth economic analysis. For a refreshing exception, see Stuart McFadyen, Colin Hoskins, and David Gillen, Canadian Broadcasting: Market Structure and Economic Performance, Montreal, The Institute for Research on Public Policy, 1980.

66. Television Broadcasting Regulations, s. 6A.

For a reassessment of these regulations, and proposals for reform, see CRTC Policy Statement on Canadian Content in Television, Ottawa, January 31, 1983.

67. Past Experiences, Future Options, above, note 61, at 24.

68. Proceedings of the Senate Banking, Trade and Commerce Committee, 91:22, June 9, 1976.

69. See, for example, Babe, Canadian Television Broadcasting Structure, Performance and Regulation, above, note 3.

For a radical critique, see Dallas Smythe, Dependency Road: Communications, Capitalism, Consciousness and Canada, Norwood, N.J., Ablex Pub., 1981.

70. See, for example, C. G. Hoskins and S. McFadyen, "Market Structure and Television Programming Performance in Canada and the U.K.: A Comparative Study," 8 Can. Pub. Policy 347 (1982).

71. CTV Television Network Ltd., Decision CRTC 79-453, August 3, 1979.

72. Canadian Radio-Television and Telecommunications Commission v. CTV Television Network Ltd., [1982] 1 S.C.R. 530.

73. Pay Television, Decision CRTC 82-240, March 18, 1982.

For the background to this decision see Woodrow and Woodsice (eds.), The Introduction of Pay-TV in Canada: Issues and Implications, Montreal, The Institute for Research on Public Policy, 1982.

74. "Groups Protest Playboy TV Deal," The Toronto Globe and Mail, January 19, 1983. In response to the public outcry, Francis Fox, minister of communications, stated, "We would not have licensed a channel if we knew it was going to be pornographic." This, even though it was known that one of the licensees proposed to show "adult entertainment" (of a mild variety: "Playboy TV Just Tame Titillation," The Toronto Globe and Mail, January 26, 1983) and an appeal to the cabinet had already been rejected. In a press release on January 25, 1983, the CRTC "invited" all pay television network licensees to discuss plans for developing "voluntary industry standards" on the distribution of adult programming.

75. Policy Statement on Canadian Content in Television, above, note 66, at 5.

76. Ibid., p. 7.

77. Ibid., pp. 18-19.

78. Ibid., pp. 27-28.

79. Ibid., p. 25.

80. Ibid., pp. 20-21.

81. This was the figure widely used in the debates leading up to the enactment of Bill C-58. See p. 49.

82. Arthur Donner and Fred Lazar, An Examination of the Financial Impacts of Canada's 1976 Amendment to Section 19.1 of the Income Tax Act (Bill C-58) on U.S. and Canadian TV Broadcasters, Ottawa, Dept. of Communications, 1979, p. iv.

Note: A revised, expanded, and updated version of this excellent study by Arthur Donner Consultants was undertaken during the summer of 1983.

83. Ibid., p. III-18.

84. Congressional Record—Senate, February 2, 1982, S.297.

85. "A Broadcasting Strategy for Canada," July 15, 1982, p. 58. The draft went on to discuss the probable adverse implication of a proposal to allow for the distribution by satellite throughout Canada of certain of the border signals. "Given the history of this issue, the up-linking of stations affiliated with the major U.S. networks on Canadian satellite facilities for which CANCOM has applied to the CRTC in order to extend the coverage of their signals to all parts of Canada beyond the reach of microwave, could trigger a significant re-appraisal of the attitude of the U.S. Administration on border broadcasting if the CRTC allowed such carriage but did not require CANCOM to enter into any contractual arrangements with U.S. program right holders." On March 8, 1983 the CRTC agreed to CANCOM's application to extend 3 + 1 (3 U.S. commercial and 1 noncommercial) throughout all remote and underserved areas in Canada.

86. Swinton, above, note 26, at 559. The CRTC has recently been struggling with the issue of religious broadcasting and has concluded in the face of freedom of the media and religion provisions in the new charter that the "balance" requirements of the Broadcasting Act prevent the issuance of licenses to particular sects or demoninations. See CRTC Public Notice 1983, - 112.

Many Canadians were shocked when the U.S. Justice Department declared a number of Canadian films (including one that was to win an Oscar, If You Love This Planet) to be foreign "political propaganda" requiring a disclaimer that they had not been approved by the American government, and delighted at the vehemence of the protest at this move. See Marshall Delaney, "Fallout: A Controversial Ruling by the U.S. Government Has Made Small-Scale Hits out of Three Canadian Documentaries," Saturday Night, May 1983, pp. 73-74.

87. For a trenchant criticism of this approach see Ithiel de Sola Pool, Technologies of Freedom, Cambridge, Mass., Harvard University Press, 1983.

88. The CTV Decision, above, note 72, at 540.

For a beginning of the necessary reassessment, see H. N. Janisch, "Emerging Issues in Content Regulation in Canada," 10th Annual Telecommunications Research Conference, Annapolis, Md., April 26, 1982, and two papers in Communications Law I (1982-83) at the Faculty of Law, University of Toronto: Geoffrey Gomery, "Is Canadian Content Legal? Regulation of the Mass Media under the Charter"; and Peter Downard, "Film Censorship in Ontario: Legality in Light of the Canadian Charter of Rights and Freedoms."

On November 4, 1982, the CRTC adopted, in principle, the report of its Task Force on Sex-Role Stereotyping, Images of Women. The task force aimed at accomplishing its goal of "a more realistic and positive portrayal of women in radio and television (both in

programming and commercials)" through self-regulation by industry.
It proposed, however, that the CRTC act as an independent body to
assess the success of self-regulatory programs. For the concerns
of broadcasters, see Robert Stephens, "CRTC Monitoring of Stereotyping Worries Media," The Toronto Globe and Mail, November 22,
1982.

89.   Re Ontario Film and Video Appreciation Society and the
Ontario Board of Censors, Ont. Div. Crt. March 25, 1983 (now on
appeal).

90.   "Censor Attacks Popular Films for Undermining Social
Values," The Toronto Globe and Mail, February 7, 1983.

91.   See Theodore M. Hagelin, "Prior Consent or the Free
Flow of Information over Satellite Radio and Television: A Critique
of U.S. Domestic and International Broadcast Policy," 8 Syracuse
J. Int. L. & Comm., 267 (1981).

92.   Paul W. Shaw, "Purging Madison Avenue from Canadian
Cable Television," 7 L. & Policy in Int'l. Bus. 655 at 656-57 (1975).

93.   Towards a New National Broadcasting Policy, New Policies and Initiatives to Provide Canadians with Greater Program
Choice and Make the Canadian Broadcasting Industry More Competitive: A Response to New Technologies and the Changing Environment, Ottawa, Minister of Supply and Services Canada, 1983. Emphasis added.

This new role for cable is not without irony. As Colin Watson,
president of Rogers Cablesystems, has noted, the industry has
moved, almost overnight, "from Trojan horse of the Canadian
broadcasting system to possible savior." "Broadcasters React
Favorably," The Toronto Globe and Mail, March 3, 1983.

The various leaked drafts of the policy document had made
reference to the cable tax, but there was no direct mention of it in
the final version; it was apparently considered inappropriate to an-
nounce a tax outside of budget procedures. See The Budget: Financial Statement of the Minister of Finance, Commons Debates, April
19, 1983, p. 24668. Note that the percentage has dropped from 8
percent to 6 percent but that it has been extended to cover "basic
cable rental, pay TV and other programming services provided by
means of telecommunications."

94.   "A Broadcasting Strategy for Canada," July 15, 1982.
This porous approach to policy-making by the Department of Communications may have been designed to scuttle a more independent
source of policy proposals, the "Appelbert Report" (after its co-
chairmen, Louis Applebaum and Jacques Hebert), more formally,
Report of the Federal Cultural Policy Review Committee, Ottawa,
Information Services, Dept. of Communications, 1982.

95. Trade Agreements Act of 1979, codified at 19 U.S.C. Sect. 301(d)(1) (1979); S. Rep. No. 96-249, 96th Cong., 1st Sess. 237 (1979).

96. U.S.-Canadian Border Broadcasting Briefing Book, on file at Preston, Thorgrimson, Ellis & Holman, 1776 G Street N.W., Suite 500, Washington, D.C. 20006; see Andrew W. Stoler, "The Border Broadcast Dispute: A Unique Case Under Section 301," 6 Int'l Trade L.J. 39, 46 (1981).

97. See U.S. v. Southwestern Cable Co., 392 U.S. 157 (1968); Cable Television Report and Order, 36 FCC 2d 143 (1972); Theodore M. Hagelin, "The First Amendment Stake in New Technology: The Broadcast Cable Controversy," 44 U. Cinn. L. Rev. 427 (1975).

98. See Stoler, above, note 95, n. 32.

99. See Public Service Responsibility of Broadcast Licensees (Blue Book), Federal Communications Commission (1946); Program Policy Statement (Network Programming Inquiry), 25 Fed. Reg. 7291 (1960); Ascertainment of Community Problems by Broadcast Applicants, 53 FCC 2d 3 (1975).

100. FCC v. Sanders Brothers Radio Station, 309 U.S. 470 (1940); WLVA-TV v. FCC, 459 F.2d 1286 (1972); see Posner, "Taxation by Regulation," 2 Bell J. Econ. 22 (1971).

101. Report and Order, Deregulation of Radio, 84 FCC 2d 968 (1981); aff'd in part, U.C.C. v. FCC (D.C.C.C.A. No. 81-1463, decided May 10, 1983).

102. 47 U.S.C. Sect. 307(d); Memorandum Opinion and Order, 46 Fed. Reg. 26236 (May 11, 1981).

103. Deregulation of Radio; U.C.C. v. FCC above, note 101.

104. See 18 U.S.C. Sect. 1464; FCC v. Pacifica Foundation, 438 U.S. 726 (1978); Home Box Office v. Wilkinson, 531 F. Supp. 987 (1982).

105. See generally Ginsburg, Regulation of Broadcasting (1979), p. 661.

106. North Carolina Utility Comm. v. FCC, 537 F.2d 787 (1976); U.S. v. AT&T, 552 F. Supp. 131, 153-60 (1982); Cable Telecommunications Competition and Deregulation Act of 1982, 97th Cong. 2d Sess., S.2445.

107. New York Times v. U.S., 403 U.S. 713 (1971); Village of Skokie v. National Socialists Party, 373 N.E.2d 21 (Ill. 1978); U.S. v. Progressive Inc., 467 F. Supp. 990 (D. Wisc. 1978), vacated (7th Cir. 1979).

108. U.S. v. Associated Press, 52 F. Supp. 362, 372 (D.C.S.D.N.Y. 1943).

109. See generally, Theodore M. Hagelin, "Prior Consent or the Free Flow of Information Over Satellite Radio and Television," 8 Syracuse J. Int'l L. & Comm. 265 (1981).

110. Ibid., pp. 293-300.

111. U.S. v. AT&T, above, note 106, at 178.

112. Ascertainment of Community Problems, above, note 99.

113. Roger Noll, M. Peck, and J. McGowan, Economic Aspects of Television Regulation, Washington, D.C.: Brookings Institute, 1973, pp. 53-63.

114. Ibid., pp. 176-78.

115. Direct Broadcast Satellite Service, 51 R.R. 2d 1341 (1982).

COMMENT
Erwin Krasnow

As W. S. Gilbert might have put it, the carping critic's lot is not a happy one. It is therefore pleasant to start by hailing Janisch and Hagelin not only for the weight and sincerity of their effort to suggest a starting point for negotiations on this contentious matter but for one proposition that I heartily endorse. For far too many years, there has been an impression on both sides of the border that it is domestically traitorous and internationally offensive for broadcasters to take the interests of their foreign audience into account in devising their programs. At least in the limited sphere of locally produced programming, Hagelin and Janisch forthrightly reject that benighted view, in favor of the plainly valid proposition that "citizens of Buffalo and Toronto share a great deal in common." I can only applaud.

For the most part, however, their analysis seems to me wide of the mark. We are told that U.S. broadcasters who have led the fight for localism domestically should appreciate the threat that U.S. border services pose to localism in Canada. Let me assure all our Canadian friends that we do indeed. The National Association of Broadcasters (NAB) has been vigorous in urging a pause in the FCC's headlong rush to authorize domestic broadcast satellites (DBS) to permit reflection on their potential effects on the American system of local television broadcasting. We are sensitive to the parallel problems that U.S. broadcast satellites and U.S. border services create for Canada. What we fail to understand or appreciate is a Canadian governmental policy of embracing and expanding the threat of U.S. service to Canadian localism (by encouraging its distribution throughout Canada) while simultaneously seeking to prevent those who provide the service from earning reasonable compensation in the marketplace.

The NAB has never urged that broadcast satellites be authorized on terms that prevent DBS entrepreneurs from earning compensation for the service they provide and the economic value they create. At its most protectionist, the FCC has never followed such a course. There was once a brief flirtation with the concept of commercial deletion by cable systems, but the seeds of that idea fell on stony ground south of the border. They flowered into actual commercial deletion only in Canada, to the loudly expressed disgust of the Toronto Globe and Mail and many other Canadians. The tax device subsequently enacted into law in Canada seems to us entirely comparable.

The American objection to that device (C-58) is not an objection to Canada's efforts to protect its own identity and promote its own culture. The concern is with the fairness and rationality of the means chosen to advance that objective. Such restrictions as the FCC still imposes on what Janisch and Hagelin call "intermarket competition" in the United States—restrictions that, by the way, they greatly exaggerate—are beside the point. If Canada chose to protect its culture by preventing its citizens from receiving U.S. services, we would have an entirely different question. The issue—and I see no reason why it does not apply to the provision of management, financial, insurance, or other services—is whether Canada or any other country can fairly seek the benefit (and invite the competition) of foreign services without permitting them to earn reasonable compensation.

"Ah," say the authors, "that is a question of property rights." They follow with what was for me a confused discussion of property rights and economic values in local, syndicated, and network programming. The upshot of that discussion is the remarkable conclusion that broadcasters who acquire the right to transmit a program to all within reach of their signal (by giving a network or syndicated program supplier cash or agreeing to carry advertising on behalf of the supplier's clients) are somehow not entitled to reap the economic value created when viewers are attracted to the program. The only apt response is a cliché: the more they explain it, the more I don't understand it. Whether the broadcasters' program rights are exclusive or nonexclusive, they are in fact making a program investment and rendering a service to willing viewers.

There is little more substance to the argument that Canadian broadcasters are placed at a competitive disadvantage by Canadian content requirements. Those requirements have not prevented the Toronto stations from broadcasting virtually all of the prime time and much of the daytime entertainment programs of the U.S. networks, together with many of the most popular U.S. syndicated shows. Moreover, in recognition of their special burdens, Canadian stations enjoy special rights to carriage and preferred channel positions on Canadian cable systems, as well as rights to employ "simultaneous program substitution" to protect the exclusivity of the U.S. programming they broadcast. No one is arguing that U.S. stations should be allowed to compete in Canadian markets on an equal basis with Canadian stations; only that, if their service is received by Canadians with the approval and aid of the Canadian government, they should not be confronted, as they are now, with the equivalent of a 100 percent tariff on their sale of advertising to Canadians.

Please observe, moreover, that when the discussion centers on the relative competitive advantages and burdens of U.S. and

Canadian commercial broadcasters, it has drifted very far indeed from the objective of promoting Canadian culture. You can (if you insist) ignore the likelihood, demonstrated by Yale Braunstein's discussion (Chapter 7), that the current Canadian tax law has not aided Canadian broadcasters or enabled them to spend more on Canadian programming. You can, like Humpty Dumpty in Alice in Wonderland, insist that words mean what you want them to mean and then define every dollar of additional revenue diverted to a Canadian broadcaster by any means as a contribution to Canadian culture. But the claim that the tax law to which U.S. broadcasters object is a substantial response to Canada's need for the development of a vibrant domestic production industry simply cannot pass the "red face" test (can the proposition in question be fully enunciated before the face turns red?).

The recent Applebaum Report says: "From the point of view of this Committee, which sees cultural policy as the promotion of creative and artistic expression as well as the access of audiences to that expression, these measures [C-58] have to be viewed as elements of an industrial policy, not a cultural policy."*

"Industrial policy" also seems the right description for the Hagelin-Janisch proposal that there be "direct network distribution" by U.S. networks in Canada. I cannot of course speak for the U.S. networks or any other affected U.S. interest, but the proposal seems to me obscure. If I understand it correctly, the idea is that U.S. television networks would distribute to Canadian cable systems at least the entertainment program service they now provide to affiliated broadcasters in the United States. The networks would compensate their program suppliers, freeing the cable systems from any need to do so, and would earn revenues by selling time to advertisers interested in reaching Canadian viewers. The network programs broadcast by U.S. border stations would be deleted by Canadian cable systems; U.S. border stations would be allowed unhampered access to Canadian viewers only in their locally produced programming (or perhaps, to some degree, in their syndicated programming).

Among many issues that come to mind, one seems to me decisive. What would become of the Canadian broadcasters who have been the objects of their government's solicitude all these years? Would they be able to purchase exhibition rights to the same U.S. network programs and then employ "simultaneous program substitution" against the new direct U.S. network service, as they do now

---

*Report of the Federal Cultural Policy Review Committee, November 1982.

against such service on U.S. border affiliates? If so, why would the U.S. networks be interested in the proposal? If not, what would the proposal accomplish for Canada?

Even if the proposal were otherwise viable, therefore, it offers little promise as a basis for negotiations. Real progress toward a resolution, in my view, demands a very different approach. I am heartened, in this regard, by the apparent recognition in the Canadian government's recent "New National Broadcasting Policy" of the proposition that the strengthening of Canada's production industry is to be accomplished primarily by the affirmative allocation of resources to that end. That is a policy which can fairly be characterized as "cultural" in nature. The next step, I suggest, is to find means of reconciling in some significant measure the desire of the Canadian broadcasters about perceived competitive advantages of U.S. border stations and the reasonable insistence of Americans that their broadcasters are entitled to compensation for services they render. I have no magic formula to offer. When one contemplates, however, the seemingly intractable problems that our world faces in places such as the Middle East or elsewhere, it seems hard to believe that it is beyond human wit to devise ways in which to resolve this particular quarrel between neighbors.

4

CONSUMER SOVEREIGNTY AND NATIONAL SOVEREIGNTY IN DOMESTIC AND INTERNATIONAL BROADCASTING REGULATION

Mark J. Freiman

> In the words of Justice Holmes, "To have doubted one's
> own first principles is the mark of a civilized man,"
> but the same wise man in Abrams v. United States
> stated that "the best test of truth is the power of thought
> to get itself accepted in the competition of the market"
> without appreciating that monopoly and oligopoly appear
> in this as in other markets.
>
> Harold Innis, "Minerva's Owl" (1947)

One of the most difficult challenges in attempting to contribute
to the current debate about broadcasting regulation in Canada and
the United States is locating a comprehensive debate to contribute
to. While much has been said and written about deregulation, about
rules for Canadian content, about the economic consequences of
regulatory supervision, about the public interest, about freedom of
the press, and about national sovereignty, taken together these
pronouncements seem more to resemble parallel monologues than
a substantive debate. Part of the reason for the desultory nature
of the discussion is probably to be found in the multiplicity of intellectual disciplines involved. Economists, political scientists,
historians, communications theorists, and legal scholars all operate within different universes of discourse and share few if any
methodological or theoretical presuppositions. Beyond this, broadcasting regulation is not simply an academic or theoretical issue.
It involves the highly tangible if often conflicting interests of governments, broadcasters, program producers, cable distributors,

and commercial advertisers. Finally, the border between Canada
and the United States, though friendly, largely unguarded, and
easily permeable by electronic signals, does nevertheless divide
two separate countries, each with distinct intellectual traditions and
each with potentially divergent economic and cultural interests.

In such a context of conflicting interests, theories, and traditions, conclusions are often easier to articulate than premises;
slogans often replace logical arguments; and one person's platitude
becomes another's radical heresy. In the area of broadcasting
regulation this phenomenon is most graphically illustrated by the
fate of the concepts of consumer sovereignty and national sovereignty as alternately touchstones and bêtes noires in the debate
about the appropriate role of government intervention in domestic
and international broadcasting. [1]

My purpose here is to look carefully at these two concepts
and to consider what, if anything, they contribute to an understanding of the current issues in Canadian and U.S. broadcasting regulation, and how, if at all, they fit into a rational regulating policy for
each country.

As general principles and in the abstract, there seems little
to object to in the concepts of consumer sovereignty and national
sovereignty as applied to broadcasting. Few would quarrel with the
idea that on the one hand people should be entitled to choose freely
which television programs to watch, and on the other, that governments have a valid interest in protecting their countries' cultural
and political autonomy. When either concept, however, is trans-
formed into an absolute standard for regulatory policy, it produces
misleading and potentially mischievous conclusions.

Let us begin with consumer sovereignty. Its basic principles
and assumptions seem simple and, at first glance, attractive. [2]
Every adult is the best judge of the relative importance and validity
of his or her needs and desires, or as Jeremy Bentham put it over
150 years ago, "Generally speaking, there is no one who knows
what is in your interest so well as yourself." [3] The index of our
evaluation of the importance of our needs and desires is to be
found in the extent of our willingness to pay to have them satisfied.
If there is any objective interest that all individuals have in common, it is the interest each has in satisfying these subjective interests at the lowest feasible personal cost, an interest more
commonly known as consumer welfare. As a corollary, therefore,
it is always a legitimate goal of government to promote consumer
welfare, since to do so is by definition to promote everyone's
interests.

Consumer welfare is promoted by harmonizing the often conflicting demands of individual consumers across a given system to

approach Pareto's optimality, that point at which no participant in
the transactions in question could be made better off without some-
one else being made worse off. Under standard assumptions, a
system that achieves Pareto's optimality in its rationing of a given
commodity is an efficient one. The lowest cost means of achieving
efficiency is through the unfettered operation of the marketplace.
Therefore, since under standard assumptions a free market will
inevitably maximize consumer welfare and thus satisfy the public
interest, wherever possible the marketplace should determine what
gets produced and for what price. In the context of broadcast regulation, this means that rather than intervening directly, regulatory
authorities ought to rely on consumer preferences as expressed
through the workings of a free market in the context of a commercial broadcasting system to produce programming that will satisfy
the needs and desires of its viewers.[4]

At least that is how the argument goes.

A threshold problem with this use of consumer sovereignty as
a gauge for the public interest in commercial broadcasting is that
it does not correspond to the current economic structure of the
medium. While at first it may appear that the broadcaster is the
producer, the viewer is the consumer, and the programming is the
commodity or product produced, this cannot be so, since if it were,
what would be missing would be the central element of any economic
transaction, that of exchange. Although viewers can be said to
"consume" the programs transmitted over the airwaves, they do
not appear to pay anything for this consumption, a startling fact
that has led some commentators to remark about the "miracle of
costless broadcasting."[5] There have been a number of attempts to
solve this apparent paradox or "miracle,"[6] but surely the simplest
solution is to point out that the real commodity being produced is
not the program but the audience watching it, who will also watch
the advertising messages that punctuate this programming. The
true consumer, then, is the advertiser who pays the broadcaster to
produce this audience. The programs being transmitted therefore
become not the products of this system but rather one of the costs
incurred by the broadcaster to produce an audience for the advertiser to buy. Viewed from this perspective, commercial broadcasting displays all the usual features of commodity production,
including consumer sovereignty, but it is the advertiser who is
sovereign in this system, not the viewer.

Moreover, the sovereignty exercised by the advertiser extends not only to choice of a suitable audience for advertising messages but necessarily to both the form and the content of the programming designed to attract this audience. Thus the "product"

that the advertiser demands from the broadcaster is an audience that is composed of individuals who might want to buy the advertiser's goods or services, that is large in numbers, and that is attentive to the advertiser's messages. To meet this demand, the broadcaster produces or buys programs likely to attract an audience that displays these characteristics.[7] This in turn means that whatever choice the viewer exercises—and undoubtedly there is viewer choice in current North American commercial television—is choice from a preselected, limited range of commercially constrained alternatives. Just how wide-ranging this preselection process is, and how limited is the range of resulting alternatives, can be illustrated with a few examples of the consequences of the advertisers' consumer sovereignty.

The first prerequisite demanded by the advertiser, that of an audience of potential customers, means that the general subject matter of the program to be broadcast will be demographically calculated to attract the correct general class of viewer. Next, the requirement to maximize this potential audience means that the treatment of the material will be at a level of complexity and sophistication that will hold the attention of the largest possible number of individuals within that group—a calculation that results in such a level that to go any lower would result in a greater loss of desired audience members than gain. While this is by no means identical with the lowest common denominator, its general characteristics become clear when one considers its equally valid obverse, namely, that the program can only be so complex and sophisticated that any increase in these qualities would result in a greater loss than gain. As for the goal of receptiveness, the advertiser's preference for an audience in a positive frame of mind leads to a general policy discouraging "controversy" in the form of programs that lead to strong emotional responses; thus, live drama disappeared from the airwaves, not because its ratings were too low, not because it was too expensive, but because it was too involving, upsetting, and thought provoking and therefore overshadowed the advertising messages that accompanied it, and they in turn failed to generate satisfactory sales.[8]

Nor do these commercial imperatives affect only subject matter and complexity. They extend to the form of programming as well. To avoid "information overload," advertisers have preferred to space their messages over the entire duration of a program. This means that the dramatic rhythm of the program must be adapted to accommodate this punctuation.[9] In contemporary entertainment programming, this means that each program segment must build to a climax in ten to twelve minutes and that this pattern must be repeated from two to five times, a structure that places incredible strain on conventional narrative techniques and encourages replacing plotting, character development, and thematic continuity with "jolts" of violence and wisecracks.

Further, insofar as the audience desired by an advertiser is not simply "there," but must actually be produced, the large sums involved in developing appropriate programming to attract the desired audience, and the consequent high cost of failure, lead both advertisers and broadcasters to look for ways to consolidate past successes and extend them into the future. This desire for stability and predictability encourages a reliance on proven forms and proven performers; hence the predominance of series production, the prevalence of the star system, the gravitation toward spin-offs and imitations of successful programs, and the emphasis on a limited number of specific genres.

These emphases put further constraints on programming. Each episode must deal with a specific problem generated by the premise of the series and must "solve" this problem without resolving the basic conflicts and tensions on which the program is based.[10] To allow casual viewing, no one episode can be contingent on the events in any other, and no character can change substantially. Thus no matter how frantic or frenetic the pacing or the action and no matter what the ostensible content of a program, all the factors favor underlying messages of "no change" conservatism and reassurance.[11]

Nor do the limitations on viewer "sovereignty" over television programming end with this fact of preselection of available program choices. Within the logic of commercial television, the ultimate purpose of programming is simply to attract the largest appropriate audience for various advertisers' messages. The actual content of programming is irrelevant as long as it encourages proper viewing habits. For each individual advertiser this means loyalty over time to programs carrying the advertiser's messages, while for the broadcaster it means expanding the total number of hours each viewer watches the programs on that station. This in turn means that the ultimate purpose of programming is not only to deliver a particular audience for a particular advertiser, but also to create a demand for more of the same program, for more of the same kind of programming, and for more of television programming in general. Like tobacco, sugar, and alcohol, commercial television programming has been developed into a highly addictive commodity that creates its own demand. The result is a North American system in which viewers characteristically switch on their sets to watch "television" rather than to watch a particular program, spend a number of continuous hours each evening watching this television, and normally do not switch the channel during that period.[12] This is a pattern that appears to be very difficult to square with the notion of free and informed individual choice, which normally underlies the notion of consumer sovereignty.

It will of course be suggested that insofar as all this indicates a problem with the concept of consumer sovereignty as applied to television programming, it is a problem that only extends to advertiser-sponsored programming, and that the solution therefore is not in government regulation but rather in the encouragement of subscription or pay television in which no advertiser comes between the viewers and their honest preferences.

This suggestion is somewhat disingenuous. First, commercially sponsored television is still the dominant mode of North American programming and seems unlikely to be eclipsed by subscription television in the foreseeable future. For that reason, subscription television, especially when it drains attractive programming away from "free television," appears to be not a cure for the problems of the dominant mode of television but rather an exacerbation. Second, the predominant form of subscription television now and for the foreseeable future is pay per channel rather than pay per program. This form is no more capable than is commercially sponsored television of registering intensity of demand[13] and is therefore subject to the same audience-maximizing pressures as is the latter. Thus, even for the limited audience willing and able to pay directly for its television programming, this inability to measure intensity constitutes an "indivisibility" or "rigidity" that makes subscription television incapable of achieving Pareto's optimality and therefore vitiates the relevance of the concept of consumer sovereignty.

Even beyond these technical problems, the concept of consumer sovereignty—even assuming it to be capable of realization—would nevertheless be objectionable as a justification for abstention from regulatory intervention in broadcasting. The core of the problem is in the identification of the public interest in broadcasting with consumer welfare and economic efficiency. By definition a system premised on consumer sovereignty treats culture as a commodity and its reception through broadcasting as a commercial transaction. If individuals are sovereign at all within such a system, they are sovereign and their choices are heeded only as consumers, and not in any of their other possible roles. This means that the satisfaction of hedonistic, individualistic, and short-term desires becomes the only valid criterion for cultural production while all other noncommercial values and needs are excluded from the system, whatever their social or philosophic justification. It also means that groups with weak consumer voices or with needs that cannot be easily quantified are effectively shut out from the cultural decision-making process.

These are results that must necessarily follow if (1) television programming is a commodity and (2) "consumer welfare" is the appropriate standard by which to measure the public interest in its production. Upon examination, however, neither of these propositions proves to be tenable. Culture and communication, even if they are often the objects of exchange, are not simply commodities, and broadcasting is not simply a service industry. The discipline of the sociology of knowledge has demonstrated that culture and communication—including broadcast communication—are important constituents of the social stock of knowledge on the basis of which people understand themselves and make important decisions both as individuals and as citizens.[14] "Entertainment" no less than factual information serves to define for the individual the central social categories of the <u>normal</u> and the <u>inevitable</u>. Through these concepts, individuals come to "understand" why things are the way they are, and to accept that this is how many of them must be. Such explanations are the social glue which holds groups together, which allows them to reproduce themselves over time, and which in special situations may also allow them to change to accommodate a changing environment. On a personal level, such explanations and the typified self-images derived from them allow individuals to make sense of their lives and to accept (and in special cases, reject) their allotted places in the sun. Most of our reality is socially constructed, and culture, including entertainment, is one of its key building materials.

This being the case, it should be clear that both the individual and his or her social group have definite interests in the process of culture and communication that go beyond the gratification of hedonistic desires on the basis of individual willingness and ability to pay. <u>Individuals</u>' interest in this process is to have access to as wide as possible a range of ideas and interpretations to allow them to make rational choices in their own lives. In a democratic society, <u>citizens</u>' interest, and hence also that of the state, is in access to a similarly wide range of both commercial and noncommercial ideas and interpretations upon which to base their decisions in the democratic process of self-government.

By definition such an adequate range of ideas and interpretations cannot be provided by a marketplace geared only to satisfy short-term hedonistic desires. In any marketplace, individuals' ability properly to valuate and hence demand a commodity depends on the adequacy of their information about that commodity. When that "commodity" is itself information, inadequacy of information becomes exponential. Not only do the individuals not know, they don't know what they don't know, and they don't know that they don't know. For this reason consumer sovereignty has never been an

accurate gauge of the individual or the public's interest in education. Similarly, for that reason there is good cause to look with
some trepidation to the increasing convergence of news with entertainment on television, since clearly the news people need to know
is not always the news they want to know. Although it is perhaps
slightly more difficult to see, the same considerations also apply
to straight entertainment, which, as indicated above, teaches even
as it amuses—or, to complete the pattern of the convergence of
news and entertainment, just as people are entertained by news and
information programs they are also informed by entertainment
programs.

The preceding arguments about individual and state interests
in the production of ideas and interpretations are based on normative assumptions, though ones that presumably few Americans or
Canadians would not share. The same conclusions can, however,
be reached without recourse to normative assumptions. Assuming
that "adequate diversity" is a positive factor in the production of
new productivity-raising knowledge, it manifests itself as a social
value incompatible with consumer sovereignty.[15] Since the benefits of such diversity are external to any possible producing firm,
this diversity will, under conditions of consumer sovereignty, not
be produced. Or, to put this into proper jargon: there is a divergence between the social marginal net benefit of diversity and the
private marginal net benefit of diversity, and in practice, the logic
of the market's operation is such that individual producers cannot
wholly internalize the externalities of diversity, causing such diversity either not to be produced or to be underproduced.[16]

The other side of the individual's and the collectivity's interest in a diversity of knowledge, information, and interpretation is
the corresponding interest in preventing monopoly, or as it is
sometimes called, hegemony, in these areas. This interest seems
clearly to have been recognized by the framers of the First Amendment to the U.S. Constitution, which sought in an eighteenth-
century context to guarantee diversity by protecting speech and the
press from government censorship. In an era of low economic
barriers to entry in journalism and publishing, and in which the
sale of 400 newspapers constituted the break-even point,[17] government was the only possible monopolist, and a literal reading of the
First Amendment provided an adequate guarantee of necessary
diversity of ideas and interpretations.

In the changed economic reality of the late twentieth century,
this is no longer the case. The costs of ownership and even of
access to the media of communications are extremely high, and
public expectations about technical quality are such that the only
messages that will be attended to are those that require a mass

audience to recoup their production costs. This means that on the one hand the capability of using the media of communications to present self-interested messages is restricted to a tiny elite of privileged individuals and corporations. On the other hand, the more usual response to the current economics of culture and communication, that of treating them as industries, leads to a monopoly of majoritarian tastes and commercial values.[18] The traditional interpretation of the First Amendment guarantees of free speech and a free press are simply incapable of dealing with either of these monopolistic situations, since they are the direct result of the free operation of the "marketplace of ideas":—a positive conception that has underlain First Amendment jurisprudence ever since Oliver Wendell Holmes' celebrated judgment in Abrams v. United States.[19]

The consequences of a reliance on the workings of this marketplace have been made apparent in a series of recent U.S. Supreme Court judgments. In Miami Herald v. Tornillo[20] and Columbia Broadcasting System v. Democratic National Committee,[21] the Supreme Court made it clear that the First Amendment did not guarantee unpaid or paid access to the media of communications—it does not guarantee the right of everyone to be heard. In WNCN Listeners' Guild v. Federal Communications Commission,[22] the court held that the public's ownership of the airwaves does not give the broadcasting audience any specific rights with regard to the material being broadcast—there is no right to hear any specific messages or classes of messages. But in Buckley v. Valleo,[23] the Court held that for those who did have access to the media of communications, the First Amendment did guarantee a right to have that access restricted only by their ability to pay for and the owners' willingness to carry their messages—the First Amendment does guarantee capital's right to be heard.

In earlier decisions relating specifically to broadcasting, most notably Red Lion Broadcasting Company v. F.C.C.,[24] the U.S. Supreme Court had taken a different tack and had identified the public interest in broadcasting as precisely encompassing the public's right to hear a broad and diverse range of messages.[25] This is functionally identical to the definition of the public interest proposed above and has important affinities with the so-called affirmative theory of the First Amendment, championed, among others, by Alexander Meikeljohn[26] and Jerome Barron.[27] The great strength of the Red Lion decision is that it recognized the potential for monopoly as the great threat to the public interest in broadcasting and saw clearly the inappropriateness of invoking the First Amendment in the defense of such monopoly. Its weakness, however, is in its identification of the source of that potential monopoly in the technological scarcity of channels in the broadcasting spectrum available to potential broadcasters.[28]

This conceptualization, which proceeds from the assumption that in a medium in which technology decrees that some messages must be excluded, it is justifiable to regulate the content of those that do gain access.[29] It stops short, however, of the realization that economics and the logic of commerce work just as effectively to deny access to some messages and allow it to others. As a result, even before its apparent change of heart about the entire doctrine in WNCN,[30] the U.S. Supreme Court confined its operation specifically to broadcasting and refused to extend it to media of communications in which there was no such intrinsic technological scarcity. More significantly, this conceptualization has led commentators and policy makers sympathetic to Red Lion to search for a solution to the potential for monopolization in broadcasting through an elimination of this technological scarcity.

This is the intellectual parentage of Judge David Bazelon's "structural solution" to the conflict of First Amendment values in broadcasting,[31] and probably to a large extent underlies FCC deregulatory policies aimed at increasing the number of on-air and off-air broadcasting outlets. However, because it is not simply technological scarcity but much more centrally the very logic of the marketplace that leads to a monopoly of majoritarian tastes and commercial values in the mass media, these "solutions" seem ill-conceived. A real solution to these kinds of monopoly cannot be found in policies aimed at reinforcing the very marketplace that promotes them in the first place.

If one takes seriously the "affirmative First Amendment" goal of ensuring that citizens have the opportunity, if they choose, to hear everything worth hearing, it is necessary to contemplate positive steps to ensure that the kinds of messages and values necessarily excluded by a system of commercial communication are made available to be heard.[32] Consumer sovereignty or the broadcasting marketplace thus cannot be synonymous with the public interest in broadcasting. At most, they can be partners—and no more than equal partners—in a system that balances satisfaction of consumer demand with protection of the noncommercial interests of both the individual and the collectivity with regard to an adequate social construction of reality.

Much the same pattern of considerations emerges when we turn to examine the concept of national sovereignty.

As a principle of international law, national sovereignty occupies a distinguished and unimpeachable position. The basic rule of international law—some would say its only rule—is that unless it is explicitly limited or renounced, every nation enjoys a sovereign right with which no other nation may interfere, to regulate as it pleases its own internal and domestic affairs, including its economic and cultural policies.[33]

Venerable as this principle may be, however, it does tend in many minds to raise a measure of uneasiness. It is hardly a secret that the principle of national sovereignty is open to abuse and has on occasion offered a convenient means for unscrupulous and unsavory governments to avoid international consequences for actions that are arbitrary, unjust, or worse. In the specific areas of broadcasting regulation, national sovereignty is most often raised to justify policies that impose quotas on foreign-produced programming exhibited on domestic channels or that control or even prevent the reception of foreign-originated broadcasting. To some, this is de facto censorship and inherently offensive, while others are simply made uneasy by the potential for arbitrary or repressive use of such regulation. Finally, in a world increasingly marked by transnational political and economic realities and in which communications and transportation technologies have effectively minimized the constraints of distance and geography, it might seem anomalous, at least to the beneficiaries of this new reality, to insist on the apparent diseconomies and dysfunctions of a nationalist perspective. In the face of these considerations, it becomes necessary to consider carefully the concept of a national identity in whose name many of the nations of the world, including some of its most stable and civil-liberty-conscious democracies, have enacted restrictive broadcasting regulations to determine whether and how far such regulation may be justified.

For many people and in many nations the concept of a national identity and the goal of preserving it are thoroughly unproblematic. Many discussions of the concept tend to be tautologous, with the goal of preserving a national identity presented as its own justification. Whatever the value of such intuitive and emotional responses, they are at least supplemented, and in some important ways qualified, by the insights of the Canadian economist and communications theorist Harold Innis. One of the focuses of Innis' work is on the dialectic between the "center" and the "margin" in economics and communications.[34] In his analysis, patterns of economics and communications tend either to be centralizing or decentralizing. Neither pattern is intrinsically preferable to the other, but an overemphasis on either will lead to serious economic or conceptual dysfunction.[35] An undue emphasis on centralization leaves the resulting system overextended and vulnerable and therefore leads to an overdependence on force and repression to maintain stability.[36] An undue emphasis on decentralization leads to narrowness, inefficiency, and an inability to adapt to changing circumstances.[37] What is necessary for a proper functioning of either an economic or a communications system is a balance between centralizing and decentralizing forces.[38]

From this point of view economic or cultural nationalism is not in itself either good or bad. It may well be dysfunctional if it leads to excessive centralization or to a monopolization of power at the center to the detriment of local decentralizing or "marginal" elements within the nation. On the other hand, in the context of transnational political, economic, or cultural empires, nationalism can be a beneficial balancing influence in the direction of decentralization. The test then for Innis of the desirability of a national identity is not in what it is, but in what it does. Thus broadcasting content regulation geared to enhance or protect a national identity makes intellectual as well as emotional sense if it corrects an existing imbalance or preserves an existing healthy equipoise. It makes no sense if its effect will simply be to exacerbate an existing imbalance.

In the specific context of Canada and the United States, this means that "American content" regulation in the United States would be superfluous and even harmful. A much more appropriate regulatory bias in the United States is one in favor of localized decentralizing programming. In the Canadian context, both centralizing and decentralizing regulatory policies are necessary. A Canadian identity, and Canadian content regulation designed to promote and protect it, are justifiable as a necessary decentralizing balance to an international U.S. cultural empire. A regulatory policy unequivocally focused on the production of a national Canadian identity, however, is not without overly centralizing dangers of its own, and must be balanced by a policy encouraging domestic decentralization in the form of programming expressing distinctive linguistic, ethnic, regional, and racial identities.

Similar considerations present themselves when one considers the question from the point of view of the specific characteristics of television as a medium. Here again, Innis' work is useful. According to Innis, the various media of communication are themselves biased either toward "space" and centralization or "time" and decentralization.[39] As a medium, television as it is currently constituted is technologically and organizationally biased toward space and centralization in its ability to spread a single message over vast geographic areas, amounting, with the advent of satellite transmission, to the ability of a single broadcaster simultaneously to address receivers everywhere in the world. When coupled with the enormous capital costs involved both in sophisticated program production and in its long-distance transmission, this centralizing bias makes feasible and perhaps even likely a virtual monopolization of international communications by economically, technologically, and demographically advantaged nations, the most prominent of which is, of course, the United States.

In such a context the notion of the free flow of information, which is often advanced to justify opposition to any attempts by receiving states to control or regulate incoming foreign broadcasts,[40] becomes a perfect analogue to the notion of consumer sovereignty and to the interpretation of the First Amendment found in Buckley v. Valleo. That, of course, means that the appropriate response is that a monopoly by one broadcaster or one type of broadcasting is as offensive to democratic notions as arbitrary censorship. The functional ideal behind freedom of information in an international context is not of a free flow, but of a free and balanced flow,[41] and to that end even significant restrictions on incoming programming can be justified as long as they are made in a regulatory context designed to prevent monopoly, preserve balance, and maximize authentic choice.

This same standard is the appropriate one for exercising indirect economic, as well as direct content, regulation designed to generate and protect domestic broadcasting production. The value of a diversity in available ideas and interpretations justifies both kinds of regulation if it is aimed at ensuring programming that commercial logic would make impossible to produce. The size of the Canadian market makes domestic program production ten times more expensive per capita than American programming of comparable technical quality. Thus, it is not simply a case of wanting Canadian programs: in purely economic terms Canadian consumers would have to demand Canadian programs ten times more intensely than American ones before it became economically rational to produce them. This, it would seem, would justify regulation, including indirect economic regulation such as that which is the actual subject of the border broadcasting dispute, as long as the purpose of such regulation was to encourage Canadian production.

Such a blanket statement would be going too far. Measures designed to shift the diseconomies of Canadian production off the shoulders of Canadian producers are justified if they result in the production not only of programs, but of ideas and interpretations that would otherwise not be produced. In general this means ideas and interpretations incapable of surviving in a purely commercial context but that would still be of potential value in the social construction of reality. The value of specifically Canadian ideas and interpretations is related to the Innisian concept of decentralization and has to do with the importance of ensuring that there will be available ideas and interpretations whose basis is in an experience that is dissimilar to that of the receiver.

Canadian content—indeed any sort of geographically or otherwise specified content—has as its justification its distinctive perspective, not simply the origin of its financing or the nationality of its producers. If what is produced is simply a domestic copy of foreign programming, none of the rationales hitherto cited is a justification for its diseconomies. Neither national sovereignty nor promotion of a national identity nor the fostering of adequate cultural diversity can plausibly justify policies whose net result is simply to provide commercial advantage to domestic broadcasting interests at the expense of domestic taxpayers and consumers or of foreign competitors. The lamentable history of the Canadian Film Development Corporation and its search for a Canadian-produced equivalent of The Texas Chainsaw Massacre[42] is a pointed illustration of the bankruptcy of such a policy.

This does not necessarily mean that "Canadian content" can only mean programming about Rimouski or Medicine Hat. What it does mean is that ultimately the justification for regulations fostering Canadian content is no different from the justification for regulations fostering the production of programming unrelated to commercial considerations in general.

This does not mean that the goal of regulation is to aim for some elitist standard of high culture. Noncommercial is not synonymous with unpopular or unpalatable. The result of the logic of the market is to identify merit exclusively with commercial profitability. As a balance to this, the goal of broadcasting regulation is to produce programming at all cultural levels, whether on national subjects or not, whose merit is intrinsic and not extrinsic.

By definition this is a goal that cannot be reached through deregulation or consumer sovereignty. Nor is it one that will be achieved by asserting the principle of national sovereignty through a scheme of quotas covering the nationality of actors, technicians, directors, and investors. It is barely possible but highly unlikely that it will be reached by a fixed system of incentives and disincentives designed to promote the public use of private interest. It might feasibly be attained through direct government involvement in program production and selection, but the dangers of such a system to civil liberties is probably prohibitive. Current fashions in regulatory policy notwithstanding, both theory and historical experience seem to indicate that by far the most practical and most likely means to achieve the valid goals of broadcasting regulation is through independent public national broadcasting systems that are generously funded and that are therefore truly independent, truly public, and truly national. It would, however, be a mistake to discount the possibility of innovative regulation accomplishing these goals in other contexts.

NOTES

1. The divergence of opinion on consumer sovereignty in broadcasting is illustrated by recent articles written or cowritten by the respective heads of the FCC and the CRTC. See Fowler and Brenner, "A Marketplace Approach to Broadcast Regulation," 60 Tex. L. Rev. 207 (1982); and Meisel, "Of Babies and Bathwater, Or, What Goes Down the Deregulation Drain," 3 C.R.R. 30 (1982). For a balanced analysis and evaluation of the arguments for and against national sovereignty in broadcasting, see Ploman, "Satellite Broadcasting, National Sovereignty, and Free Flow of Information," in Nordestreng and Schiller (eds.), National Sovereignty and International Communication (Norwood, N.J.: Ablex, 1979).

2. See Robbins, Political Economy Past and Present: A Review of Leading Theories of Economic Policy (London: Macmillan, 1976). Much of the summary that follows is based on Lord Robbins' sympathetic account of the theory of consumer sovereignty in Chapter 2, entitled "The Political Economy of Consumption."

3. Bentham, "Manual of Political Economy," quoted in Robbins, supra at 15.

4. This is precisely the point made by Brenner and Fowler, supra note 1.

5. See, e.g., Hagelin, "Prior Consent or the Free Flow of Information over Satellite Radio and Television: A Critique of U.S. Domestic and International Broadcast Policy," 8 Syracuse J. Int'l L. & Comm. 265 at 309 (1981).

6. Fowler and Brenner, supra note 1 at 232, identify the commercial sponsor as the "representative" of the ultimate consumer or class of consumers.

7. For an excellent description of the role of advertising and advertisers in commercial television, see Barnouw, The Sponsor: Notes on a Modern Potentate (New York: Oxford University Press, 1978).

8. Kotcheff, "How Can the Quality of Canadian Popular Programming be Improved?" in CRTC, Symposium on Television Violence (Ottawa: Ministry of Supply and Services, 1975), at 130-31.

9. Id. at 132.

10. The Korean War can never end on M*A*S*H, Gabe Kotter's class can never graduate, and Ann Romano can never remarry on One Day at a Time without simultaneously ending these series.

11. Thompson, "Moloch or Aquarius: Strategies for Evaluating Future Communications Needs," in Robinson and Theall (eds.), Studies in Canadian Communications (Montreal: McGill University Press, 1975) at 66.

12. Ellis, "Remarks," in Symposium, supra note 8 at 147. There has been no research yet into how, if at all, these patterns may have been affected by the remote central channel changers that are necessary for multiple-tier cable television viewing.

13. In ordinary market situations, a consumer with an intense desire for a given commodity can make good this intensity by bidding higher for it than other consumers who also want the same commodity but not as much. Under the present structure of both commercial and subscription television there is no way for viewers to indicate the intensity of their demand for a given program. In the case of commercial television, standard audience measurement techniques cannot differentiate between active enjoyment and passive acquiescence. In the case of subscription television, the single monthly fee pays for the entire schedule of programs and provides no reflection of the viewers' likes and dislikes of particular aspects of the schedule.

14. See Berger and Luckmann, The Social Construction of Reality (Garden City, N.Y.: Doubleday, 1966), upon which much of the following summary of the social role of culture is based.

15. This is an extension of the argument in Scitovsky, The Joyless Economy (London: Oxford University Press, 1976).

16. Credit for this "economese" formulation goes to Professor Ian Parker of the Department of Economics, University of Toronto.

17. Innis, "An Economic Approach to English Literature in the Nineteenth Century," in Political Economy in the Modern State (Toronto: Ryerson University Press, 1943) at 35.

18. Once broadcasting is conceptualized as an industry, standardization of programming and of formats becomes inevitable. Robert Babe has demonstrated econometrically that for most markets diversity does not become demographically rational until the achievement of a degree of audience fragmentation that makes the production of quality programming no longer commercially rational. See Babe, Canadian Television Broadcasting Structure, Performance and Regulation (Ottawa: Minister of Supply and Services, 1979), at 56-61. This is the hard economic reality behind the failure of "quality" pay-television services like CBS in the United States and C-Channel in Canada.

19. 250 U.S. 616 (1919). The most pithy critique of this doctrine is to be found in the quote from "Minerva's Owl," which serves as the epigram for this chapter.

20. 418 U.S. 241 (1971).
21. 412 U.S. 94 (1973).
22. 450 U.S. 582 (1981).
23. 424 U.S. 1 (1976).

24. 395 U.S. 367 (1969).

25. Id. at 390.

26. Meikeljohn, Free Speech and Its Relation to Self-Government (New York: Harper, 1948).

27. J. Barron, Freedom of the Press for Whom? (Bloomington: University of Indiana Press, 1973).

28. Red Lion, supra note 24 at 388.

29. This is the basis of the U.S. Supreme Court's classic broadcasting decision, National Broadcasting Company v. United States, 319 U.S. 190 (1943) per Frankfurter J. at 226.

30. Significantly, the decision of the court in both Red Lion and WNCN was delivered by Justice White.

31. Bazelon, "FCC Regulation and the Telecommunications Press" [1975] Duke L.J. 213. This analysis was first articulated by Judge Bazelon in his dissenting opinion in Brandywine-Mainline Radio Inc. v. Federal Communications Commission 153 U.S. App. D.C. 305 (1971) at 73-76.

32. See the conclusion of this chapter.

33. See, e.g., Brownlie, Principles of Public International Law (Oxford: Clarendon Press, 1979) at 287.

34. Representative works in the area of economics include "An Introduction to the Economic History of the Maritimes," "Liquidity Preference as a Factor in Industrial Development," in Essays in Canadian Economic History (Toronto: University of Toronto Press, 1956) at 27-42, 327-57, and 252-72, respectively. Innis explored the same themes in communications in, inter alia, "Minerva's Owl" and "The Bias of Communication," both in The Bias of Communication (Toronto: University of Toronto Press, 1951) at 3-32 and 33-60, respectively.

35. This is the major thesis propounded in Empire and Communications (Toronto: University of Toronto Press, 1950).

36. See, e.g., "The Problem of Space," in The Bias of Communication, supra note 34 at 92-131, and "Paper and the Printing Press," in Empire and Communications, supra note 35 especially at 143-46.

37. "The Wheat Economy," in Essays, supra note 34 at 273-79.

38. See "Decentralization and Democracy" and "Imperfect Regional Competition," both in Political Economy in the Modern State, supra note 17.

39. An excellent elaboration of this element of Innis' communications theory is to be found in Carey, "Canadian Communications Theory: Extensions and Interpretations of Harold Innis" in Studies in Canadian Communications, supra note 11.

40. See, e.g., Buergenstal, "The Right to Receive Information Across National Boundaries," in Aspen Institute Program on Communications and Society, <u>Control of Direct Broadcasting Satellite: Values in Conflict</u> (Palo Alto, Calif.: Aspen Institute, 1974).

41. See Ploman, supra note 1.

42. See Knelman, <u>This Is Where We Came In: The Career and Character of Canadian Film</u> (Toronto: McLellan and Stewart, 1977).

COMMENT
Glen O. Robinson

CONSUMER SOVEREIGNTY

At the outset I should admit to some ambivalence on the subject of consumer versus national sovereignty. I do not believe that
the First Amendment of the U.S. Constitution has extraterritorial
application. (I take it that statement will invite no <u>legal</u> quarrel
even from the most ardent defenders of the faith.) I do note that
Article 19 of the Universal Declaration of Human Rights embraces
a similar principle, that everyone has a right to "freedom of opinion and expression," which is expressly defined as the right to
"seek and impart information and ideas through any media and regardless of frontiers." I do not, however, put much weight on
this grand principle as a restraint on individual nations imposing
various types of restrictions on speech, and on the receipt of information by their citizens. Just as we in the United States have
interpreted our First Amendment to allow various restraints on
speech and on receipt of information, I impute to Article 19 a
similar flexibility. Indeed, a decent respect for the sovereignty of
nations obliges one to acknowledge the broad discretion of national
governments to regulate communications and information.

A decent respect for the sovereign prerogative to regulate
information and communications, however, does not require respect
for all excuses in which that sovereign prerogative is clothed.

This brings me to my central objection to Freiman's discussion. First and foremost, I think his flailing commercial broadcasting for its "addictive" and "manipulative" quality is a rhetorical
refuge from the reality of democratic choice. Freiman apparently
would have us believe that consumers' commercial choices are
somehow not free simply because they are commercial—intended to
serve the interests of capitalist entrepreneurs as opposed to consumers.

In part I take this notion to be a simple application of the ever
popular view that consumers' tastes are artificially shaped by commercial interests, what John Kenneth Galbraith calls the "revised
sequence" of supply and demand. However, Freiman's discussion
is also a critique of commercial television broadcasting and the
fact that programming is dictated by the interests of advertisers and
not by the direct vote of viewers.

Let us look at the second point first. We can call it a "market failure" problem. There is a range of different kinds of market failures. Unfortunately, Freiman's discussion here is a bit vague so I have to take some liberties in responding to what I think he implies.

Two types of problems appear to be suggested. One is the fact, peculiar to advertiser-supported broadcasting, that programming choice depends, in the first instance, on advertisers, not viewers. Of course, advertisers do not buy advertising time to please themselves; they buy it to reach an audience. Indirectly, therefore, viewer choices influence advertiser choices. As everyone familiar with this business knows, there can be variance between what the viewers would choose for themselves and what the advertisers choose for them. It is mostly a matter of demographics and so on. Despite this possible variance, I am unaware of reliable evidence that demographics or any other factor causes a large gap between what advertisers want to expose to viewers and what viewers want to see. Of course, a commercial, advertiser-supported program market does not "fairly" reflect minority tastes, since every viewer gets an equal vote regardless of the intensity of his or her preference. This problem can be eliminated by introducing a subscription system.

That solution, however, does not satisfy Freiman, who believes that consumer sovereignty is somehow tainted by its commercial character. Herein we find the Galbraithian revised sequence problem. This is a big subject, which we cannot go into here in detail. Suffice it to say that it is true that advertising has an influence on demand creation, but so too does one's childhood, education, reading habits, place of residence, degree of travel, associates—the list is endless. So what? If a friend buys a new Porsche, and out of envy I decide I must have one as well, my demand for it is the same as if desire for the Porsche has been influenced by watching television ads. In both cases my demand is the product of an external stimulation unrelated to my "innate needs," whatever that means. I infer from Freiman's discussion that this "artificial" demand is not entitled to the same respect as that which reflects some "true"—some "free"—consumer choice. On his account, as I understand it, regulation of program choices does not really interfere with true freedom.

It is necessary only to state this proposition to see where it leads. What is a real consumer need? What consumer choices are free in the sense that they are uninfluenced by an environment that is in some sense artificial ?* By a simple progression of such questions we quickly reach the point where we have relegated consumer sovereignty to a very small sphere: consumer sovereignty is limited to the minimal essentials required to sustain life. That seems to me a dismally narrow view of what individual choice is all about.

Now I do not say that free choice is always, or even often, the best choice, best in some sense of edified, enlightened choice. Nor will I say that it is the only choice possible in a democratic society. I am prepared to be moderately imperialistic about overriding majoritarian consumer choice, not only to prevent the majority from smothering the minority with its preferences, but also to expose the majority itself to something it would not choose left to its own unaided preference. † I make no pretense that this imperialism cum paternalism is justified in the name of freedom. That is too Orwellian for my taste, and it has precisely the Orwellian vice that it removes from the regulators an honest consciousness of what they are doing and how far they are justified in going in supplanting individual choice in favor of the more "enlightened" preferences of their leaders.

NATIONAL SOVEREIGNTY

Let me switch from the general problem of consumer sovereignty versus regulation to the more specific problem of promoting national cultural identity.

---

*Students of philosophy will see that free in this sense of being unaffected by environmental conditions inevitably becomes a concept of metaphysical substance only, as with Kant's concept of the "noumenon" or "thing-in-itself. "

†This could be defined as a "market failure" problem insofar as informational and cultural programming of the kind with which we are concerned is a "public good" that cannot be adequately supplied by private markets. While public goods may have real value to people, individual consumers will not reveal their true preference through market purchases.

Incidentally, I do not insist that we address this problem in the framework of welfare economics. On the other hand, it might clarify matters if we focused specifically on what are the conditions that give rise to, and justify, coercive intervention by the state. Analyzing the problem in terms of market failure may help to do this.

I am more sympathetic to this objective than my previous remarks might suggest. I acknowledge the right of governments to
attempt to promote or to preserve the individuality of national cultures against the corrosive forces of outside cultural influences. I
say "attempt" advisedly because I think that self-conscious efforts
by governments to protect indigenous cultures are almost invariably
doomed unless they can draw on a very deeply rooted cultural identity. In most cases the very fact that the government intervenes
to protect local culture from erosion is a fair indication that the
cultural heritage is too shallow, too weak, or too dysfunctional to
sustain itself in a modern society. There is, then, a kind of
Canute-like quality to most of these efforts—like trying to keep
blue jeans out of the Soviet Union, or the Beatles out of America.

In the case of Canada, I do have to wonder what precisely is
the threat? I do not mean to imply that Canadians don't have an
independent culture. I merely put it to defenders of that culture,
what precisely do you seek to protect,* and what in the communications and information that you get from across the border is so
threatening? Is it American cowboy or cops-and-robber films?
American sitcoms? American soap operas? Freiman's discussion
alludes throughout to the peril of commercialism; perhaps then it
is American commercials? Or maybe it is simply the tawdry commercial style of American programming in general. If the commercial orientation of the programming is the objection, I am left in
wonder as to how this has anything to do with Canada's traditional
cultural identity. Is Canada a purer, less commercial, society
than the United States? That is a possibility, but you will forgive
me, I hope, if I put the question on the table for debate.

Perhaps it is nothing so specific as a particular genre, but
merely the fact that the stories tend to be about U.S. events or
places and thus divert Canadians' attention from an interest in their
own events and places. I can understand that, and sympathize, up
to a point.

I think, however, the problem is vastly overdrawn and would
be more properly confronted by other measures. If Canada believes

---

*I cannot suppress some bewilderment at Freiman's emphasis
in protecting "distinctive linguistic, ethnic, regional, and racial
identities." The linguistic identity of French-speaking Canadians
I can appreciate, the ethnic distinctiveness perhaps also. But regional identity has no meaning to me: are Toronto and Buffalo in
different regions? Finally, I was surprised to learn that Freiman
apparently perceives racial differences between Canadians and
Americans.

it is really essential to its national pride and culture to have more films made about Canada, or about the Canadian experience, or simply about Canadian events and people, I would not think of criticizing it for subsidizing such a worthy purpose out of general tax receipts or specially earmarked taxes on media. Such subsidies have been given in various forms to the CBC and to other groups. A policy has recently been announced of subsidy to other program production enterprises generally. From what I read, however, it appears that "Canadization" of program content in this way has not altogether succeeded in eliminating "the problem." Nor, to all appearances, has the government's regulatory policy of requiring Canadian broadcast stations to air a certain percentage of "Canadian content" programs (a concept that, as far as I know, is not precisely defined). The fact remains that Canadian viewers, in impudent disregard of their government's wishes, seem to prefer foreign programs, at least as far as entertainment is concerned.

CANADIAN CULTURAL IDENTITY

I wonder whether Canada has really faced up to the hard question: what precisely does cultural identity mean in concrete terms of specific program content? My doubts are suggested in part by the fact that some of the measures taken to date ostensibly to promote Canadian culture seem to me very weakly related, if related at all, to the problem. Consider, for example, the celebrated tax legislation denying tax deduction for advertisers who buy time on foreign (U.S.) broadcast stations (and in foreign [U.S.] newspapers or periodicals). The immediate purpose is to redirect advertising dollars to Canadian stations (and print media). The long-term effect, we are told, is to promote Canadian culture. Maybe, but I am skeptical. Why should one believe that it will have that effect? CRTC requirements that Canadian stations carry certain percentages of "Canadian content" presumably do affect what the viewer sees, in some undefined sense, and the forced transfer of advertising revenue to those stations is a modest means of helping commercial stations pay for it, but to suppose this will change significantly the kind of programs produced is to suppose that the Canadian advertisers will buy commercial time to support programs that Canadian viewers do not value enough to demand.

The chief effect of Canada's tax measure seems to be that a Canadian broadcast station rather than an American station gets a share of the rents generated by presenting M*A*S*H reruns to Canadian audiences. I do not object to that: an American station in Buffalo is inherently no more deserving of those rents than its

counterpart in Toronto.* I also regard the hysteria created on this
side of the border to be mindless; nothing illustrates this better
than the fact that the United States is proposing mirror legislation
to retaliate. Canada shoots its advertisers in the foot by denying
them cheap access to audiences, therefore the United States proposes to shoot its advertisers in the foot to retaliate. It is a script
that might have been written for the Marx Brothers or the Three
Stooges. This does not have much to do with cultural identity or
any of the high-minded spiritual values that interest Freiman, however.

The same point can be made about the erstwhile practice of
deleting commercials from U.S. programs carried on Canadian
cable systems. Whether or not this action was theft, as U.S.
broadcast interests described it, it seems to me to have been high-
handed in any case. But that is neither here nor there. The point
is that it is hard to explain as cultural protection. I agree that U.S.
commercials can be pretty offensive, but I find it incredible that
one could conceive them to be any more threatening to Canadian
cultural interests than the programs they accompany—programs
that were readily, even eagerly, consumed sans commercials—or
with Canadian commercials substituted for U.S. commercials.

If Canada is serious, truly serious, about protecting its cultural values against the corrosive effect of foreign influence, as
embodied, say, in foreign television programs, I have a simple
solution: set up a board of censors to screen the foreign-made
programs that are carried on Canadian broadcast stations and cable
systems. If Freiman is really faithful to his own principles of
balancing the interests of national sovereignty against consumer
sovereignty, he and other like-minded colleagues should not hesi-
tate to embrace such a measure, or at least something like it. I
do not see any such specific proposal in his discussion. Nor have I
seen such proposals by others expressing similar concerns. Possibly that is because the critics want to win agreement on the moral
merits before advancing particular proposals. However, I also de-
tect a certain squeamishness among the defenders of cultural integrity, an uneasiness in coming out with specific measures that
expose the full implications of the principles they are expounding.

---

*Though it is not important to the question of principle, the
amount of money being transferred is trivial relative to total advertising expenditures in the United States or Canada. The Clyne
Report in 1979 estimated the revenue transferred from American
to Canadian stations was $9.7 million, compared to total U.S.
television advertising revenues of $6.8 billion and Canadian reve-
nues of $376 million.

Do not mistake my message. I emphatically do not want to promote censorship. I do not believe it would be in Canada's own long-term interest, nor would it serve larger world interests of promoting understanding through open relationships and free information flows. Still, I am prepared to concede that I cannot really know this for certain. The gains to Canadian cultural sanity of not being bombarded by inane Hollywood sitcoms and soaps might outweigh the loss of consumer freedom and the inevitable curtailment of valuable information and ideas that censorship threatens. I could respect a candid Canadian decision to face this question squarely with censorship, perhaps on an experimental basis (in an open society every measure is, in a sense, experimental). That would at the very least provide us skeptics with a more credible measure of Canadians' political preferences than rhetoric alone can supply.

5

AN AUDIBLE SQUEAK:
BROADCAST REGULATION IN CANADA

John Meisel

Lightning strikes in the most unexpected places and at odd times. As I was beginning to collect my thoughts for this presentation, First Choice, one of Canada's two national pay-television programmers, and Playboy Enterprises announced that they would jointly produce $30 million worth of "adult" programming in Canada, and that these programs would be shown late at night on the First Choice pay-TV channel.

Then the sky fell. Within 48 hours, a national demonstration was planned. Thousands of people in 19 centers from Victoria, British Columbia, to St. John's, Newfoundland, marched to protest the plans for this programming. Over 400 gathered on Parliament Hill, in bitterly cold weather. The newspapers and broadcast media could not leave the issue alone. The CRTC's correspondence secretariat was buried in an avalanche of more than 7,000 letters and petitions.

In considering all this frenzy while also preparing this discussion, I was struck by the fact that this public outburst was probably more revealing than the proposed programs. So-called adult programming has been available in the United States for some time. In this fabled land of plenty, there are at least three national adult services (Playboy, Eros, and Penthouse's electronic annex), as well, I am told, as more raunchy fare available on stand-alone STV or MDS systems in various metropolitan areas, such as the "Night Owl" programs in Los Angeles.

Yet I can recall hearing of no American protest in any way comparable to the uprising in Canada. Playboy's senior vice-president, Joel Katz, reported that the corporation was stunned by the response, and Playboy went so far as to agree not to organize a promotion campaign. One cause for the anxiety sprang from the fact that the proposal may violate the spirit of Canadian content regulations imposed on the pay-TV licensees. A more important part of the reaction sprang from the concern of feminist groups that, once again, women would be symbolically diminished. But the major stream of criticism derived from the holders of traditional moral values, who feared yet another slip in the long and seductive slide into national depravity.

What was really telling about the public response to the Playboy affair was the eminently Canadian assumption that broadcasting—even the explicitly commercial medium of pay television—is a matter of collective concern. Those who objected to the proposed programming were not for a moment satisfied with the option of not buying the offending service. Television programming is more to them than simply a consumer good to be provided to individual purchasers by unrestricted programmers in accordance with the free play of market forces. The incident shows that this assumption, which has been the basis of Canadian government policy from the days of the Aird Commission in 1928, still holds in the present.

All of which brings me to the main point I wish to make: the context of broadcast regulation in Canada is fundamentally different from the context of regulation in the United States, and for that reason the substance and scope of regulation are bound to be distinct.

It is easy to overlook the difference between the two countries when we review their many similarities in language, political traditions, work habits, and economic structures. Our interrelatedness in the communications field is vividly and directly symbolized by the arrangements approved last year for two U.S. pay-television services to be carried on a Canadian broadcasting satellite and by Canada's most recently launched satellite being deposited into its orbital slot by NASA's space shuttle.

Moreover, for a considerable time our traditions in broadcast regulation followed a similar evolution: the judgments of the Federal Communications Commission in the United States as well as those of the CRTC and its predecessors in Canada revealed a common concern for standards of service to the public in news and public affairs, in the free expression of differing points of view, in balance and variety in programming, and in limitations on the amount of commercial advertising. Nevertheless, there have been very significant differences, the chief of which is the presence of the CBC as the cornerstone of Canadian broadcasting, and the existence of several provincially funded educational networks. Furthermore, Canadians have gone to extraordinary lengths to ensure that the main public and private networks are available in remote and sparsely settled areas.

Disparities between the two countries in broadcast regulation have become even sharper in recent years. There has been a strong movement in the United States toward dismantling regulatory restrictions in favor of reliance on market forces to achieve the goals of broadcasting policy. We have seen measures to loosen federal restrictions on cable television and allow it to compete with broadcasters (although municipal control, absent in Canada, is important in the United States); we have observed the steps being taken to license hundreds of low-power television stations to enhance competition. In an op-ed article in The New York Times in November 1982, FCC Chairman Mark Fowler listed the restrictions and requirements he would like to see removed: the fairness doctrine, ascertainment requirements, guidelines to ensure provision of news and public affairs programming, restrictions on the resale of broadcasting stations. All of this would be in support of the position he argued in U.S. News and World Report the previous April: "In broadcasting, consumers, through the marketplace, subject the broadcaster every hour to a national plebiscite. When you turn that dial, advertisers and broadcasters get the message. Those programs that most people want to watch will be supported by advertising, those they don't want to watch will generally not be."[1]

There is no mystery as to why reliance on market forces has such appeal. Any economist can enlighten us at a moment's notice about the sensitivity of the marketplace to consumer preferences and about its capacity for quickly and effectively exploiting the implications of technical innovation and translating them into products and services that benefit everyone. We are all familiar, too, with the more abstract contention that the free operation of market incentives will yield the best feasible match between scarce resources and individual tastes, and thus create the greatest possible wealth for the economy as a whole. Of course, for industry, there is great attraction in casting aside the iron glove of government intervention in favor of the silken caress of Adam Smith's invisible hand.

With respect to the broadcasting industry in particular, vigorous arguments have been made in favor of turning over more decision making to the open market. It has been suggested that the technological developments of the past decade have so multiplied the channels for public communication that old assumptions about the limited number of frequencies are no longer valid. Hence, it is argued, there is no longer any basis for regarding the use of broadcast frequencies as a public trust, subject to requirements of public service. The fundamental democratic need for the expression of a broad range of viewpoints on matters of public concern will be met through the existence of a multiplicity of broadcast outlets. In the words of Walter Block, a Canadian economist at

Vancouver's Fraser Institute, the answer is to allow free competition to create a veritable tower of Babel of different voices . . . a sort of Hyde Park Corner of the airwaves. Under this approach, so the claim runs, the dangers of state intervention in the broadcast media are avoided, the needs of democracy are met, and consumers get what they want.

I must confess to a certain skepticism in the face of this line of thought. I question the assumption that free markets lead inevitably to unrestricted choice. We have all witnessed the influence that heavily financed advertising campaigns can have on consumer preferences and the way this can be used to justify the producer's prior selection of items for mass production. We have all seen, too, examples of how the efficiencies of mass production are achieved at the price of a reduction of consumer choice.

Markets may be appropriate mechanisms for the allocation of luxuries and resources that are in ample supply. In a caring society, where individuals are seen to have an intrinsic worth, markets alone cannot be allowed to determine how rich the rich shall be and how poor the poor. Nor can they be resorted to alone in determining the levels of health care or education available to the public. There are other aspects, as I noted in an address in Annapolis in 1982: "Would the United States, for example, snuff out domestic production of oil and gas even if it knew that, in economic terms, it would be cheaper to purchase all requirements from the USSR?"[2]

The routine anomalies in the workings of the marketplace are particularly important in the field of broadcasting, which is so sensitively linked to the basis of a democratic society. Can we really expect broadcasters to address the needs and tastes of minority audiences rather than compete for domination of the mass audience? Genuine program choices are not made by audiences in a free market but by network executives responding to their advertising strategies. History has shown them to have been notoriously cautious, imitative, and unwilling to select programs dealing with issues in a manner that avoids stereotyping. No less a person than a former head of the FCC has, in a celebrated speech, characterized the result as a wasteland. It therefore seems to me that multiplication of broadcasting sources will not lead to a broadening of the scope of public debate, and that the market mechanism, so deft at incorporating technological innovations, will prove less receptive to innovations in political and social ideas. A Hyde Park Corner where you can speak only if you lease the property at going commercial rates will lead to a tower of Babel where the host of voices clamors to say the same things!

I claim no novelty of insight in making these observations. In Channels magazine in 1982, Benjamin Barber drew attention to the danger that the heterogeneity and pluralism of communications technologies may not enhance or even permit an informed public consideration of national issues. Dozens of other writers and speakers have expressed concern at the move toward dramatic reductions of regulation. Mark Fowler himself acknowledged in his New York Times article that certain program needs may not be met by an unregulated broadcast marketplace. He mentioned specifically that children's programs, in-depth radio news, and high culture may not be provided by the free-enterprise broadcasters, and suggested that fees charged by government for spectrum use might support a public broadcasting effort to meet these needs.

Whatever the merits of the theoretical arguments about broadcast content regulation, they are unlikely to lead to the same resolution in Canada as in the United States. To be sure, they have found an echo in Canada, where the broader impetus for deregulation or unregulation has also been felt. On the official level alone, several major publications have addressed problems of regulation: the reports of a joint standing committee of the House of Commons and the Senate, the Lambert Royal Commission on Financial Management and Accountability, the Law Reform Commission, the Special Parliamentary Task Force on Regulatory Reform, and the Economic Council of Canada. But the emphasis has been on regulatory reform rather than on deregulation. In the area of broadcasting, pressures to lighten the regulatory load are of course generated, notably in the public positions taken by the Canadian Cable Television Association and the Canadian Association of Broadcasters and in the direct actions of consumers, especially in remote and northern areas, who have circumvented the regulated broadcasting system by installing their own satellite TV receiving dishes.

There are important differences in the context of debate in the Canadian setting, however. For one thing, Canadians do not seem to have developed the finely honed suspicion of government that marks the attitude of many Americans. For decades social scientists have found the reasons for this difference a titillating subject of speculation. Why did the forces of law and order—personified in the Royal Canadian Mounted Police and its predecessors—play such a prominent role in the settlement of the Canadian west, while the settlement of the U.S. frontier was much more free-wheeling? Why does Canada's constitution speak of "peace, order and good government" while that of the United States promises "life, liberty and the pursuit of happiness"? Why do Canadian

responses to attitude surveys consistently reveal higher levels of
trust and confidence in government? A variety of explanations have
been suggested for this phenomenon: the absence of a revolutionary
past, the dispersion of our small population over vast distances,
a sensitivity to society as a community, perhaps enhanced by the
presence of a self-conscious and distinctive French Canadian population in our midst.

Canadian attitudes entail more than an absence of distrust.
Canadians have consistently seen fit to use the state positively as
an instrument for common purposes to a much larger extent than
the United States. Our use of public enterprises spans a long
period, from the building of the Canadian Pacific Railway, the
establishment of public electrical utilities, the founding of Trans-
Canada Airlines, to the formation of Petro-Canada. In the broadcasting sector, as I have already noted, this proclivity to adopt
public enterprise is reflected not only in the existence of the CBC,
but also in the emergence of an array of public broadcasting services at the provincial level.

Heavy government involvement in the building of railways was
in large part prompted by the need of a vast, sparsely settled country for an effective transportation system. Similarly, broadcasting and telecommunications are seen as vitally important in forging
and maintaining links among the various regions and groups making
up the country. The extension of broadcast services to remote and
underserved areas has therefore been the goal of public policy, a
goal pursued steadfastly in the face of unfavorable market conditions.

Canadian attitudes and traditions, then, suggest that our solutions to the regulation-deregulation dilemma will be different from
those in the United States. Perhaps more importantly, though, the
nature of our response will reflect the differing problems we face.
It may turn out that the operation of market forces will realize
what Americans want their broadcast media to achieve. It is in-
conceivable that market forces could address the central concern
of Canadian broadcast regulation—the need to promote a Canadian
presence on the airwaves. To build upon our prime minister's
vivid analogy, the Canadian mouse must not only sleep beside the
American elephant, but also grow, build, and find self-expression
in its looming shadow.

From the outset, this elemental fact has oriented Canadian
policies toward broadcast regulation. The legislative framework
for communications regulation in the United States sets out as its
purpose "to make available . . . a rapid, efficient, nationwide
and world-wide . . . service with adequate facilities and reasonable charges."[3] The Canadian Broadcasting Act, by contrast,
speaks of the need "to safeguard, enrich and strengthen the cultural, political, social and economic fabric of Canada."[4]

You are big and strong enough—and your markets are big and strong enough—to enable you to support an indigenous, unthreatened broadcasting system. We and our markets are only one tenth as strong and so we must seek means you do not even think about to ensure that we can continue being ourselves.

In introducing the first Broadcasting Act in 1932, Prime Minister Bennett told Parliament that "this country must be assured of complete control of broadcasting from Canadian sources, free from foreign interference or influence. Without such control, he argued, "radio broadcasting can never become a great agency . . . by which national consciousness may be fostered and sustained and national unity still further strengthened. . . ." This theme is still paramount in considerations of Canadian broadcasting, as reflected in the recently published Applebaum-Hébert report on federal cultural policy and the cabinet's broadcast strategy, released in 1983.

If we want to have Canadian voices on the airwaves, market forces will not do it. Market forces pull entirely the other way. Canadian broadcasters can purchase expensively produced U.S. programs for a fraction of the cost of creating a comparable original program. Moreover, they can frequently derive higher advertising revenues from showing these tried-and-true American products, so that the economic incentives to buy American are reinforced. It can be argued, and I have made the argument myself, that Canadian productions, if they are any good, will find their way onto the U.S. and world market. Indeed, we have already seen examples of this, as the explosion of programming services in the United States and elsewhere creates a requirement for more and more material. But the fact remains that the path of least risk for a Canadian broadcaster is to buy American. One can put this even more strongly: rational, exclusively economic decision making may dictate virtually total reliance on U.S. entertainment programming.

The statistics amply reflect this. While the United States imports only a minuscule amount of its TV programming (the figure for the networks in 1978 was 2 percent), Canadian private television programmers on the whole provide only the minimum required amounts of Canadian programming. In the peak viewing hours, between 7:30 and 10:30 in the evening, only about 30 percent of programming on these stations is Canadian in origin, and only 5 percent of the drama shown in this period is Canadian produced.

These figures reflect programming by Canadian broadcasters: they do not reveal the massive influx of U.S. services available directly in border areas, or via cable elsewhere.

The history of television regulation in Canada has been a history of attempts to reconcile the national cultural objective of strong indigenous programming with the desire of Canadian viewers for an ever-greater variety of programming, and the need for Canadian commercial broadcasters to make ends meet. The tension between these imperatives has suffused every major television issue the CRTC has had to consider in recent years—the expansion of cable television, the extension of TV services to remote areas, and the introduction of pay television.

There is no doubt that the technological environment is changing rapidly in Canada as well as the United States. There is no doubt, either, that regulation comes at a price in terms of flexibility, innovation, and simplicity. The CRTC is attempting, in a variety of ways, to reduce the regulatory load on its broadcast licensees. It is also experimenting, in the context of its pay-TV licensing decision, with building in some of the competitive benefits associated with a free market system. In that decision, the CRTC deliberately rejected the notion of a monopoly pay-TV service, even though this option enjoyed widespread support, in favor of a competitive market structure. Our expectation, which will soon be put to the test, was that competition in this domain of discretionary services would enhance the prospects for high quality programming, both Canadian and foreign, and would provide greater variety for consumers.

The CRTC has recently taken other initiatives to lighten the regulatory burden, with respect to FM radio, for instance. In the Canadian context these moves cannot aspire to deregulation, as I noted earlier, but to better regulation. One of the consequences of our particular geographic setting and of our demographic realities is that we must devise political institutions and procedures that differ from those of the United States, despite so many seeming similarities between the two countries. It has often been noted, in fact, and with reason, that these similarities sometimes ill prepare us for dealing with our differences, particularly when these may lead to conflict. The border station advertising controversy is a case in point.

As long as Canada aspires to maintain its political and cultural distinctiveness, and this is not only in its own interest but equally in that of the United States, and as long as it continues to see television broadcasting as an integral part of this effort, there will continue to be a place for active governmental concern, for broadcast regulation—and broadcast content regulation—in the Canadian system. Canada may not wish to be known as the mouse that roared, but amidst the thunderous trumpeting of the American elephant, we like to hear ourselves squeak.

NOTES

1. U.S. News and World Report, April 1982.
2. John Meisel, "Of Babies and Bathwater, or What Goes Down the Deregulatory Drain," 10th Annual Policy Research Conference, Annapolis, Md., April 1982.
3. U.S. Communications Act, 1930.
4. R.F.C., 1970 c. B-2.

COMMENT
Stephen A. Sharp

Let me sketch very briefly, for those who are not familiar with the U.S. Federal Communications Commission, what it is and the role it occupies. We are seven members appointed by the president, confirmed by the Senate, serving fixed terms. Our functions include some of those that are exercised both by the CRTC and the Department of Communications. We are an independent regulatory agency, which means that we do not report to the president or take direction from him and that we are subject to legislative oversight by the Congress and to direction through statute when the Congress can get a statute passed and signed by the president.

We operate under the Communications Act, which, with respect to broadcasting, is an outgrowth of the Radio Act of 1927. That act is fairly flexible. We have 56 years of regulatory baggage. Most of the regulations we have at the FCC are authorized by the act but by no means are required by it. As a result we have begun an examination of specific regulations to determine whether or not they are working, whether they are needed, whether they should be replaced with different regulations, or whether they should be abolished entirely. It is important to recognize that we are not deregulating willy-nilly. We are looking at all regulations with an eye toward deregulation, but we are not doing so in every area. We have a number of studies under way and, in some cases, we have determined not to deregulate. In some cases, we simply have changed the mechanism of regulation. Let me deal with the concept of deregulation generally.

Deregulation is a realistic response to technological drive. Technology is pushing us in a number of ways. Certainly the recent decision of the Canadian government is a clear reflection of the power of technology and how it affects policy. We operate in the Fowler Commission on the premise that in certain circumstances economic self-interest can perform many regulatory functions, so that government need not do so. It is done by using the leverage of economic forces in society, which will continue to exist no matter what you do in terms of regulation. You use those forces for the public good rather than taking resources of government to tinker with the marketplace.

We have found in our experience since 1927 that regulation often gets in the way of good service and that often it does not achieve the goal for which it was intended. In those cases, it is time to look at those regulations again and decide whether or not you keep them. That is what we are doing. The FCC's general policy is to create competitive opportunities for delivery of information. I look at information as a whole. I do not look at broadcasting. I do not look at radio or television, multipoint distribution system, or any particular medium. I look at information transfer as a whole and make sure in my own mind when I make a decision that the public is able to receive information of all types, through all different types of media. Perhaps some information would be conveyed in one way, other information would be conveyed in another, according to the speaker's view as to the best means of transmitting his or her viewpoint.

In the video area, we wish to create competitive opportunities. Deregulation requires competition in order to work; that is the important trade-off that a lot of people have forgotten about. We must recognize that we are not going to be protectionists to broadcasting, for instance. Broadcasters will have to fend for themselves in dealing with new, competing technologies. The focus of deregulation is for the broadcaster to be free to engage in a flexible response to new technology.

These competitive means of video delivery include television, as we know it—subscription television, low-power television, cable television, multipoint distribution system, direct broadcast satellites, master antenna systems—and exploding video cassette and video disc sales. All of these are means by which information is transferred. Our real concern is that the viewer have a choice of programming. The viewer gets this choice by having multiple opportunities for delivery, and we hope those multiple opportunities will in fact have multiple programs. This is not necessarily a guarantee. We have all heard about how much ABC, NBC, and CBS look alike, and I think that is a fair characterization.

I think that the concept of the marketplace of ideas is also a part of this. We seek a marketplace of ideas and try to use competitive economic forces to make the suppliers of these program delivery systems accommodate public needs and interests out of their own economic necessity. In the process—in news, public affairs, and entertainment programming—content will be recognizably different and will convey different viewpoints to whoever wishes to hear them. The "Hyde Park for lease" problem raised by John Meisel is one that focuses on the over-the-air advertiser-supported commercial broadcasting system. I suggest that as we find more programming and channels available, the economics begin to change. This is what is heralded by Allan Gotlieb's discussion of narrowcasting (Chapter 1). He points out that, because of the exceedingly rapid growth in channels of delivery, there is a real opportunity for the development of programming. The United States market for programming is a hungry one, hungry almost to the point of desperation. It is a market that has yet to be tapped in any significant fashion by the Canadian production industry. Gotlieb's observation that the advent of narrowcasting offers a great opportunity for Canadian program production is, I think, correct. I think, also, that the cabinet's new broadcast strategy reflects that. I think we are looking at a major change in the structure of information delivery. As this change occurs over the next five to ten years, many of the problems that we have faced in the past may well fade away.

Americans, as is generally recognized, are not aware of Canada's culture, nor are they aware of Mexico's culture, or most any other, including their own. They do, however, understand the culture issue. I think some of the discussion at this conference concerning moral values, lifestyles, and how programming treats these things brings to the fore a problem the American public has had for some time. Many Americans want to defend their culture, but they are defending their culture—the culture of Illinois, Nebraska, and Alabama—against a culture that is alien to them. It is called "Hollywood," and it exports a different type of lifestyle, a different type of moral and social value. Many in the American public do not like what they see on television because they believe it undermines their culture, and I suggest to all of us that this is a problem that does not have a border. This is a problem that is endemic to the entertainment business. The real question is whether or not the entertainment business can accurately reflect reality in terms of variety of lifestyles and at the same time reflect a majority view of what the majority sees as a moral and social fabric. I am not sure that the tension will ever be resolved because the creative forces generally lead the masses in social change. Nevertheless, I think the important thing is for all of us to realize that this is a problem shared by many and not just Canadians.

6

THE POSITION OF THE BORDER BROADCASTERS

Leslie G. Arries, Jr.

As one of the U.S. broadcasters who has participated extensively in the effort to resolve the lingering border dispute, I feel
compelled to submit this statement. I have testified before congressional committees and before the Section 301 committee in-
vestigating the complaint filed by 15 U.S. border stations, I have
spoken to my Canadian audiences and individual broadcasters. I
have suffered the effects of this misguided Canadian policy. It is
important to me that the record of this conference accurately reflect the experience and perspective of the U.S. broadcasters. I
will review the history of the border broadcast dispute, examine
the response of the United States and Canada, describe the impact
of the Canadian law, discuss the underlying cultural issue, and
suggest a framework for resolving the problem.

BACKGROUND

U.S. broadcast signals have been widely received in Canada
since the early 1950s. Television signals are received over the
air in conformity with the Canadian-U.S. Television Agreement of
1952, an arrangement negotiated by the two governments to allocate
television channels between the two countries. Subsequently,
Canadian cable television systems began to carry U.S. signals.
This has enabled most residents of all major Canadian cities and
many smaller cities and towns to enjoy high quality, publicly demanded American broadcast programming.

The U.S. broadcasting industry developed much faster than
its Canadian counterpart because the size of the U.S. population

justified greater financial investment in U.S. stations by program sponsors. Canadian viewers and Canadian industry benefited greatly from the rapid development of U.S. broadcasting. Canadian viewers received quality U.S. programming at no direct cost. As Canadians grew increasingly fond of watching U.S. broadcast programs, the Canadian cable television industry developed rapidly to spread U.S. signals throughout Canada.

The U.S. border broadcast stations received no remuneration for the television and radio broadcasts Canadians were enjoying until Canadian advertisers recognized the popularity of American programming with Canadian audiences. Then they began purchasing advertising time on U.S. stations to reach Canadian audiences. The total dollar flow was small compared to the overall Canadian and U.S. television industry revenue base, but it became significant to the U.S. border stations, facilitating the provision of quality service to their U.S. and Canadian audiences.

Since 1955, KVOS-TV of Bellingham, Washington, has been liable for Canadian taxes on all its income from advertising revenues received from Canadian sources (these taxes are based on a negotiated allocation between the two countries). The station also operated the largest full-line film production enterprise west of Toronto until it was forced to dissolve this business at the end of December 1977 to economize in the face of the severe adverse financial impact of Bill C-58.

The government of Canada has adopted several laws and regulations to discourage advertising by Canadian businesses on U.S. television and radio stations. The two most notable and most repugnant policies are commercial deletion and C-58.

Canada announced the practice of commercial deletion in 1971. Cable operators who picked up U.S. signals would be encouraged or required to delete the commercials carried by U.S. stations before transmitting the programming. The effect of this policy, had it been fully implemented, would have been to sharply curtail and probably eliminate advertising by Canadians on U.S. stations. One of Canada's most distinguished newspapers, the Toronto Globe and Mail, characterized commercial deletion as piracy in an editorial published in 1976.

In January 1977, after negotiations conducted by Secretary of State Henry Kissinger, Canada suspended further implementation of commercial deletion and limited the practice to three cities: Toronto, Calgary, and Edmonton. Even so, commercial deletion still restricts the ability of some U.S. broadcast stations to market their advertising product in Canada. Commercial deletion remains particularly costly to several Spokane, Washington, stations whose signal is relayed by microwave to Calgary area cable systems, some 450 miles to the north.

The respite provided by the understanding reached with Secretary Kissinger was short lived. The Trudeau government proclaimed Bill C-58 into law in September 1976. The law became fully effective in 1977. The critical provision of this law is:

> In computing income, no deductions shall be made
> in respect of an otherwise deductible outlay or ex-
> pense of a taxpayer made or incurred after the
> section comes into force, for an advertisement
> directed primarily to a market in Canada and
> broadcast by a foreign broadcast undertaking. [1]

The effect of this law has been to impose a 100 percent tariff on the export of U.S. advertising services to Canada. As the Vancouver _Province_ explained, "Most corporations operate at roughly a 50 percent tax level. In the old days, if a company spent $1 to advertise on KVOS, 50 cents of it would be paid for by taxes, or rather the lack of them. Now the whole dollar comes out of the client's pocket. "[2]

RESPONSE

The United States government responded quickly to this problem, and in September 1977 the Senate adopted a resolution, introduced by Senator Patrick Moynihan and 16 cosponsors on April 26, 1977, calling on President Carter to "raise with the Government of Canada the question of impact of the recent provision of the Canadian tax code on the U.S. broadcasting industry with a view toward adjusting outstanding differences. "[3] The State Department told the Foreign Relations Committee it intended "to keep this matter and its adverse impact on U.S. broadcast interests before the Canadian Government as opportunities to do so arise. "[4]

Various high level government contacts between Canada and the United States have included discussions of this issue. It has been raised in the context of negotiations on a new tax convention between the United States and Canada, at various interparliamentary group meetings, at meetings between high-level cabinet and subcabinet officials, and even at the presidential level. On May 23, 1978, the United States sent a formal diplomatic note to the Canadian government protesting the unilateral imposition of broadcast controls via Bill C-58. Canada has consistently and bluntly rejected all U.S. requests for serious negotiations.

From early 1977 to late 1980, Bill C-58 was a significant factor in the refusal of Congress to modify the Tax Reform Act of

1976 to provide a North American exemption from the restrictions on tax deductibility of expenses incurred in attending business conventions held in foreign countries. For example, on April 27, 1977, the Senate rejected an amendment allowing such deductions by a vote of 48 to 45. Similarly, the House Ways and Means Committee reported H.R. 9281 in the fall of 1978 with an amendment that a North American exception to the foreign convention provision should not apply to Canada as long as C-58 continued in effect.

On December 13, 1980, Congress passed H.R. 5973, which revised the tax treatment of the expenses of attending foreign conventions. The law includes an exemption for Canada and Mexico from restrictions applicable to conventions held in other foreign countries. This privilege was granted to Canada only after Representative Barber Conable urged Canada to reciprocate the goodwill demonstrated by Congress by being more forthcoming on the C-58 issue and eliminating the discrimination against U.S. television stations.

Canada has ignored Conable's request and remains intransigent on C-58.

Although the U.S. negotiators raised C-58 during negotiations on the bilateral tax convention between the U.S. and Canada, they were unsuccessful in pursuing the matter. In September 1981, during hearings on the tax treaty, Senator Charles Percy, chairman of the Committee on Foreign Affairs, questioned the Treasury Department about the Canadian intransigence on C-58 during the aforementioned negotiations. Subsequently, Senator Robert Dole, in a letter to Percy, expressed disappointment that the tax treaty ignores this issue and urged the Foreign Relations Committee to include the need for its prompt resolution in weighing whether to report the treaty favorably. Dole stated:

> It is unfortunate whenever a tax treaty, particularly one with a developed country, fails to resolve tax discrimination problems between the treaty partners. The dispute with Canada over C-58, Canada's indirect tax discrimination against U.S. broadcasters, is exactly the sort of dispute it was hoped the new Canadian treaty would resolve. I am disappointed that the new treaty, at the insistence of the Canadians, ignores this dispute.[5]

The failure, at least so far, to resolve C-58 in as logical and appropriate a context as the tax treaty negotiations further illustrates the unreasonable stance of the Canadians and explains some of the frustrations felt by the U.S. broadcasters.

SECTION 301 CASE

On August 29, 1978, 15 U.S. border broadcast stations filed a formal complaint under Section 301 of the Trade Act of 1974 with the then Special Trade Representative. Eight other stations, though not signatories to the formal complaint, filed comments in the 301 proceeding stating their concurrence in the charge that C-58 was an unfair trade practice. The complaint alleged that C-58 was discriminatory, unreasonable, unjustifiable, and burdened U.S. commerce. In November 1978, the STR held hearings on the complaint, at which Canadian broadcasters appeared in opposition. The Canadians argued that Section 301 did not encompass trade in services such as border broadcast advertising. In 1979 Congress amended Section 301 and thereby removed any legal argument as to the applicability of Section 301 to border broadcast advertising service. The 1979 amendment also introduced a one-year statutory deadline for resolution of Section 301 complaints.

In February 1980, the U.S. Trade Representative informed the Canadian government that a final resolution to the complaint must be reached before the statutory deadline of July 1980. On July 9, 1980 the USTR held hearings on possible remedies. Two members of the Senate Committee on Finance, Senators H. John Heinz and Patrick Moynihan, submitted testimony on behalf of the broadcasters. The broadcasters suggested that the president select a combination from among four remedies: duties or quantitative restrictions on exports of Canadian feature films and records to the United States; mirror-image legislation; continued linkage to the foreign convention issue; and general linkage to other U.S.-Canadian interests.

On July 31, 1980, President Carter, after considering the recommendation of the USTR and the evidence developed in the extensive investigation and hearings, determined that the Canadian tax practice embodied in C-58 "is unreasonable and burdens and restricts U.S. commerce within the meaning of Section 301."

On September 9, 1980, more than two years after the filing of the Section 301 complaint, President Carter sent a message to Congress calling for the enactment of mirror-image legislation. The Ninety-sixth Congress did not have time to consider the proposal.

President Reagan, recognizing that the remedy proposed by President Carter had died with the Ninety-sixth Congress, reviewed the case and resolved to solve the problem. On November 17, 1981, after thorough study and careful consideration within several agencies and departments, President Reagan issued a message to Congress about C-58. After noting that a good-faith effort by the

USTR had failed to eliminate the offending practice, President
Reagan recommended legislation similar to the amendment proposed
by President Carter. This so-called mirror bill would deny an
income tax deduction for the expense of advertisements placed by
U.S. businesses with a foreign broadcast undertaking and directed
primarily to a market in the United States.

Most significantly, President Reagan recognized that this
amendment by itself might not cause the Canadians to resolve this
dispute. He noted his right to take further action to obtain the
elimination of C-58 on his own motion under the authority of Section
301(c)(1). The border broadcasters welcomed President Reagan's
determination to solve this problem.

CANADIAN RESPONSE

The Canadian government consistently has been intransigent
on C-58. Even before the Parliament enacted the bill, Canadian
officials adamantly refused to discuss with the United States the
strenuous objections of the State Department. United States Ambassador Thomas Enders took the U.S. case to Parliament during
its debate on C-58, asking for negotiations to attempt to reconcile
the interests of both countries. Although the Canadian Senate Banking Committee proposed conciliatory amendments to Bill C-58, the
Canadian Senate rejected those recommendations after intense public debate.

The stated Canadian goal is to keep advertising revenues in
Canada to develop its film and broadcast industries. The Canadian
government claims to view the matter as a cultural issue and seems
to believe the issue represents so few dollars in the mix of Canada-
U.S. trade that Canada can succeed by simply refusing to negotiate.

The Canadian government has ignored the recommendation of
a commission it established in 1978 to develop a strategy to re-
structure the Canadian telecommunications system to help safeguard Canada's sovereignty. After analyzing the border broadcast
situation, this commission, the Consultative Committee on the
Implications of Telecommunications for Canadian Sovereignty,
concluded:

> The treatment of the U.S. border stations by Canada
> has created serious friction between the two coun-
> tries, which could result in retaliatory measures in
> other fields of enterprise, and it is clear that there
> can be no solution that would satisfy the interests of
> all parties. The subject has been a matter of

discussion between officials of the Canadian Department of External Affairs and the U.S. State Department, and in 1976 Canada made proposals for, _inter alia_, a bilateral treaty on cross-border advertising, but these were unacceptable for the United States. At this point we should like to quote from the brief submitted to us by the U.S. border stations:

> . . . we urge that the problems of the Canadian broadcasting system (in this particular matter) can only be resolved in the context of an amicable understanding between the two countries. [6]

We concur in this statement.

The commission recommended that "the federal government should renew the discussions with the United States with a view to resolving the border television dispute at an early date."[7]

More recently, both the legitimacy and the success of the Canadian policy have been questioned by Canadians. One of the most prominent Canadian cable company executives, Edward Rogers, has called for a review of Bill C-58 by the Canadian government. Referring to Bill C-58 and simultaneous substitution (a policy requiring cable operators to blank out the U.S. signal and substitute the signal of local Canadian stations when a U.S. station broadcasts the same program at the same time), Rogers stated:

> Right now the broadcasters have got their increased cash flow from these restrictions, but the increase in program choice and the deregulation of optional and discretionary services has not been forthcoming.
>
> Bill C-58 should be reviewed by the Canadian government. It has caused great misunderstanding in the United States. Yet there has never been a public accounting by the privileged few companies who financially benefited from this very sensitive legislation. There should be such a public accounting and soon. If the cash flow gains to these relatively few private companies is not going to produce enhanced Canadian programming—then the bill should be repealed. [8]

The Canadian press also has been critical of C-58. In an editorial headlined, "Heads We Win, Tails Too," the Toronto _Globe and Mail_ criticized the Canadian attitude that produced C-58. The editorial concluded:

Canada can bluster all it wants about U.S. pressure tactics, but it does so on very shaky moral grounds. Either we recognize that both sides can play at protectionism, and accept the game on those terms, or we should simply stop imposing protective policies.

The United States is not about to let us have it both ways—and, more to the point, we don't deserve to.[9]

The Hamilton, Ontario, Spectator denounced C-58 as piracy. It stated:

The objection the U.S. stations have is valid. Canadian cable-TV companies are, as charged, pirating U.S. programs and inserting Canadian commercials. In essence, they are robbing the U.S. networks and stations. Because the 1975 tax law doesn't allow Canadian advertisers to deduct the cost of advertising on a U.S. station if that advertising is aimed at Canadians, the cable companies are getting paid for pirating U.S. programs because Canadian advertisers buy time from the cable companies. . . .

And piracy is piracy. If U.S. cable companies were doing the same as the Canadian companies are, Canadians would complain even louder than they do already.[10]

IMPACT ON U.S. BROADCAST STATIONS

President Carter found that Bill C-58 "denies the U.S. border broadcasters access to a substantial portion of the advertising market in Canada, amounting to approximately $20 to $25 million annually, to which they previously had had access."[11] The implementation of Bill C-58 has reduced by at least two thirds the cross-border advertising revenues of U.S. television stations.

Total Canadian advertising revenues derived by U.S. television stations dropped by approximately 50 percent from 1975 to 1977; from $28.9 million in 1975, the last full year before implementation of Bill C-58, to $16.8 million in 1976, and to $9.2 million in 1977. Canadian expenditures on border stations declined further in 1978, to a total of $6.5 million, according to a study by Donner and Lazar.[12]

A study undertaken for the government of Canada indicates that Bill C-58 has reduced the cross-border flow of advertising.

The study projects that there would have been $29.5 million of advertising placements in 1978. By subtracting the actual cross-border flow of advertising from this figure, the study estimates that by 1978 the loss of advertising was $23 million.

Apart from the loss in annual advertising flow is the decline in the asset value of the U.S. stations along the Canadian border due to Bill C-58. The $23 million decline in advertising flow may have reduced the asset value of such stations by a multiple of three, or $69 million. This reflects the rule of thumb in broadcasting that the asset value of a station is approximately three times the level of annual advertising proceeds.

Bill C-58 also applies to radio broadcasters. Due to apparent laxity in enforcing Bill C-58, the impact on some U.S. radio stations has been delayed. However, a broadcaster in Calais, Maine, whose station is the only broadcast outlet for neighboring St. Stephen, New Brunswick, conservatively estimates that he will lose $100,000 annually on the basis that approximately one third of his advertisements are directed primarily at Canadians by Canadian businesses.

SOLUTIONS

The border broadcasters appreciate the deep concerns about national identity and cultural sovereignty that underlie Canadian policies such as Bill C-58. But such concerns do not justify a policy so pointedly unfair and one-sided.

Moreover, it is difficult to understand how Bill C-58 reduces the U.S. cultural presence in Canada. It does not affect in any way the ability or predisposition of Canadians to watch the U.S. programming of U.S. television stations. As the Hamilton Spectator observed:

> It's one thing to build up pride, to persuade people that a Canadian TV show or a Canadian product is a good buy. That's legitimate in any free-market system.
>
> It's quite another to legislate so that consumers have no choice about what they may or may not purchase, watch or otherwise consume.[13]

The Canadian government apparently has begun to recognize the potential for using cable system profits from popular U.S. programming to develop the Canadian program production industry. Supporting Canadian production rather than unilaterally handicapping popular U.S. stations is reasonable. Given the substantial demand for programming generated by cable television, significant opportunities exist for marketing of Canadian programming in the United States. We welcome such a free flow of programming between our countries. As broadcasters, we are highly sensitive to the cherished values we attach to the free flow of communications. Unilateral obstacles to this free flow, such as Bill C-58, are a particularly repugnant form of trade barrier.

Finally, we agree with the statement made by former Canadian Ambassador to the United States Peter M. Towe before leaving Washington. He said: "These problems—ours and yours—will not be solved by mere finger pointing, much less exaggerated claims and counterclaims. We must strengthen our commitment at the highest level to finding appropriate solutions."[14]

CONCLUSION

We think that Senator John Danforth, the chairman of the Senate Finance Committee, Subcommittee on International Trade, aptly summarized our situation when he introduced S.2051:

> In the face of our declining balance of trade, it is
> crucial that Congress stand behind American export
> interests. The communications industry is one of
> our important service industries and the service
> sector is becoming an increasingly important growth
> area on our export ledger. Thus, it is vitally impor-
> tant that we reenforce one of the few legal mechanisms
> which U.S. service exporters can invoke to gain re-
> lief from foreign trade barriers.[15]

The border broadcasters do not seek "victory," but rather only a quiet resolution of this issue on terms that allow a fair opportunity to earn compensation for services rendered.

NOTES

1. Bill C-58, An Act to Amend the Income Tax Act, September 1976.
2. Vancouver Province, June 30, 1977.
3. U.S. Senate Resolution 152, September 1977.
4. U.S. Senate Report 95-402.
5. Letter from Senator Dole to Senator Percy.

6. Consultative Committee on the Implications of Telecommunications for Canadian Sovereignty.

7. Ibid., pp. 45-46.

8. Edward Rogers, speech to annual meeting of shareholders of Canadian Cable Systems Ltd., January 26, 1981.

9. The Toronto Globe and Mail, July 24, 1980.

10. Hamilton Spectator, July 15, 1980.

11. 45 Fed. Reg. 51173.

12. Arthur Donner and Fred Lazar, An Examination of the Financial Impacts of Canada's 1976 Amendments to Section 19.1 of the Income Tax Act (Bill C-58) on U.S. and Canadian TV Broadcasters (Ottawa, Dept. of Communications, 1979).

13. Hamilton Spectator, July 15, 1980.

14. Congressional Record, S.12647, October 30, 1981.

15. John Danforth, Congressional Record, S.297, February 2, 1982.

7

THE ECONOMICS OF ADVERTISER-SUPPORTED TELEVISION IN ADJACENT COUNTRIES: CONSUMER SOVEREIGNTY, ADVERTISING EFFICIENCY, AND NATIONAL POLICY

Yale M. Braunstein

The dispute over Canadian laws and regulations aimed at Canadian purchasers of advertising time on U.S. broadcast television stations that are viewed by Canadian audiences is not simply a disagreement between governments. The current Canadian tax regulation is designed to divert income from U.S. broadcasters to Canadian stations. There are few comprehensive analyses of the effects of these regulations, however, and advertisers and broadcasters on both sides of the border, as direct participants in the battle, often have different views from that of their governments.

U.S. border stations are described as viewing the issue as "a matter of bucks," while an official in the office of the U.S. Special Trade Representative has been quoted as saying the money involved only amounts to "peanuts."[1] From the U.S. government's perspective there are two major issues: the precedent of a barrier to unhindered trade in "services"[2] and the "viability of Section 301 [of the Trade Act of 1974, which authorizes responses to 'unreasonable' trade limitation practices]."[3]

Among the Canadian parties, one can identify at least four sets of interests: those of the Canadian broadcasters, the Canadian program producers, the viewers, and the government. The government's position, as described by Broadcasting, is: "The Canadians say their tax law is not subject to negotiations. They also express concern about cultural sovereignty; the advertising revenues diverted from American stations are intended to help develop Canada's broadcasting industry."[4]

This discussion will develop a model of advertiser choice among media and use it to highlight the economic forces that have helped to create this dispute. A set of stylized facts will be devel-

oped from the trade press and government documents that have
discussed recent rounds in the border war. We will see that the
effects can be analyzed by the traditional economic decomposition
of a response to a price change into income and substitution effects.
Specifically, although recent Canadian tax law changes have reduced
advertising on U.S. stations, there is no evidence that there has
been any significant effect on the revenues of Canadian stations.

THE UNIQUE CANADIAN BROADCAST MARKET

If one had to summarize the cause of this "border war," it
could be argued that it arises from an unfortunate interplay of political geography, language, and the technical aspects of broadcast
television. Nations license television broadcasters, and the signals
have a limited effective range. Unlike short-wave radio, the broadcast television signal does not reach far distances; but unlike cable
television, it is impossible to create precise limits. Because of
interference problems, adjacent television "markets" generally do
not use the same frequencies (channels), and, as a result, there is
often an overlap in coverage areas. These technical aspects are
compounded by several factors: (1) Canadian and U.S. television
sets are perfectly (technically) compatible; (2) the vast majority
of Canadians live close to the border; (3) English is the dominant
language in both countries; and (4) there are several U.S. cities
with television broadcast stations that can be received easily by
Canadian households.
Although different sources disagree on exact numbers and
there has been some change over time, the situation in Canada has
been officially described as a dilemma:

> Every generation of Canadians, over the last 50 years
> or so, has had to face up to the dilemma of broadcast-
> ing in this country. In many ways Canadians have been
> well served by their broadcasting system. A combina-
> tion of Canadian stations has always meant a greater
> diversity of choice for most of us than any other coun-
> try in the world. But in other ways, it has always
> fallen short of the ideals expressed by most objective
> critics. The present statistics on television viewing
> state the facts baldly. Canadians spend much more
> time watching foreign, mostly American programs
> than they do watching programs produced in their own
> country. As in the past, they are watching the world
> through borrowed eyes. [5]

Specifically, there are approximately 17 million English-language television viewers in Canada, and two-thirds of the English-language programs are foreign. The two-thirds figure understates the problem, however, as these programs account for 74 percent of total viewing (81 percent in peak time) and 83 percent of the viewing time of English-speaking children.[6] Although these percentages include both U.S.-produced programs broadcast by Canadian stations as well as the programs of U.S. broadcast stations, the twin problems of geography and the widespread use of cable television seriously limit the practical effects of domestic-content policies.

There have been two major responses by the Canadian government to this situation. In the mid-1970s the Canadian Radio-Television Commission (CRTC) ordered Canadian cable television systems carrying signals received from broadcasting stations not licensed to serve Canada (i.e., from U.S. broadcasters) to delete commercials randomly from these signals. It is generally believed that the random deletion policy was at least partially successful.[7] Nevertheless, there was strong and vocal opposition, and this policy was dropped.

The second action was the 1976 passage of Bill C-58 amending Section 19.1 of the Canadian Income Tax Act. This amendment, still in effect, denies Canadian firms the right to deduct, for tax purposes, the cost of advertising in U.S. media from their income. One estimate puts the annual revenue loss of U.S. broadcasters in the $10-million range; this is approximately half of the dollar volume that had previously existed.[8] Since the Canadian corporate profits tax rate is 52 percent, the effect of C-58 was to double the effective cost of advertising on U.S. stations. While it should not be surprising that there was, in fact, a reduction in U.S. border stations' advertising receipts, it is not obvious whether the tax-adjusted expenditures of Canadian advertisers in either the U.S. or Canada increased or decreased. We shall return to this point later.

AN ECONOMIC MODEL OF ADVERTISING
IN OVERLAPPING MARKETS

It is important to realize that Canadian firms do not choose to advertise on U.S. television stations solely because the advertising rates of the U.S. stations are lower. Although this is the situation for the Vancouver, British Columbia-Bellingham, Washington market, the reverse is true in the Montreal, Toronto, and Windsor regions. (Comparable 1980 advertising rates for several VHF broadcasters are shown in Table 7-1.) If one were to adjust for the fact that a Canadian advertiser often pays for the right to reach many U.S. viewers who are not prospective customers, the "effective" advertising rates on U.S. stations would be significantly higher. (Here, "effective" means "per Canadian household reached by the signal.")

TABLE 7.1

Selected Advertising Rates
(30-Second Spots, Highest Rate, 1980)

City Pair	Station (VHF)	Advertising Rate (U.S. Dollars)
Bellingham, Wash.	KVOS	300
Vancouver, B.C.	CBUT	410
"	CHAN	725*
Buffalo, N.Y.	WGR	1,850
"	WIVB	1,700
"	WKBW	1,800
Toronto, Ont.	CBLT	675
"	CFTO	850
Detroit, Mich.	WDIV	3,500
"	WJBK	3,311
"	WXYZ	3,393
Windsor, Ont.	CBET	170
Burlington, Ver.	WCAX	500
Plattsburgh, N.Y.	WPTZ	500
Montreal, P.Q.	CBMT	320
"	CFCF	320

*Combination rate with CHEK, Victoria.
Source: Television Factbook, Stations Volume, 1980.

Since price-per-minute comparisons or even price-per-minute-per-household comparisons do not explain the purchases of U.S. advertising by Canadian firms, we must look further. The missing element is the relatively heavy Canadian viewing of U.S. border stations both over the air and via Canadian cable television carriage of U.S. stations. With this background, we can now develop a model of the decision-making process of Canadian advertisers.

The standard models of optimal advertising expenditures by a firm have been developed from the 1954 work of Dorfman and Steiner.[9] They find that an advertiser maximizes profits by setting the marginal revenue from advertising equal to the marginal cost of advertising as well as by setting the traditional marginal revenue from sales equal to the marginal cost of production. These conditions are equivalent to having the share of revenues spent on advertising equal to the ratio of the advertising elasticity of demand to the price elasticity of demand. (See Appendix A for the derivation of these results.)

For the purpose of this discussion, it is necessary to modify and extend the Dorfman-Steiner model in three ways: (1) two different advertising media need to be included; (2) corporate profits taxes need to be included; and (3) advertising expenditures need to be decomposed into advertising volume (in physical terms) and the price of a unit of advertising.

The firm chooses the levels of output of Q and the level of advertising in the two media (a_1 and a_2) to maximize profit:

Maximize: $\pi = (1 - t) [PQ(P, a_1, a_2) - C(Q) - g_1(a_1)] - g_2(a_2)$

where: t = corporate profits tax rate
  P = price of output
  $Q (P, a_1, a_2)$ = demand function
  $C(Q)$ = production cost function
  $g_1(a_1)$ = advertising cost function in medium 1.
    (Advertising expenses in medium 2 are
    not deductible for tax purposes.) (1)

The optimum level of advertising in each medium is:

$$a_1^* = \frac{e_1}{e_d} \cdot \frac{PQ}{MC_{a1}} \tag{2}$$

$$a_2^* = \frac{e_2}{e_d} \cdot \frac{PQ(1 - t)}{MC_{a2}} \quad ; \text{where } e_1 = [(\partial Q_1/\partial a_1)/(Q_1/a_1)] \tag{3}$$

The optimal advertising ratio (if the firm advertises in both media) is:

$$(\frac{a_1}{a_2})^* = \frac{e_1}{e_2} \cdot \frac{MC_{a2}}{MC_{a1}(1 - t)} \tag{4}$$

where: e_1 = advertising elasticity of demand in medium 1
  MC_{a1} = marginal cost of a unit of advertising in
    medium 1.

Equations 2, 3, and 4 indicate that for profit maximization the ratio of advertising in medium 1 to that in medium 2 is proportional to the ratio of the advertising elasticities, inversely proportional to the marginal costs, and proportional (but not directly) to the corporate tax rate. Depending on the values of these parameters, it is possible, of course, for the efficient firm to advertise in only one of the media.

The marginal cost and tax rate terms in equations 2, 3, and 4 are relatively easy to interpret and measure with actual data. Unfortunately, this may not be the case for the advertising elasticity terms. To gain insight into the meaning of (e_1/e_2), assume that sales can be "assigned" to the advertising that generated them. With this assumption, Q can be decomposed into two parts, Q_1 and Q_2, and the response of sales to advertising is $(\partial Q_1/\partial a_1)$ in medium 1 and $(\partial Q_2/\partial a_2)$ in medium 2.[10] We can further decompose Q_1 into two parts: sales per viewing household (Q_1/v_1) and viewing households (v_1); therefore, $Q_1 = (Q_1/v_1)(v_1)$.

Since it is reasonable to assume that $(\partial v_1/\partial a_1) = 0$ for any one advertiser, we get:

$$\frac{\partial Q_1}{\partial a_1} = v_1 \left[\frac{\partial (Q_1/v_1)}{\partial a_1} \right] \tag{5}$$

The last term can be interpreted as a measure of the advertising effectiveness in medium 1, as the change in sales per viewing household results from a change in advertising level. If this effectiveness is the same in the two media (or if one is a constant fraction of the other), then

$$\left(\frac{\partial Q_1}{\partial a_1} \right) / \left(\frac{\partial Q_j}{\partial a_j} \right) = \left(\frac{v_1}{v_j} \right) \tag{6}$$

Equation 6 shows that the ratio of the advertising elasticities is equal to the ratio of the viewers, where j is any other medium. Specifically, since $e_1 = (\partial Q_1/\partial a_1)/(Q_1/a_1)$, we can rewrite equation 4 as:

$$\left(\frac{a_1}{a_2} \right)^* = k \left(\frac{v_1}{v_2} \right) \left(\frac{MC_{a2}}{MC_{a1}(1-t)} \right) \tag{7}$$

(where k is a constant), and we see that the optimal ratio of advertising in the two media is proportional to the ratio of viewers.

IMPLICATIONS OF THE MODEL

It should be obvious that medium 1 represents Canadian television stations and that medium 2 represents U.S. stations that reach Canadian viewers. Equation 7 shows that the ratio of advertising on Canadian stations to that on U.S. stations can be increased by any of the following: (1) increasing relative viewing by Canadians of Canadian stations or decreasing that of U.S. stations; (2) increasing the relative cost of advertising on U.S. stations; or (3) increasing the Canadian corporate profits tax rate.

Since items 2 and 3 together can be rewritten as "increase the after-tax relative cost of advertising on U.S. stations," it is obvious why C-58 has been effective in reducing advertising purchases on U.S. media. Similarly, if we remember that v_1 refers to the viewing of advertising messages, the effects of the now discontinued commercial deletion policy could be analyzed if the appropriate data were available. In other words, C-58 has increased the cost of Canadians' advertising on U.S. stations both in relative and absolute terms. However, it is important to remember that equation 7 only explains the optimal advertising <u>ratio</u>. The effective cost (post-C-58) of advertising to the firm is now:

$$A = (1 - t) g_1(a_1) + g_2(a_2) \tag{8}$$

whereas, before the adoption of C-58, it was:

$$\hat{A} = (1 - t) [g_1(a_1) + g_2(a_2)] \tag{9}$$

if the tax rate and advertising rates have not changed. (Obviously we are ignoring inflation; however, it is possible that g_1 and g_2 have also changed in response to the advertising demand shifts.) Furthermore, it is also possible that the change in advertising levels and mix might have caused the overall advertising elasticity to change; this would then cause a shift in the optimal ratio of advertising expenditures to sales. (See equation A3 in Appendix A.)

Can we determine the effect a law such as C-58 will have on the purchases of <u>Canadian</u> advertising alone? First assume that the <u>total</u> advertising budget of the firm is not influenced by C-58 (i.e., assume there is only a relative change in prices). In this case, $A = \hat{A}$ or:

$$(1 - t) (\hat{A}_1 + \hat{A}_2) = (1 - t)A_1 + A_2 \tag{10}$$

where A_1 = advertising expenditures in medium 1 after C-58
$\hat{A}_2$ = advertising expenditures in medium 1 before C-58.

Rewriting equation 10 we see that:

$$A_1 = \hat{A}_1 + \hat{A}_2 - (\frac{1}{1-t}) A_2.$$

If the Canadian firm (in percentage terms) reduces its expenditures on U.S. advertising by more than the corporate tax rate, it will spend more for advertising on Canadian media (and vice versa). Although estimates vary, most sources indicate that the drop in aggregate U.S. television advertising sales to Canadian firms has been approximately the same as the corporate tax rate (52 percent).[11] If these estimates are correct, C-58 has not led to an absolute (as opposed to a relative) increase in the purchases of Canadian television advertising by Canadian firms. However, it has increased the Canadian government's tax revenues and the effective cost of advertising by Canadian firms.

In other words, the "substitution effect" (in favor of Canadian media) may be completely offset by the "income effect" of the tax increase. If the assumption of no change in advertising budgets is valid, C-58 has resulted in increased tax revenues for the Canadian government but little or no additional revenue for Canadian broadcasters. On the other hand, if advertising budgets have changed, the effect of policies such as C-58 on the revenues of Canadian broadcasters will depend on the relative advertising elasticities as well as the advertising volumes and the tax rate.

CONCLUSION

If the purpose of C-58 is to aid Canadian broadcasters and to enable them to spend more on programming produced in Canada, it is unlikely that this objective has been or could be accomplished by increasing the effective cost of a certain type of advertising. On the other hand, both the tax policy (C-58) and the earlier commercial deletion policy will reduce the outflow of Canadian dollars, and C-58 has increased the Canadian government's tax revenues.

If one had to identify the single major source of the "problem," it is the propensity of Canadian television viewers to watch non-Canadian programming. Many people have addressed the dilemma facing the Canadian policy-maker: how does one balance a desire for more Canadian programming with a respect for freedom of choice and expanded options for the audience?[12] I have shown that policies directed at the advertising medium are not likely to have significant effect on program funding or production.

APPENDIX A

The Dorfman-Steiner Model

Maximize: $\pi = P \cdot Q(A, P) - C(Q) - A$
where: P = price of output
$Q(A, P)$ = demand function
$C(Q)$ = production cost function
A = advertising expenditures

Maximum profit is found by taking partial derivatives with respect to Q and A:

$$\frac{\partial \pi}{\partial Q} = Q \frac{\partial P}{\partial Q} + P - \frac{\partial C}{\partial Q} = 0 \tag{A1}$$

$$\frac{\partial \pi}{\partial A} = P \frac{\partial Q}{\partial A} - \frac{\partial C}{\partial Q} \cdot \frac{\partial Q}{\partial A} - 1 = 0 \tag{A2}$$

These two equations are equivalent to:

MR = MC (production) $\tag{A1'}$

MR (advertising) = MC (advertising). $\tag{A2'}$

Combining these equations gives:

$$\frac{\partial C}{\partial Q} = Q \frac{\partial P}{\partial Q} + P = P(1 - \frac{1}{e_d}) = P - \frac{P}{e_d}$$

$$\text{or} \quad \frac{1}{e_d} = (\frac{P - MC}{P}) \; ; \; P \frac{\partial Q}{\partial A} \quad \frac{\partial C}{\partial Q} \cdot \frac{\partial Q}{\partial A} + 1$$

$$\text{or} \quad \frac{PQ}{A} e_a = \frac{Q(MC)}{A} e_a + 1$$

Therefore $A = PQe_a - Q(MC)e_a$

$$\text{or} \quad \frac{A}{PQ} = e_a (1 - \frac{MC}{P}) = (\frac{e_a}{e_d})$$

where: $e_a = (\partial Q / \partial a)/(Q/a)$

and $e_d = -(\partial Q / \partial P)/(Q/P)$ $\tag{A3}$

NOTES

1. Unidentified sources quoted in "Another U.S. Volley in Border War," Broadcasting (March 30, 1981), p. 27.

2. Ibid.

3. Senator Jack Danforth (R-Missouri) discussing bill S. 2051; quoted in "Mirror Tax Law Introduced in Senate," Broadcasting (February 8, 1982), p. 103.

4. Broadcasting (March 30, 1981), p. 27.

5. Draft of federal ministers' report on communications (July 15, 1982), p. 3. Emphasis in original text; final version of report expected in 1983.

6. Ibid., pp. 7-8.

7. See, for example, ibid., p. 57, and Wall Street Journal (December 1, 1977), p. 12.

8. Broadcasting (March 30, 1981), p. 27.

9. R. Dorfman and P. Steiner, "Optimal Advertising and Optimal Quality," American Economic Review (December 1954).

10. This implicitly assumes $\partial Q_1 / \partial a_j = 0$, for $1 \neq j$, i.e., advertising in one medium does not influence the sales in the other.

11. The estimates include (U.S. dollars per year):

Before C-58	After C-58	Change	Source
20 million	9 million		Business Week 11/6/78
20 million		10 million	Broadcasting 3/30/81
		12 million	Broadcasting 11/2/81
		20 million	Broadcasting 2/8/82

12. See, for example, K. Wyman, "Rationales for Cable Regulation: A Canadian Perspective," in O. H. Gandy et al., Proceedings from the Tenth Annual Telecommunications Policy Research Conference (Norwood, N.J.: Ablex, 1983).

MODELS OF REALITY AND
REALITIES OF MODELS: A COMMENT

Ian Parker

The use of formal economic models of "reality" is part of the lifeblood of the contemporary economics profession. On occasion such models can even provide insights into aspects of the historical reality they attempt to portray. The usefulness of formal economic models for understanding and policy formulation, however, depends critically on a recognition of their nature, limits, and potential dangers. The essence of models is that they abstract from the full range of complexity of sociohistorical processes. The hope in constructing applied economic models is that to some extent they accurately capture the basic features of the situations they are intended to represent, and that the simplifying assumptions on which they are grounded are strategic simplifications, which highlight the principal economic relations and forces at work in the historical system under study, without undue distortion or reductionism.

Mathematical formulation of an applied economic model is potentially of considerable value, because it requires precise specification of the set of assumptions a researcher has adopted, and from which (provided that the calculations are correctly done) his or her conclusions tautologically follow. In effect, it obliges the economist to show others familiar with the mathematical code how the rabbit that gets pulled out of the hat in the conclusion of the model got into the hat in the first place.

There are, however, certain potential limitations or dangers, for both empirical analysis and communication, in the use of such models. Analytically, simplifying assumptions are often introduced less because they are "strategic" simplifications, in the sense noted above, than because they render the theoretical problem more tractable mathematically. The pressure for mathematical precision and determinate results can thus introduce a bias toward neglect of the problem of the referential adequacy of the model. Alternatively put, concern with ensuring the mathematical correctness of the conclusion, taking the assumptions as given, can divert attention from the appropriateness of the assumptions for a particular empirical context, and in the process can also narrow the range of questions asked from those that are interesting to those that seem mathematically manageable.

Operational researchers tell the story on themselves of the chess-addict king of a far-off realm who called in a team of operational researchers to provide him with an optimal strategy for playing chess. The team asked the king to explain the rules of the game to them, and on this basis, developed a "model" of chess. In constructing the model, they found it necessary to make some minor simplifying assumptions, to increase the mathematical tractability of the model: the model, for example, had only 12 pieces a side, instead of 16; the pieces were to move only on the black squares; and all pieces were to move identically, to eliminate the complications produced by the "nonstandard" pieces, such as the bishops and knights. They then returned to the king with some proposals on the "optimal" strategy . . . for a game that by now resembled checkers! There was nothing wrong with the model, except that it was irrelevant to the problem it had been designed to solve.

The use of mathematical models also has consequences for the communication of conclusions, particularly between those who are at home with the mathematical code (and who hence are conscious of the considerable gap that often exists between model and reality) and those who are not (for whom the mathematical symbolism, with its combined impenetrability and aura of scientific objectivity, constitutes a mystifying "barrier to entry" that tends to ensure that the conclusions of a model have to be accepted or rejected principally on faith).[1]

Yale Braunstein has produced a simple and interesting model extending the Dorfman-Steiner optimal advertising model[2] to the case of two markets with differential taxation provisions in each market, and has derived the optimization conditions for this case. In so doing, he has contributed to the theoretical literature on the economics of advertising. Unfortunately, he has also attempted to apply this theoretical model in an inappropriate empirical context, to evaluate the "success" (defined narrowly in terms of the diversion of Canadian advertiser revenues from U.S. border broadcasters to Canadian broadcasters) of the Canadian tax policy contained in Bill C-58. That policy disallows as a business expense deduction advertising directed primarily to a Canadian market purchased by Canadian-based advertisers on non-Canadian stations and periodicals. Braunstein does not provide significant empirical evidence to test the model, but he argues that the model suggests theoretically that the policy was probably ineffective.[3]

Braunstein's theoretical conclusion contrasts sharply with much available empirical evidence on the financial implications of Bill C-58, some of which is presented below. Yet his discussion is significant for both policy and theoretical reasons. From a policy standpoint, the C-58 tax provision has proven to be a contentious issue between the governments of Canada and the United States. If Braunstein's theoretical conclusion, that the C-58 policy has been relatively ineffective, is empirically correct, the effective cost to

Canadian broadcasters and to the Canadian government of eliminating the policy would be negligible. On the other hand, if the tax measure has been an effective component of Canadian government cultural and telecommunications policy, its elimination would constitute for them a genuine loss.

Braunstein's model is also interesting in theoretical terms, because it provides an illustration of the application of a "checkers-type" model to a "chess-type" problem: Braunstein's model contains several crucial misspecifications as applied to the border broadcasting question. When the model is respecified so that it more accurately reflects the realities of the situation, Braunstein's conclusion about the ineffectiveness of the C-58 tax provision is reversed. As will be shown, there are substantial theoretical reasons for supposing that the provision has channeled a large proportion of Canadian advertiser revenues diverted from U.S. border stations to the Canadian broadcasting stations serving the same markets, and that the "distortionary" effects relative to advertiser preferences have been lower than Braunstein's model implies.

The remainder of this discussion therefore provides a respecification of the Braunstein model that indicates how the wrong rabbit got into the theoretical hat; raises some theoretical and policy issues relatively neglected by Braunstein; presents some of the empirical evidence that suggests that Bill C-58 has been successful in diverting Canadian advertiser funds to Canadian broadcasters; and indicates the types of further empirical data that could increase the precision of our estimates of the policy's success.

REMODELING THE BORDER
BROADCASTING DISPUTE

The Braunstein model, as applied to assess the effects of Bill C-58, involves some serious oversimplifications. In this section, a simple model paralleling Braunstein's in most respects is developed initially, and then some complexities excluded by Braunstein are introduced to enable a still closer approximation of the model to the economic realities of the situation.

Recall that Braunstein's (partial-equilibrium, comparative-static) model is intended to describe the advertising-placement decision of a Canadian advertiser attempting to reach potential Canadian consumers of his or her product and able to use two basic means of reaching them, Canadian broadcasting stations and U.S. border stations reaching the same market by broadcast or cable. Braunstein abstracts by assumption from issues such as the demographic composition of the audiences of different programs, the nature of the advertiser and of the product being advertised, and the advertising rate structure (as distinct from the single quoted rates used by Braunstein) of different broadcasters, all of which (as will be shown below) have implications for the actual advertiser decision-making process and hence the effectiveness of the C-58 taxation policy, although for model comparability his assumptions will be temporarily adopted.

The fundamental misspecification of the Braunstein model, however, arises from the apparently innocuous assumption that "sales can be 'assigned' to the advertising that generated them," and that sales in the single Canadian market can therefore be partitioned into two components, which are (uniquely and exclusively) attributable to advertising on a Canadian station broadcast or to advertising on a U.S. station broadcast.[4] From this assumption stems the potentially different advertising elasticities of sales attributed to the two media and the subsidiary assumption that "advertising in one medium does not influence the sales in the other."[5] The mathematical proof of the "ineffectiveness" of the C-58 policy hinges critically on this "partitionable sales" assumption.

Once it is appreciated, however, that the two notional media of Braunstein's model reach not two separate markets, with distinct behavioral characteristics, but in fact a single market, insofar as the aim of a Canadian-based advertiser to reach a given Canadian market is concerned, the appropriate specification of the model becomes transparent. The decision problem for the advertiser is the standard "optimal media-mix" or "advertising portfolio choice" problem of minimizing the cost of getting a given level of exposure for his or her product, or alternatively of maximizing the impact per advertising dollar, with the single difference from the standard problem that advertising on one of the media (U.S. border stations taken as a group) is treated differently for tax purposes after the institution of the C-58 provision.[6]

Given this perspective on the advertiser's decision problem, the effectiveness of the C-58 tax policy turns on a somewhat different consideration than that emphasized in the Braunstein model: namely, the extent to which advertising on U.S. border stations and on the Canadian stations reaching the same Canadian markets are more or less perfect substitutes for each other. If (for the moment) we abstract from the demographic and other considerations noted above, and assume that there is a reasonable (though not necessarily "perfect") degree of competition among broadcasters on both sides of the border, competition among broadcasters, advertising agencies, and media-placement services should ensure that the effective cost per consumer contact-minute tends to be virtually identical across stations, regardless of whether they broadcast from north or south of the border: advertising rates, corrected by a program ratings factor, should be more or less identical for all stations reaching the market. [7]

If this were not the case, advertisers would tend to shift their advertising from the relatively high-cost to the relatively low-cost broadcasters, which would produce pressures on the high-cost broadcasters to lower their advertising rates and on the low-cost broadcasters to raise their rates (at least, once temporal excess advertising capacity had been exhausted or reduced). The conclusion that emerges clearly from the foregoing analysis is that if market forces were effectively operative in the television advertising market before the institution of the advertising taxation provision of Bill C-58, advertising via Canadian broadcasters to a particular Canadian market and advertising via U.S. border stations reaching the same market should have been virtually perfect substitutes, on Braunstein's assumptions.

This conclusion has significant implications for the analysis of the policy effectiveness of Bill C-58, its effect on Canadian government tax revenues, and its potential "distortionary" effects on Canadian advertiser preferences. If advertising north and south of the border were perfect substitutes, even a small change in the relative ratings-corrected cost of advertising north and south of the border in favor of Canadian broadcasters should have induced a virtually complete cessation in the flow of Canadian advertising dollars to the U.S. border stations and their diversion to the corresponding Canadian stations. The C-58 income tax provision, which (given the Canadian corporate tax rate) effectively doubled the relative cost of advertising to Canadian markets via U.S. border broadcasters, was more than a small change.

Braunstein is aware of the sharp drop in U.S. border broadcasters' revenues from Canadian advertisers[8] after the institution of Bill C-58. What his model prevents one from seeing, however, is that if (as the assumptions of his model imply, once the partitionable sales fiction has been eliminated) advertising on Canadian and U.S. border stations were virtually perfect substitutes, when the C-58 provisions came into effect virtually all of the Canadian television advertising dollars would have flowed to Canadian rather than U.S. border broadcasters, and the increase in Canadian government tax revenues from advertisers would have been negligible. Moreover, the distortionary effects of the policy on Canadian advertiser preferences would have been minimal, since with a demographically homogeneous market for advertisers' products, it would initially have been a matter of indifference for advertisers (provided that broadcasters' advertising rates per customer contact-minute remained unchanged) whether they advertised on the Canadian or the

U.S. border stations. Hence the cost incurred by the advertisers in shifting from U.S. to Canadian broadcasters, the distortionary effect, would have been negligible.

What requires explanation in the modified Braunstein model described above is why any Canadian advertisers aiming at Canadian markets would still advertise on U.S. border stations after Bill C-58 came into effect. At this point the need for a more realistic approximation to the actual situation faced by Canadian advertisers than the Braunstein model provides becomes evident. In the first place, the viewing audiences of different programs (say, an afternoon soap opera in contrast to a public affairs program, or a boxing match, or Sesame Street, or a rock and roll TV-FM radio simulcast) can have markedly different demographic structures, in age, sex, education, income, and other characteristics. Thus even if the aggregate audience size and advertising rate per minute are identical for two programs, for an advertiser targeting a specific demographic subgroup, the payoffs to advertising on one or the other differ substantially. In related fashion, the payoffs to advertising on a given program will vary considerably between advertisers. When this factor is operative and strong, it both helps to explain why some advertisers would continue to advertise on U.S. border stations after Bill C-58 came into effect and indirectly suggests that the distortionary effect of Bill C-58 could be somewhat greater than the negligible amount implicit in the Braunstein model as revised above. [9]

A second factor that could help to explain why certain Canadian advertisers might continue to advertise on the U.S. border stations after the institution of Bill C-58 involves relaxing the assumption that the advertisers are interested solely in contacting the Canadian audience reached by the U.S. border stations. For a national or multinational advertiser based in Canada but selling the same product in Canada and the United States, even if the principal advertising target is the Canadian market reached by the U.S. stations, contacting the related U.S. market involves an additional payoff for the advertiser or its parent company or subsidiary. Similarly, tourism-related Canadian advertisers hoping to attract U.S. as well as Canadian visitors could be expected to be more likely to pay the "premium" involved in advertising on a U.S. station than, say, a Canadian local used-car dealer. [10]

A third and less important factor that could account for the presence of some Canadian advertising on U.S. border stations has to do with periods during the day when the U.S. stations are the only ones, or virtually the only ones, broadcasting to the Canadian market. Particularly since this situation is most likely to occur during the midnight to 6:00 A.M. time block, when advertising rates per minute tend to be relatively low, a Canadian advertiser wishing to reach a "night-owl" audience might well advertise on a U.S. border station simply because of the absence of a suitable Canadian broadcast alternative during this time block.[11]

A final factor that would affect the trade-off for Canadian advertisers between advertising on U.S. border stations and Canadian stations has to do with changes over time in relative advertising rates. The Braunstein model implicitly takes these rates as given, as a consequence of the partial-equilibrium, microeconomic, single-firm, marginal-change framework that it assumes. In some contexts, this partial-equilibrium framework might not be misleading, but in the present context its applicability is open to question. The decidedly non-"marginal" nature of the changes brought about by Bill C-58 for broadcasters on both sides of the border is underlined by the approximately 100 percent increase in the effective cost to Canadian advertisers of advertising on U.S. border stations; the sharp contraction in the Canadian advertiser revenues (which, for example, in 1975 were reported to be about 20 percent of gross revenues for Buffalo's WGR-TV, WBEN-TV, and WKBW-TV[12]) of U.S. border stations; and the fact that Canadian advertising dollars spent on U.S. border stations before Bill C-58 represented about 10 percent of total Canadian television advertising expenditures, and a significantly higher percentage of the revenues of those Canadian stations in markets reached by the U.S. border broadcasters.

Other things being equal, if competitive market forces were operative for the broadcasters, it would be expected that after the enactment of Bill C-58 the decrease in Canadian advertiser demand for time on U.S. border stations and the increase in demand for time on Canadian stations, given the nonmarginal nature of the shift, would tend to produce pressures eventually raising the advertising rates charged by Canadian stations relative to those of U.S. border broadcasters, in comparison with a situation where Bill C-58 had not come into effect.[13] If such pressures on relative advertising rates materialized (particularly after the end of the Canadian Anti-Inflation Program in 1978), for Canadian-based advertisers the effects of Bill C-58 on advertising placement decisions would be partially offset. Hence the positive effect of Bill C-58 on Canadian broadcaster revenues and the negative effect on U.S. border broadcaster revenues would differ somewhat from a situation where relative advertising rates had remained constant.

The preceding discussion has indicated that the Braunstein model contains some serious limitations as a means of analyzing the economic effects of the Bill C-58 legislation, and has outlined an alternative model that corresponds more closely in a number of respects to the actual decision situation of Canadian-based advertisers. The conclusion that emerges from that model is that in the

absence of Bill C-58, U.S. border stations and their Canadian counterparts were in practice reasonably close substitutes from a Canadian advertiser's point of view. The model also indicates certain
probable characteristics of those Canadian advertisers who have
continued to advertise on U.S. border stations since Bill C-58 came
into effect, in terms of factors that could render advertising north
and south of the border less than perfect substitutes. The revised
Braunstein model therefore provides significant theoretical support
for the view that the significant drop in U.S. border station revenues
from Canadian advertisers under Bill C-58 was accompanied by a
corresponding (though not an equal) increase in the revenues of
Canadian broadcasters, while at the same time accounting for the
continued presence of some Canadian advertising on U.S. border
stations.

"Best-guess" estimates made by Donner and Lazar for 1978
(the first year in which Bill C-58 was fully in force and the last year
for which a comparable publicly available estimate exists) suggest
that on reasonable assumptions regarding the trend growth rate of
Canadian advertising, in 1978 the after-tax revenue (in Canadian
dollars) of U.S. border broadcasters declined by $12.8 million,
that of Canadian advertising agencies declined by about $0.7 million,
and that of Canadian broadcasters rose by $10.2 million, compared
to a situation in which Bill C-58 was not in effect. [14] Their calculations also imply for 1978 a net increase in Canadian government
tax revenues of just under $10 million, a net decrease in U.S. gov-
ernment tax revenues of roughly $9 million, and a decline in total
Canadian advertisers' television advertising expenditures of about
$6 million, as a result of the introduction of Bill C-58. [15] These
findings are consistent with the advertising portfolio-choice model
mentioned above, but they sharply contradict the conclusions derived
from the Braunstein model, particularly insofar as the impact of
Bill C-58 on Canadian broadcaster after-tax revenues is concerned.

CONCLUSION

It was suggested at the outset of this comment that the Braunstein model not only involves some serious misspecification problems, but also predisposes one to a neglect of certain important issues regarding the economic implications of Bill C-58. [16] Some of
those issues, relating to both theory and empirical measurement,
have been raised in the preceding section. This concluding section
outlines six additional economic factors not fully dealt with in the
Braunstein model that require integration in a more comprehensive
analysis of the economics of Bill C-58.

Aggregate Advertising Expenditure and Media Mix

One of the purposes and effects of Bill C-58 was to raise the cost to Canadian advertisers of advertising on U.S. border stations. This factor would thus produce a negative income effect for Canadian advertisers. If their aggregate expenditure (on a "net of tax" basis) remained constant, there would be a contraction in their total advertising expenditures. Whether their after-tax total advertising expenditures would remain constant after the imposition of Bill C-58, however, depends critically on the trade-off (in changes in demand for commodities advertised) between, or relative effectiveness of, greater advertising expenditures or lower commodity prices in the new situation.

Moreover, at a different level of aggregate advertising expenditure, it is possible that a different media mix (measured by the proportion of total advertising expenditures going to television or to other competitive advertising media) would be adopted by advertisers. Without specification of the relevant income elasticities of media demand and elasticities of substitution among Canadian stations, U.S. border stations, and competing alternative media at different levels of aggregate advertising expenditure, it is not possible to say whether the net effect of these two factors would be to reinforce or weaken the impact of Bill C-58 on Canadian broadcaster revenues. Yet the exclusive focus on TV advertising within the Braunstein model means that the media-mix question cannot properly be posed in it, as it stands.

Disposition of Government Tax Revenues

As is not infrequently the case with partial-equilibrium models, the Braunstein model treats increased government tax revenues solely as a withdrawal from the system. Yet if the level of the government deficit is to remain constant, these monies have to be spent and can thus increase broadcaster and advertising agency revenues directly (when some of them are spent on government advertising) and indirectly (when "multiplier"-type processes are effective and advertising expenditures are positively correlated with the general level of economic activity).[17] The magnitude of such effects should not be exaggerated, but neither should they be ignored.

Indirect Taxation versus Direct Subsidization

Braunstein hints that direct subsidization of activities desired for policy reasons is preferable to the more indirect method of favorable Bill C-58-type tax treatment, although the argument does not follow directly from his model in itself. Abstracting from the different fiscal implications of the two types of policy, however, in the first place (for reasons suggested in Policy Determination under Uncertainty the two types of policy are not mutually exclusive, and there are theoretical reasons for using both (if each is beneficial in itself and the two types of policy are not contradictory). Secondly (apart from narrowly political questions), the Bill C-58 method maintains a greater degree of administrative simplicity and flexibility for both the Canadian government and Canadian broadcasters than a number of the obvious types of direct subsidization would entail.

Time, Learning, and Processes of Reciprocal Causation

The Braunstein model is a comparative-static model, which assumes perfect information and an unchanged structure of economic relations. In any industry, however, and particularly for industries such as broadcasting and advertising (whose existence is predicated on the production of information and the absence of perfect information), there is a self-contradictory aspect to this conventional assumption of standard economic theory. There are three ways in which this theoretical contradiction could assume empirical importance in the case of the Bill C-58 legislation.

1. To the extent that there was a habitual or "satisficing" element (in Herbert Simon's sense) to Canadian advertiser media-mix decisions before Bill C-58, and to the extent that the policy shock induced search or learning behavior by advertisers, which increased advertising efficiency, the gross "costs" of the policy would be overestimated, and hence the net benefits underestimated, by standard estimating procedures.

2. The assumption that the advertising and broadcasting industries were in equilibrium before the introduction of Bill C-58 (or at any time after) is analytically convenient but empirically dubious, given the elements of uncertainty concerning macroeconomic factors, program development, ratings estimates, and qualitative and quantitative aspects of advertising effectiveness; the significant gestation periods necessary to produce new programs and audiences for new programming, the resultant substantial time lags between expenditures on inputs and sales revenues, and the associated rigidities inhibiting rapid adjustment;[18] and the importance of liquidity constraints in determining broadcasters' policies, in the absence of "perfect capital markets."

3. In the foregoing context, the assumption of a given structure of economic relations inhibits recognition of the efforts of

broadcasters to increase their market shares, and of the interaction between revenues, program quality, and ratings—if increased revenues are devoted to raising average program quality, which raises absolute or relative ratings, which enables an increase in advertising rates, which raises revenues, a "virtuous cycle" of program improvement can occur, whereas liquidity constraints can produce the opposite vicious cycle.

Policy Determination under Uncertainty

In the case of smoothly functioning markets and perfect certainty assumed in the Braunstein model, the theory of policy under certainty pioneered by Tinbergen, Meade, and Mundell shows that for small adjustments, a given number ($\underline{n}$) of policy objectives can be reached through the use of $\underline{n}$ independent policy instruments, so that if a policy instrument is less effective than $\underline{n}$ other independent policy instruments, it can be discarded.[19] Yet policy determination rarely, if ever, occurs in such an environment, and the theory of economic policy under uncertainty demonstrates that when there are uncertainties about the precise effects of different policies, it is preferable to use a range or "portfolio" of policies to achieve each policy objective.[20] In this context, even if the Bill C-58 tax provision were not the best means of achieving the objective of strengthening Canadian television programming (and, for reasons suggested earlier and below, the revised Braunstein model provides no basis for such a position), it could still be an important component in a portfolio of policy instruments directed at this objective.

Bill C-58 and the Theory of Second-Best

The Braunstein model analyzes the effects of a single policy-induced "distortion" an an otherwise market-determined environment. Yet it is clear that a number of Canadian government and CRTC cultural, communications, and economic policies have conditioned the economic environment in which Canadian broadcasters operate. Most notably, the "Canadian content" regulations have imposed a significant responsibility for the production of in-house programming on Canadian networks, affiliates, and independent stations. Perhaps because of an undue extrapolation from the United States, where the number of hours of in-house production per week is lower than in Canada, and where there is a greater average degree of separation between programming and broadcasting, the Braunstein model appears to assume that direction of funds toward broadcasters is an ineffective way of affecting programming. It is true that if the increased broadcaster revenues were channeled solely into increased dividends for station owners and not into programming, this argument would have some force, but empirically this does not appear to have been the case.[21]

A familiar proposition from the economic theory of second-best[22] is that if there are a number of distortions in an economic subsystem, elimination of only one of the distortions can lead to a reduced level of social welfare. Given the importance of the "Canadian content" and other provisions that are part of Canadian government cultural policy, the consequent necessity of adequate funding to produce Canadian programming, and the empirical evidence on the success of Bill C-58 by this criterion, the theory of second-best appears to apply, and Bill C-58 hence appears to be a significant component of a portfolio of Canadian government cultural policies, the elimination of which could produce both a reduced capacity to achieve cultural objectives and a reduced level of social welfare.

The preceding analysis has not been intended to underestimate Braunstein's contribution to the economic theory of advertising. It has, however, indicated that his discussion contains some crucial misspecifications as applied to the border broadcasting dispute and that a revised version of the model more closely approximating the realities of the situation provides theoretical support for the argument that Bill C-58 has been relatively successful in achieving its objectives. Empirical evidence consistent with the conclusions of the revised model but inconsistent with those drawn by Braunstein has been presented. Finally, some basic economic factors not dealt with in the Braunstein model have been sketched, all of which would need to be taken into account in a more comprehensive analysis of the economics of Bill C-58.

NOTES

1. There is considerable psychological truth in the anecdote about the eighteenth-century confrontation between the atheistic French philosophe, Diderot, and the mathematician Euler at the imperial Russian court, even if the story is apocryphal. The Empress decided that Diderot's vocal atheism required refutation, and Euler was ordered to produce an algebraic proof of the existence of God for the nonmathematical Diderot. Euler is reputed to have said, "Sir, $a + b^n/n = x$, therefore God exists; reply," whereupon Diderot fled the field and asked to return to France.

2. Robert Dorfman and Peter O. Steiner, "Optimal Advertising and Optimal Quality," American Economic Review (December 1954), pp. 826-36, esp. pp. 826-31.

3. "[If] the assumption of no change in advertising budgets is valid, C-58 has resulted in increased tax revenues for the Canadian government but little or no additional revenue for Canadian broadcasters. . . . I have shown that policies directed at the advertising market are not likely to have any significant effect on program funding or production." Yale Braunstein, Chapter 7 of this book, p. 159.

4. Braunstein, op. cit., p. 157.

5. Braunstein, op. cit., note 10: "$\partial Q_1 / \partial a_j = 0$." Notice the implications of these assumptions. First, they effectively convert all members of the Canadian viewing audience into schizophrenics, who "belong" to one medium or the other depending on whether they watch the same advertisement on the same program at the same time in the same numbers on a U.S. border station channel or a Canadian broadcast channel. Moreover, their behavior as viewers of each medium is potentially different (characterized, for example, by differing elasticities of demand), and there are no cumulative or "repetition" effects on them of multiple runs of the same advertisement between media, although there presumably can be within each medium. The essential problem here lies in a confusion between "media" and "markets." The Braunstein model would be appropriate for an advertiser marketing a commodity in two spatially separated markets, each of which was reached exclusively by a single advertising medium (ignoring distribution costs), since in this case the implicit identification of media with distinct markets and the partitioning of sales would be intelligible; where the two media reach a single market, however, an alternative specification such as that outlined in the text is required.

6. A technical note: the question of the optimal level of aggregate advertising expenditure must of course be solved simultaneously with the "media portfolio choice" problem. Drawing on the standard portfolio choice literature, however, it is possible to treat these two decisions as analytically separable, in that the aggregate advertising level decision will be made from the set of "dominating" media-mix strategies (those that provide the greatest advertising impact for a given level of expenditure). The aggregate advertising expenditure decision can then be made in terms of the type of criteria set out in the Dorfman-Steiner model or more sophisticated models of optimal advertising choice.

7. The operative word here is "tends." There are various rigidities (in addition to the demographic and other factors reintroduced below), such as broadcaster costs of changing rate structures, advertising contract lengths, differing quantity-discount

policies, advertising "package" sales, differing salesforce effectiveness, transactions costs of various types in shifting advertising from one broadcaster to another, informational gaps, nonmarket factors such as friendship, and so on, which can give rise to minor divergences from equality at any point, but the logic of the competitive process is such that these divergences are unlikely to persist indefinitely under unchanged circumstances.

8. Braunstein, op. cit., p. 158 and note 11.

9. Since Braunstein's original model has no place for this "complication," implicitly (by assumption) it cannot occur there. A technical note: since it is for all practical intents and purposes impossible to measure the "consumers' surplus" accruing to Canadian advertisers on U.S. border stations before Bill C-58 without further (effectively unverifiable) assumptions about "the elasticity of Canadian advertiser demand for U.S. border station advertising time," a precise dollar estimate of the magnitude of the distortionary effect using the standard techniques would be extremely difficult to obtain and of questionable meaning. A second note: the text has abstracted from the practice of "advertising package sales." Of course, such sales require analysis of the aggregate size and weighted demographic composition of the audience reached by a package, before the implicit average rate structure can be determined.

10. Empirical investigation in comparative terms of the composition, by type of company and product, of Canadian advertising on U.S. border stations and on Canadian stations reaching the same markets before and after Bill C-58 could provide a more secure basis for assessing the importance of this factor. The investigation would also require data on actual advertising rates charged and on Canadian and U.S. program audience size and demographic structure, to ensure that the comparison was not distorted by these other factors. Some data relevant to such an analysis are contained in Arthur Donner and Fred Lazar, "An Examination of the Financial Aspects of Canada's 1976 Amendment to Section 19.1 of the Income Tax Act (Bill C-58) on U.S. and Canadian TV Broadcasters" (Toronto, 1979), but they would need to be supplemented by more detailed information to arrive at reasonably precise estimates.

11. Again, this possibility could be investigated empirically, although on a priori grounds it has likely been quantitatively less significant over most of the period since 1976 than the other factors. Donner and Lazar (op. cit., pp. I-6, I-7) suggested that up to late 1978, "the bulk of Canadian advertising on the Buffalo stations" was placed in the 4:00 to 6:00 P.M., 7:00 to 8:00 P.M., and Saturday morning time slots, although they do not indicate the precise extent to which this pattern was affected (if at all) by the introduction of Bill C-58. It would be worthwhile to extend their analysis in both detail and temporal coverage.

12. Jack Miller, "Buffalo TV vs. CRTC," Broadcaster (January 1975).

13. "Other things," of course, were not equal during the period from 1976 onward, to mention only national and local market differences in inflation rates (both during and after the Canadian Anti-Inflation Board program), interest rates, levels of real economic activity and unemployment, aggregate advertising expenditures, television programming and broadcasting cost-structures, and other broadcast-policy changes by broadcasters and regulators, as well as changes in the Canadian-U.S. dollar exchange rate. Observed advertising rate and volume data over the period reflect the influence of all of these factors and of rigidities such as those mentioned in note 7 above, in addition to the economic impact of Bill C-58 itself. It would therefore be necessary to factor out their combined effect to isolate the effects on advertising rates and volumes of Bill C-58 alone.

Certain published data (such as those available in Television Factbook and used by Braunstein) are insufficiently detailed to provide the basis for such a comparison over time, even if they are adjusted in terms of the BBM "weekly circulation" or other aggregate market-penetration data contained in Television Factbook, because they do not provide information on ratings per program and broadcaster advertising-package sales rates. The crucial point, however, is that the relevant empirical estimate of the effect of Bill C-58 on advertising rates and volume cannot rely solely on trends in actual observed rates and ratings, but must correct for the influence of the other factors above. Alternatively put, even if U.S. border station advertising rates actually charged were observed to rise more rapidly than the corresponding Canadian station rates over all or part of the period, the relevant question is how much higher they would have risen in relative terms in the absence of Bill C-58, if competitive market forces were operative for stations on both sides of the border. The discussion of trends in relative advertising rates and volumes in the text presupposes that this adjustment has been made.

In their generally balanced and careful empirical study, Donner and Lazar (op. cit., pp. III-24-25) briefly discuss the question of the effect of Bill C-58 on the price of advertising time, but their discussion omits explicit quantitative consideration of the effects of most of the factors outlined in this note, and to that extent has certain limitations from a theoretical standpoint. In providing reasonable order-of-magnitude empirical estimates of the economic impact of Bill C-58, however, the Donner-Lazar study still remains unsurpassed.

14. Donner and Lazar, op. cit., pp. vi, III-1 ff., Tables 2 to 6.

15. These calculations (based on Donner and Lazar, op. cit., Table 6) take into account the higher cost to Canadian advertisers (and the associated increase in Canadian tax revenues) of placements with U.S. border stations, the drop in U.S. border broadcaster and advertising agency pretax income, the increase in Canadian broadcaster pretax revenues, and the decline in Canadian taxes paid by KVOS-Washington, under Bill C-58. They are intended to provide solely order-of-magnitude estimates of the changes involved.

16. The Braunstein discussion is not concerned with cultural and international political-economic issues raised by Bill C-58, and for that reason this comment does not address them either. Such issues are dealt with in other contributions to the volume.

17. Note that these effects do not depend on any earmarking of tax revenues from specific sources to specific types of government expenditure.

18. On uncertainties and rigidities, see notes 7 and 13 above.

19. A technical note: the theory essentially derives from a mathematical theorem on the properties of full-rank square matrices; the importance of the small-adjustment assumption is that in such cases a linear approximation of the actual instrument-objective adjustment process may not diverge excessively from reality, and questions on the speed and stability of the adjustment process can therefore be suppressed.

20. See W. Brainard, "Uncertainty and the Effectiveness of Policy," American Economic Association Papers and Proceedings, Vol. 57 (May 1967), pp. 411-25.

21. See Donner and Lazar, op. cit.

22. See R. Lipsey and K. Lancaster, "The General Theory of Second-Best," Review of Economic Studies, Vol. 24 (1956-57), pp. 11-32.

COMMENT
Robert E. Babe

Yale Braunstein's intent is to ascertain the effects of Bill C-58 on advertising revenues to Canadian television stations. The author deduces his conclusion mathematically from an initial set of premises, including the following: "An advertiser maximizes profits by setting the marginal revenue equal to the marginal cost of advertising as well as by setting the traditional marginal revenue from sales equal to the marginal cost of production."[1]

As is the case in any purely logical or deductive approach, the conclusion one reaches is only as sound as the premises upon which it is based. While it has been argued that realism in assumptions is not required if they yield predictions that are subsequently verified,[2] in Yale Braunstein's discussion there are no predictions that are subjected to testing. Therefore, we are required to address the assumptions themselves to assess how convincing a case has been made. In particular, I question whether marginal cost and marginal revenue of advertising are unambiguous and stable enough to be useful grounds on which to construct an elaborate model of business behavior.

The notion of marginal cost of advertising is fraught with ambiguity. There are two distinct but interrelated categories of advertising cost—production cost and distribution cost. Production costs for a 30-second commercial can range from a few hundred dollars to several hundred thousand dollars. Moreover, each commercial message can be considered as a unit unto itself, or as a component of a sequential series of television commercials that themselves may constitute an element in a well-conceived multimedia advertising campaign. Insofar as there is ambiguity in the incremental unit of commercial production, there is also ambiguity in the costs associated with incremental production. Marginal cost could be defined on the basis of using one less cameraperson for an isolated TV spot to the use or nonuse of television itself as part of a multimedia campaign; from using one less commercial message in a planned sequence of messages to using or not using highly sophisticated and expensive techniques within a given message. None of the aforementioned incremental units of production is truly isolatable from the preceding units; unlike the production of commodities such as tables, where a reduction in the volume of production will not necessarily change the production characteristics of units that are produced, each incremental reduction in commercial pro-

178

duction will change qualitatively what remains. There is high inter-dependence among the units of production.

Marginal distribution cost is troublesome, too. It could refer to procurement of a single time slot on a single television station, exposure in a single television market area, exposure on a single television network, or even use of a given advertising medium. Furthermore, commercial production decisions are not made in isolation from commercial distribution decisions; rather, the opposite is true, compounding the ambiguity of the notion of marginal advertising cost.

In neoclassical microeconomics the notion of marginal revenue is developed under the assumptions of fixed tastes or consumer preferences, fixed incomes, and constant prices of related goods and services. If the demand curve for a final commodity shifts because any of the foregoing fixed factors has changed, so does the marginal revenue schedule. Obviously, if tastes and preferences are continually in flux, so are the demand and marginal revenue schedules.

Marginal revenue from advertising has meaning only if there is either (1) a demand curve that shifts and comes to rest as a result of advertising, or (2) a demand curve whose precise movement is known over time and whose movement attributable to advertising is known. These conditions are unlikely to exist or to be ascertainable. For example, the consumer effects of a single exposure to a commercial are likely to vary over time and to be influenced by exposure to other advertisements for the same product. Another example of the limitations of using inherently static concepts such as marginal revenue to analyze a dynamic process concerns rivalry in advertising. Whatever the effects of a single firm's advertising practices on sales may be, these effects are subject to change if the advertising practices of competitors change. Competitors' strategies will probably change in response to their perception of the effects of the advertising practices in question.

More generally, I believe economists are all too frequently naive when it comes to studying information industries. Information, by its very essence, implies dynamic analysis, for it is the property of information to change whatever it comes in contact with: whether we are speaking of the encoded instructions in a molecule of DNA coming in contact with nutrients or a professor's lectures influencing the thought patterns and behavior of students. Nor is information quantifiable insofar as, _inter alia_, there is no information in the absence of both an originator and a recipient to process it; it entails an interactive process and cannot be understood by looking at the originator or receiver in isolation, assuming either to be unchanged after producing and processing information.[3]

The main problem I have with the present analysis and those of a similar nature is that the form, while seemingly scientific and rigorous due to the use of mathematics, can obscure (perhaps unintentionally and unbeknown to the author) many oversimplifications. Such analyses can intimidate policy makers who lack the skill required to decipher the basis on which important policy conclusions are reached.

A more fertile avenue of research into the question at hand would be to interview the advertisers whose behavior Parliament hoped to influence by passing Bill C-58 to ascertain the bill's actual effects on their advertising practices.

NOTES

1. Yale Braunstein, Chapter 7 of this book, p. 156.

2. Milton Friedman, "The Methodology of Positive Economics," in Essays in Positive Economics (Chicago: University of Chicago Press, 1953), pp. 3-43.

3. Robert E. Babe, "Information Industries and Economic Analysis: Policy-Makers Beware," in Oscar Gandy et al., Proceedings from the Tenth Annual Telecommunications Policy Research Conference (Norwood, N.J.: Ablex, 1983).

8

THE IMPACT OF NEW TECHNIQUES AND FUTURE TECHNOLOGIES ON U.S.-CANADIAN BROADCAST RELATIONS

Thomas H. Martin

It is next to impossible to predict the impact of new technologies and techniques for television production and distribution on cultural relationships between Canada and the United States. The reason for this is that one has to be able to predict (1) technological changes, (2) ways in which the television industry responds to the changes, (3) ways in which the regulators on each side of the border respond to moves by industry, and (4) ways in which entrepreneurs respond to discrepancies in regulatory initiatives by the two countries. Considering the historical origins of the dispute over importation of U.S. television signals into Canada, it was clear that technology made possible the use of coaxial cable and microwaves to import distant signals. It was less clear, although predictable, that cable television companies would not want to edit incoming signals. It was surprising that Canadian radio and television regulators would allow cable television to remain unregulated for so long. Finally, it was not surprising at all that the Canadian cable television industry would take advantage of the opportunity, would grow prolifically with the implicit assistance of U.S. border broadcasters, and would eventually be subjected to retaliatory regulation in Canada. This discussion examines the technologies, industry responses, governmental responses, and potential border conflicts.

TECHNOLOGICAL CHANGES

There are significant changes occurring in the technologies underlying television production and distribution. It used to be that producing a program was like producing a film. Today the quality,

portability, and resolution of video equipment make it equal to or
superior to film. Computerized editing of tapes makes it possible
to create magic unimaginable a decade ago. Computer-generated
images can be interspersed with instant replays and collages of
simultaneous images. Management, if it were not hampered by
union regulations, could change production quality and cost from
week to week as the ratings changed. Do-it-yourself television programming never caught on in small cities and countries because the
"talking head" could not compete with talented artists before and behind the Hollywood cameras. Those who have tried to duplicate
Hollywood quality have found the cost to be extremely high. Even
though cameras and cassette recorders are now affordable, the cost
and skill required to do state-of-the-art editing insure dominance by
a few production centers. In the next decade there will be a progressive transition from analog to digital equipment. This means that
resolution will have to be extremely high and storage density per
second of footage will have to increase one hundredfold. The advantage of digital is that all sorts of transformations of the signal can
be carried out. Colors can be cleaned up, abrupt transition can be
smoothed out, and animation can be inserted. Digital originals do
not decay over time as do old film prints. A whole new generation
of technicians will create novel new looks and formats with this expensive equipment. While it is true that tomorrow a low-cost studio
will be able to buy today's equipment, that equipment will only be
able to generate a today-quality image, which by tomorrow will look
old-fashioned. Production will continue to be dominated by the
major studios.

The technologies for distribution of signals are also changing.
Distribution from producers to stations, which always used to be
done either through telephone lines or by mailing films, is now done
via satellites. High resolution signals can be transmitted at much
reduced cost to stations regardless of location. This has led to the
superstations and ad hoc networks that use satellites to patch together a distribution scheme. It is unlikely that any other technology
will displace satellites as the preferred distribution vehicle to stations.

Distributors may bypass stations, however, and go directly to
cablecasters or consumers. The reason has to do with high resolution signals. Over-the-air television as it currently exists is starved
for bandwidth. Cable television makes possible more bandwidth per
signal. Direct broadcasting from satellites at high frequencies also
makes possible greater bandwidth. As laser technology improves
and drops in cost, we will probably see cable systems replace coaxial with fiberoptic cable, and direct broadcasters from the geo-
stationary orbit replace transponders with laser beams. One of the

driving forces behind a 20-year move into laser technology will be a desire for the vast amounts of bandwidth possible with lasers. Bandwidth is attractive because it is needed to send high resolution images and to send digital signals. Digital signals are attractive because perfect quality can be maintained and signals can be protected through encryption. The move away from over-the-air broadcasting will be slow and painful. Everyone has a television set that receives over-the-air signals, and transmission over the air is very inexpensive. The new distribution technologies are all expensive and require massive rewiring, purchase of new equipment in the home, and expensive platforms in space. Just as radio still retains a market, over-the-air television will still exist, serving background needs for many people at very low cost. It will not, however, be expected to carry the full load of cultural obligations. The ideological battles are likely to be waged over the new transmission channels and over who has control of the content pumped through them. The new channels will probably serve the needs of the large urban areas and the most affluent in those urban areas. They can afford to underwrite rewiring, space platforms, and new equipment in the home.

The range of home television equipment is likely to be much greater than it is now. Today all equipment is limited by the 525-line standard, which is 1950s technology. The cathode-ray tube can produce much higher resolution, which the home computer needs. The home electronics industry needs to find ways to get people to trade in their old sets. Large-screen sets are useless without high resolution images. But high resolution sets are not needed unless there is high bandwidth transmission. Computer games seem to be a way to break out of the chicken-or-egg cycle. High resolution videodiscs or videotapes might be another.

The games or computer-related uses of television are exciting because they introduce digital processing and storage capacity into the home. For a long time videodisc and videotape storage will be analog because of limited storage capacity. Home computers, however, will rely on large-scale integrated circuits that can be mass produced at low cost with more and more capacity on chips each year. If everyone could be encouraged to buy intelligent television sets, a lot of things might be possible. Over-the-air transmission might be drastically changed so that sets picked out frames, filled in the dots, and otherwise allowed compressed signals to be transmitted over low bandwidths that expanded into high bandwidth end products. Teletext is just such a primitive example of what could be done if people had processors in their sets and keyboards in their hands. Telidon provides another example of how intelligent sets can be used to paint interesting images out of simple signals. Because producers will be thinking digital and distributors would love to transmit digitally, there is every reason to believe that consumers will be strongly encouraged to buy digitally oriented receivers.

The receiver in the set is likely to have multiple sources for inputs and outputs. There will be some signals one wants to receive using various antennas. Today cable television is expected to carry local over-the-air signals, but as it increases in power it probably will fight to escape from this burden, especially if over-the-air shifts to background broadcasting for marginal audiences. Sets will have switching boards that will allow inputs to come from satellite down converters, antennas, cable television, videodisc, videotape, the personal computer, or the telephone. The videotape is likely to become an essential component for use in allowing viewers to watch what they want at hours of their own choosing. Today it serves as an input and output source as well. This leads to easy pirating, which increases in undesirability as the value of programming improves. There may be attempts, similar to the Betamax case, to outlaw the videotape and replace it with internal discs or chips that act as a temporary store for time shifting. It may, however, be too late to prohibit videotape machines, since they have so many benefits for users.

Videodiscs currently are meant to serve as a distribution but not reproduction technology. Many people feel that videotape and disc cannot coexist, yet they serve different functions. Few people use tape for long-term storage, but an ideal application for videodisc is a visual encyclopedia or reference work. Where people now have shelves of books and records they may want to have classic movies or operas or how-to manuals. These discs will probably be used in conjunction with the home computer to teach skills or to provide answers to questions. Whereas almost everyone will have videotape recorders, a smaller portion will have videodiscs.

Some commentators have argued that the wave of the future is interactive television. Certainly when the television set is used as part of the home computer, it is used in an interactive manner. Most cable television systems have been built with the potential for two-way traffic. If television sets come to have modular plugs so they can be used with telephone jacks, interaction is even more possible. However, human and production costs pose limits to interaction. People expect television to be relaxing and entertaining. They do not want to think and answer questions. Also, if interaction is going to be more than a gimmick, programming has to change in response to the viewers' reactions. This implies either branching or production for small audiences. Both are extremely expensive. The most likely way in which interactive services might develop is as meter readers, transaction handlers, or selection devices. People might look at their checkbook balance on the screen, order up a movie, or enter a contest. In almost all cases feedback would not have an immediate effect on production.

This then constitutes a possible range of technological options for production, distribution, and reception of television. Production under these projections remains high cost, innovative, and dominated by a few sources. Distribution alternatives multiply and over-the-air programming fades in significance, with high-resolution cable and direct broadcasting rising in importance. Equipment in the home differs from home to home, ranging from simple sets with antennas to elaborate complexes of signals, processors, and storage devices. The home computer and videotape are likely to become essential aspects of the set, but not for utilitarian reasons. Rather, they simplify controlling the timing of viewing and facilitate game playing.

INDUSTRY RESPONSES

Many forces in the industry have led television to become what it is today. The costs of production have been high. Distribution used to be tied up by networks through dedicated telephone lines. Reception over the air is free. Advertisers underwrite programming to attract audiences. Quality needs to be only high enough to keep people tuned in. People view television as free and so do not take much interest in what they get. People generally do not think about it very much, or if they do, feel there is little they can do about it. Because channels are scarce and not much can be produced, those who control content and local distribution wield great power. The fact that politicians are beholden to them to gain coverage during campaigns only increases their power. It is unlikely that new technologies would be allowed to get so out of hand that the broadcasters might lose control.

Cable television and direct satellite broadcasting pose threats to broadcaster control. Cable television has fought since the early 1960s against restraints imposed by broadcasters and regulators. The cablecasters have made possible importation of distant signals. Cable, along with companies like Home Box Office, have pioneered pay television. As the networks have failed in their attempts to suppress cable, they have changed tactics and used it. The cable experience has shown that pay television can be made to work and that special-interest programming may be viable. The advantage of pay television is that viewers pay for what they get, making it possible to give them what they want. Pay television does not have to be totally without advertisements, and in fact some advertisers may be interested expressly in those audiences who will pay for special-

purpose programming. The mixed pay and advertising format probably will be developed extensively in coming years. As technology
for monitoring home usage is put in place, it will be possible to
switch from general monthly pay charges to specific pay-per-view
billing. Systems similar to coded mailing lists will be developed so
that special-purpose audiences can get programming intended for
them partially underwritten by advertisers who want to sell to them.
This is called narrowcasting. The networks have developed news,
sports, and cultural narrowcasting channels to test the concept.
Currently it is hard to attract advertisers because audiences are
small or unmeasured. Audiences cannot be charged until they become habituated to the new services. If narrowcasting works, it
probably will be transferred to regular broadcasting as well.

The economics of production and distribution suggest that for
costs to be kept low there have to be lots of viewers. In the past
the expectation was that they would all view at once. With narrowcasting it is possible to follow a tiered approach. A small audience
pays a high price to view the product first, and later it can be distributed for less to a larger audience. Still later it can be sold
abroad to a still larger audience. A tiered approach conceivably
allows the most interested audience to be the most influential on the
producer.

Currently, the relation is too indirect for the producer to get
feedback from the pay audience. Cable systems do the buying of
channels and audiences pay for a whole channel or bundle of channels. In the future, it is more likely that audiences, through interactive billing, will be able to exercise more control over what they
pay for. The price of viewing may also change from showing to
showing. If this happens it will mirror very closely the cycle followed in the film industry. A consequence will be that producers
will produce products that viewers value. A negative impact will be
that the temptation to pirate will increase. Policing to prevent
theft will be extremely expensive, and in some cases will inhibit
producers from taking the chance.

A strategy that is being adopted to minimize the losses inherent in pirating is to organize multimarket distribution strategies,
as, for example, to produce a film, a television series, a book, and
a line of dolls or clothing. In this way, profits can be made in a
number of markets even if one or two other markets lead to loss due
to pirating.

Another multimarket distribution strategy, this time by cablecasters, is to find a variety of services that will attract people to
the cable system. Pay movies have been extremely successful in
attracting subscribers. There are now efforts to provide security
systems, energy monitoring, videotex services, and interactive

computerized games. As cable seeks out these services to extend its market, it runs the risk of direct competition with the telephone companies.

In summary, the most likely trends in industry practices are a shift toward narrowcasting with broadcasters bypassing local broadcasters and going through pay cablesystems. Both the producers and cablecasters probably will use tiered multimarket strategies and devices to protect themselves from piracy in any one market.

REGULATORY RESPONSES

I will say very little about how the regulators in each country are likely to respond to the trends since Janisch and Hagelin (Chapter 3) deal with regulatory options in great detail.

In the United States there is likely to be great concern about the diminished importance of local broadcasters. Attempts will be made to impose local obligations on cablecasters. There will be concern about direct broadcasting as a further threat to the local broadcaster. Legislators will threaten to prevent popular programming such as sports from being shown first on cable. However, the strong trend toward deregulation and competition probably will give cable and direct broadcasting the chance they need to make significant advances.

In Canada, where concern revolves around promoting national culture, cable has been viewed as a Trojan horse bringing in U.S. programming. The pay concept is only beginning to be tried out, and the narrowcasting concept is viewed as extremely risky. Canada's dilemma is that the market size is so small that fragmentation poses real problems. Direct broadcasting has been used with the ANIK satellites, but more as an extender of the national cultural fare to the remote areas than as a device to increase diversity. There is definite interest in using interactive services such as Telidon to serve local needs for information. As Canada tries to keep the television production and distribution system simple and widespread, there is a strong tendency for individuals to try to take advantage of what is happening in the United States.

RESPONSE TO REGULATORY DISCREPANCIES

In suggesting how clever entrepreneurs might take advantage of discrepancies, I have chosen to present three scenarios. Each scenario is based on the trends already described, reasons are given for the scenario, and suggestions are made as to how the scenario might turn out differently if the U.S. and Canadian governments were to coordinate their policy making. I make clear throughout that the cause for discrepancies is idealism on both sides of the border as to (1) how audiences will behave, (2) how industry will behave, and (3) how profits are made in the television industry. Experiences in both countries since the 1950s have shown that attempts to use television to enhance local culture have run into difficulties. My personal bias is to have local groups use the media for community building. This would require concerted efforts by local groups, low-cost production, and audiences who wish to be involved rather than stimulated. My vision has been expounded by intellectuals worldwide for television and for cable television. It again seems to inspire proponents of videotex. There is no evidence that the vision has yet materialized or ever will. Instead, television audiences tend to be passive recipients of high-cost stimulation. The industries involved have worked hard to maximize the audience per show and minimize the cost of production. The advertising industry, which has played so significant a role in underwriting production and distribution, is more interested in effectiveness of advertisements than in the cultural worth of the "bait" used to attract the audience. Government has an obligation to protect its citizenry from exploitation and to invest in public goods that otherwise would not be developed. When the idealism of one government is not shared by the other opportunities are exploited and border disputes result.

Scenario 1: The Thwarting of Telidon

It had been thought in the late 1970s that videotex would become the next mass medium. Canadians had made a substantial investment developing Telidon and almost all critics agreed that Telidon was significantly better than videotex systems developed in England and France. Canadian scholars felt strongly that the low cost of producing Telidon screens would lead to local production of informative material. Potential adopters of Telidon were identified in the United States, and the major threat—AT&T—was precluded from entering the home information market for a number of years. What, then, kept Telidon from being a success?

For Telidon to be widely adopted, home viewers had to have a microcomputer that took signals off telephone and television lines and processed them for display on screens. The microcomputer was easy to produce and if mass marketed would cost little more than any other microcomputer. Yet the mass market never developed.

The Canadian government tried to stimulate the market through massive trials and underwriting production, but gave up after a ten-year effort resulted in only a 10 percent adoption rate in Canada and less than a 2 percent adoption rate in the United States. There was much anger in Canada when a few years later the Japanese routinely introduced circuitry for image creation into sets they marketed in North America. The circuitry was used for enhancing reception on high-resolution sets and was used interactively for game playing, but was neither referred to as Telidon nor used for any prosocial purposes. Attempts were made in Canada to block importation of the sets and to sue for patent violation, but to little effect. Eventually commercial interests in the United States, in conjunction with American Bell, began marketing information utility services, and the Canadian government found itself in the position of either allowing importation of signals or else prohibiting use of the very type of interactive services it had been promoting so long in Canada.

The reasons behind the initial failure of videotex had much to do with telecommunication regulatory decisions in the United States. In spite of warnings by the electronics industry during the 1970s that the Japanese were eliminating American manufacturers of television sets, little was done to protect U.S. industry. The standards for television sets had been frozen in the 1950s, the market was saturated with sets in the 1970s, and the Japanese could produce replacement sets at lower cost and with higher quality than could U.S. producers. Consequently, by the 1980s the Japanese played a dominant role in the production of television sets for North America. Other trends were active at the same time. The Federal Communications Commission favored deregulation and letting the market decide what new technologies would succeed. The cost of producing sophisticated electronic circuitry continued to drop and made possible the introduction of major new uses of home electronic equipment.

Japanese industry for a long time had been very interested in finding ways to encourage Americans to buy high-resolution television sets. The reason was that the current 525-line standard gave too low a quality image for the Japanese market, where it was often necessary to insert Japanese subtitles, and the resolution was too low for complex characters. Japanese manufacturers felt that if U.S. consumers would underwrite the cost of converting to high resolution, the Japanese consumer would not have to. The opportunity came in the early 1980s with fascination over video games. The games were greatly limited by low-resolution sets, and the U.S. companies promoting game playing were excited when the Japanese started marketing high-resolution sets. Because they had the initiative, they were able to introduce a whole line of sets. One could go to a single supplier to purchase a screen, portable keyboard/tuner, source switcher, and videocassette recorder. The models that were introduced offered such exciting potential that over a seven-year period most people who replaced old television sets chose the Japanese models and the potential for attachments that went along with them. The Japanese line did not favor Telidon, for there were Japanese videotex systems, such as Captain, that would have been adversely affected. When the U.S. regulators finally began responding to electronics industry pressure to protect new home electronics markets from Japanese dominance, it was already too late. The best that could be done was to reinstitute formal standards setting at the FCC and to try to keep out new equipment that had not yet been authorized.

The Canadians tried every means available to keep Telidon alive in the U.S. market. Read-only software packages had been sold that were compatible with many personal computers. Cable-television operators had been licensed to generate the Telidon images at the head end and distribute them to receivers on their systems. Many advertisers and electronic publishers had been assisted in developing attractive and useful databases. Immense amounts of advertising and public relations activities were funded. By the 1990s market studies showed that most Americans had heard of Telidon, some had seen demonstrations of it, but very few had ever considered getting it. When asked, people explained that they really didn't know what they would use it for, that it cost a lot of money, and television was already too complicated. The people with Telidon receivers thought it would be far more useful if more information were in the databanks. Yet the databanks could not grow because the receiving market was limited in size.

Telidon was unable to enter the home through the telephone line as had been initially intended. This had much to do with the reorganization of AT&T. Most homes were served by local loops from Bell operating companies. These companies, due to the revised consent decree, found it very hard to raise enough capital to maintain high quality service to home subscribers, and the telephone companies found it hard to attract and retain high quality employees. The capital that was attracted went into the business-user market, since direct transmission services threatened to attract away the Bell operating companies' most lucrative market. State regulators were under heavy pressure from consumer groups to keep home service rates low. The consequence of low home rates was that new digital services were delayed, noise on lines increased, and occasional power fluxes periodically damaged electronic receivers. The Japanese and Canadian companies competing with American Bell in selling electronic telephone instruments found consumers complaining about faulty equipment and intolerable errors in data communications. Telidon over the telephone in the United States simply did not work. When outraged vendors and consumers protested poor service to the public utility commissions, the operating companies argued that they could not maintain high quality service if they were unable to attract capital, and that much of the degraded service was due to faulty electronic instruments sold by non-Bell companies. The operating companies also argued that their primary obligation to the home market was in voice communication, which, while not as attractive as formerly, was still tolerable. Consequently, sales of novel home electronic telephone instruments diminished and American Bell retained a dominant position in the sale of ordinary telephone sets. In the early 1990s, when it was ready, American Bell introduced its own line of electronic equipment that got around most of the difficulties in digital service. The equipment was similar to what had proven successful in the business market and was finely tuned to the types of capabilities U.S. businesses wanted consumers to have in their homes. Even though the modern telephone set and television set were similar internally, the public did not perceive them as substitutable. They used their interactive television sets for entertainment and their graphic display telephone sets for transacting business. Almost all of the capabilities promoted as videotex in the 1980s were being used in the late 1990s by at least 25 percent of U.S. citizens and 40 percent of Canadians without Canadians receiving the credit they deserved, and with control over equipment based firmly in Japan and the United States.

There are actions that could be taken now to keep the Japanese from dictating the nature of the home entertainment set. One action would be to establish standards for plugging chips into television sets. The RS 232 coupler has made it possible for a wide variety of computer terminals to be connected to communication lines. There is a small number of plug standards for allowing signals into television sets. Yet to have all add-ons external to the television set is causing homes to turn into wiring nightmares. Just as a large number of people buy integrated stereo systems, many people will buy integrated sets that include modems, cable reception boxes, videocassette options, and remote keypads. To minimize the cost to society, an effort might be made now to make certain that public standards for upgrading machines are uniform from vendor to vendor. In this way there can be competition in the attachments industry. Telidon reception equipment can then be sold as a small upgrade kit through service centers and does not have to attempt to compete directly with the television receiver industry.

A more extreme move would be to require that all receivers sold in Canada and the United States have built-in microcomputers for processing Telidon signals. This move would act like the UHF tuner to reduce entry barriers to videotex. The Japanese would of course oppose either approach, arguing that it is too early to know which videotex standards are needed and that inserting boards by other vendors would degrade the quality of television sets. A push for standards might be supported by U.S. and Canadian industry as a strategy for weakening the dominance of foreign electronics companies and insuring a niche in the market from which they could work to regain control of the home video reception industry. The forecasted difficulty in home telephone service is a far more difficult problem to resolve since it is inherent in the revised telephone industry structure.

Scenario 2: The Rebirth of Border Broadcasting

By the early 1980s the U.S. border broadcasters felt that their market was being undercut. The Canadian government had taken actions limiting the number of U.S. stations the Canadian cablecasters could transmit, there was an effort under way to force cablecasters in Canada to pay royalties to the U.S. royalty tribunal for signals received from the border broadcasters, and the U.S. networks were beginning to sell programming directly to Canadian cable systems rather than lose control of their product by providing it to U.S. stations that then gave it away to the Canadians. The Canadian cable systems viewed the same sequence of events with discomfort, for they saw the trends as increasing costs to the cablecasters without resulting in any new added benefit. If they entered into agreements with the U.S. networks the commercial broadcasters in Canada would be upset. There would be more accusations of cablecasting being in collusion with the Americans and not serving Canadian interests. A few Canadian cable systems and border broadcasters entered into discussions and came up with an independent network approach for solving their mutual problems at the expense of the U.S. networks.

Canadian cable companies were limited in the number of U.S. signals they could carry, so if border broadcasters were to drop network programming and the Canadian cablecasters were still to carry their signals, the border broadcasters would not have to compete with the U.S. networks in Canada (except for those U.S. programs Canadian broadcasters chose to air). Provided that the programs border broadcasters produced were as attractive as U.S. network television, this would mean that the border broadcasters would have a large captive Canadian audience. The Canadian cable systems agreed to underwrite production provided the costs were very low and the end product attracted a large Canadian audience. Since production would take place outside Canada, it would be possible to avoid Canadian regulations requiring Canadian content and jobs.

The border broadcasters did not like the idea of getting involved in production, but felt they had no choice. They formed a consortium, hired a former network television vice-president, and settled on a strategy. It was well known that there were many creative people in Los Angeles and New York City who wanted to be involved in television production but could not find acceptance by the networks. Many times these creative people had formed ad hoc networks for distribution of their programs. These ad hoc networks could not be sustained for long because the high costs of production, promotion, and distribution resulted in economic feasibility only with guaranteed money makers. The solution the border broadcaster consortium found was to set up production facilities in such countries as Jamaica, Mexico, and Taiwan, where the cost of production was as low as possible. The content of the programming was kept as American as possible, all actors and actresses were American or Canadian, and unions were strictly forbidden. Off-camera crews and production staff were recruited from all over the world, but at low pay scales. The most modern production techniques could be employed because there were no entrenched bureaucracies to overcome. The actors and actresses did not like leaving Canada and the United States, but many of them had had to leave before during production of movies. There were severe threats by the unions and networks that creative people who left would never find work in the United States again, but many people felt that if their work were produced and caught on, they could return to Los Angeles or New York City as stars and demand large salaries.

Not only were production costs a tenth of what they were in the United States, but distribution costs were also relatively low. In Canada the distribution costs were essentially borne by the cable systems. Viewers were in the habit of watching the border stations and the content was even more directed to their tastes than it had been before. In the United States the consortium purchased time on a satellite transponder for distribution to subscribing U.S. cable systems. Many of them subscribed because the content was new and highly attractive. The major source of revenue anticipated by the Canadian and U.S. underwriters was syndication rights both from U.S. independent television stations and overseas broadcasters.

The final cost was promotion, since most of the material was unfamiliar to the audience. Advertisers on the border stations had

long been in the habit of promoting their programs in Canada to attract Canadian audiences. Canadian advertisers now saw the independent network as an excellent vehicle for penetrating the U.S.
market. They consequently agreed to enter into large-scale promo-
tional campaigns to build up U.S. audiences for the programs they
supported. In exchange, they were guaranteed test-marketing of
programs in Canada and northern U.S. states to make certain that
they attracted the right audiences. Many U.S. advertisers who sold
heavily in Canada and northern U.S. states also joined in underwriting and promoting particular programs.

The consortium rapidly became known as the Atlanta of the
North or the Northern network. Its programming was targeted at
viewers of Anglo-Saxon, Slavic, Germanic, and Scandinavian origin. Gradually, it became necessary to orient content and shooting
locations around northern settings. Eventually, many English-
speaking Canadians came to feel that the independent programming
was more Canadian than the U.S. network series carried by the
Canadian broadcasters.

The primary groups opposed to the arrangement were the
Canadian and U.S. creative communities. The Canadian creative
community argued that jobs were being lost to Canadians and that the
Canadian cablecasters and advertisers had no right to contract
abroad for production. The advertisers and cablecasters responded
that the creative community would be hired if they were willing to
come up with attractive ideas, use the latest production techniques,
and not hamper production with union restrictions. They also legiti-
mately argued that they were creating a U.S. market for Canadian
products while at the same time serving the needs of the Canadian
audience. French Canadians were particularly outraged that the
whole arrangement was English-oriented, but could do little about
it. The U.S. creative community, unlike the Canadians, had no-
where to turn to express their outrage. They tried to get Congress
to pass retaliatory legislation, but to no effect.

The reason that the scenario is possible is that (1) creative
communities in both countries seek to maintain control over production, leading to high production costs, and (2) national borders split
a potentially large northern viewing audience into a U.S. portion
that has no control over what is produced and a smaller Canadian
portion that does have control but cannot afford to produce much.
Action that could be taken now that might reduce the unpleasant aspects of the scenario include setting up U.S.-Canadian joint production ventures and establishing a U.S.-Canadian independent northern
network. If producers, actors, advertisers, and distributors from
both sides of the border felt that they had a voice in the activity, it

would probably be well received by both countries. The most difficult part would be to accept content that was attractive to audiences rather than to intellectuals.

Scenario 3: The Pirating of Satellite Signals

During the 1980s the primary means of distributing television programming to cable systems and television stations in the United States and Canada was via stationary satellites. For high-quality reception, large receiving antennas were used by the stations and cable head ends. Many enterprising companies started selling smaller antennas to private individuals along with down converters. In this way individuals could receive over 100 different programs. With mass production and self-assembly kits, the prices of receiving systems for individuals dropped to about $1,000. Receiving dishes were particularly popular in the Rocky Mountain states, where reception of over-the-air signals was particularly difficult.

Television distributors protested strongly to the FCC and brought suits in court to outlaw the use of receiving dishes, arguing that reception of their signals was equivalent to wiretapping and violated copyright in the programs transmitted. Users argued that the airwaves belong to the public and that everyone has a constitutional right to own and use a receiving dish.

At the same time that receiving dishes were popping up in the United States, they were being installed in Canada. Again they were most popular in rural areas where television reception was poor. The Canadian government was even more upset than the U.S. because satellite reception constituted direct broadcasting across borders, which the Canadian government did not condone. Occasionally the Canadian police tried to tear down receiving dishes as they were installed, but the Canadian public also argued they had a right to receive signals coming onto their own property.

The U.S. programming distributors decided that the only way to stop direct reception of satellite signals was to encode the signals so that only authorized receivers having decoder boxes could decode the signal. This put an end to most unauthorized reception of signals. However, there developed a small trade in duplication and sale of decoder boxes. In the United States the television signal distributors vigorously prosecuted anyone they discovered possessing signal decoders. There was an active market in pirated decoders in Canada, which the police tried to confiscate at the border. The government did not like having so publicly to enforce a prohibition.

It became clear that a major decoding operation was under way in midwestern Canada. A large firm had produced its own decoder, was receiving the signals, and was producing videotapes of much of the programming. The videotapes were of very high quality and were all expressly labeled that their use in Canada was not permitted. The company that produced the tapes operated a mail order catalogue through which it sold the tapes outside Canada. The company did not sell any tapes in the United States, but sold many in Latin America, Europe, the Middle East, and Asia.

U.S. producers began to discover that their overseas distribution markets were drying up because broadcasters had already purchased tapes from the Canadian company. The U.S. companies sought to take the Canadian firm to court, claiming violation of copyright. The Canadian company countered that the satellite signals violated Canadian airspace and that programs illegally brought into Canada without passing through customs did not deserve to be protected by copyright. The company also pointed out that if its activities were outlawed in Canada it could move to Mexico or operate on a ship in international waters.

A bill was introduced to make signals transmitted into Canada without authorization unprotectable by copyright. There would be a permit tax to operate a receiving dish and ordinary income taxes and sales taxes on any profits made from selling copies of programs, but making copies would not be illegal. Another bill was introduced that would authorize signals to be transmitted into Canada and extend copyright protection, provided that import taxes were paid by the originators of the signals. The U.S. satellite users lobbied heavily against both bills and threatened retaliation against Canadian satellite transmissions, but the bills were approved by Parliament.

This scenario is almost inevitable somewhere, if not necessarily in Canada, unless conventions are agreed to by all neighboring countries that satisfy their need to keep out unwanted signals in exchange for active prosecution when there is piracy. Lack of agreement about spillage of signals across borders should not be allowed to continue. The quantity and economic value of programming transmitted via satellites is likely to increase. The problem is still somewhat manageable because receiving dishes are expensive. However, direct broadcasting satellites will aggravate the problem of countries like Canada that want to limit reception of American programming. Either reception must be authorized or police actions are required to ferret out offenders. Certainly having originators encode their signals makes unauthorized reception more difficult, but not impossible. As long as authorized receivers have decoders, there will be a black market in unauthorized receivers. In the scenario, the massive offender serves almost as a Robin Hood and helps bring the issue of unauthorized transmission to the fore. Technology may some day provide a solution, such as laser transmission from space, that is so tightly beamed that it does not cross the border. However, the parties should not wait for this long-term solution. Instead, an agreement must be reached that balances the dual interests of the originators in making a profit and protecting their property rights against the rights of countries that do not want their citizens receiving foreign signals.

CONCLUSION

There are many more scenarios that could be developed, involving such exotic technologies as videodisc, pay-per-view subscription television, cable computer networks, or direct broadcasting satellites. However, the nature of the technological impact should be clear. Both Canada and the United States are interested in free enterprise. Companies in every country will try to structure evolution of the technologies to serve their own purposes. They will set up programming practices that minimize costs and maximize profits. They will view governmental action as a hindrance when it enforces noneconomic objectives, but as a necessity when private action threatens their own economic objectives. Both the Canadian and U.S. government have a legitimate right to promote prosocial technologies, cultural programming, and creative communities. There is no guarantee that wide-open competition and entrepreneurial spirit will lead to happiness, but it is very difficult for noneconomic objectives to be pursued by one government alone without at least tacit cooperation by the other. The extensive border between Canada and the United States is too permeable to television signals to pretend that each country can ignore the existence of the other. For practices that offend either party to be prevented, bilateral agreements must be worked out in advance so that businesses find cooperation more fruitful than sabotage and so that government officials find it in their best interests to coordinate actions rather than block each other.

INDEX

ABOUT THE CONTRIBUTORS

AMBASSADOR GOODWIN COOKE is Vice-President of International Affairs at Syracuse University. He was graduated from Harvard University in 1953 and joined the U.S. Foreign Service in 1956, serving in Pakistan, Yugoslavia, Italy, Belgium, Canada, the Ivory Coast, and the Central African Republic before his retirement in 1981.

LESLIE G. ARRIES, JR., is President of Buffalo Broadcasting, Inc., and has had an extensive career as a broadcasting executive. He was graduated from Northwestern University in 1945 and has worked with television firms in New York, Boston, and Cleveland.

ROBERT E. BABE is an Ottawa-based consultant and Associate Professor in the Department of Communications at the University of Ottawa. He received his Ph.D. in Economics from Michigan State University and is the author of two books and a number of articles on Canadian communications policy.

YALE M. BRAUNSTEIN has been Professor of Economics at Brandeis University since 1977. He received a B.A. from Rensselaer Polytechnic Institute in 1966, and an M.A. (1968) and Ph.D. (1975) from Stanford University.

BARRY COLE is a Professor at the Annenberg School of Communications and the School of Law at the University of Pennsylvania. He has been an advisor to the FCC and a congressional consultant, and is the author of several works on communications policy.

MARK J. FREIMAN is currently teaching in the Canadian Studies Department at the University of Toronto. He holds a Ph.D. from Stanford University and has taught in departments of literature and communications in England, the United States, and Canada.

THE HONORABLE ALLAN E. GOTLIEB has been Ambassador of Canada to the United States since 1982. He received his B.A. from the University of California at Berkeley, was a Rhodes Scholar at Oxford in 1953, and received a law degree from Harvard in 1954. He has had a distinguished career in the Department of External Affairs and was the first Deputy Minister of the newly formed Ministry of Communications in 1968.

THEODORE HAGELIN was graduated from the Wharton School at the University of Pennsylvania in 1965, and holds law degrees from Temple (1970) and Harvard (1975) Law Schools. Specializing in communications law, he taught at Boston University and the University of Cincinnati before becoming Professor of Law at Syracuse in 1978.

HUDSON JANISCH was born and brought up in Capetown, South Africa, and educated at Rhodes University, Cambridge University, and the University of Chicago, from which he received his Doctor of Law (JSD). He has held teaching positions at the University of Western Ontario and Dalhousie University and is currently a professor in the Faculty of Law, University of Toronto, where he teaches communications, public, and administrative law.

ERWIN KRASNOW received his B.A. from Boston University in 1958 and law degrees from Harvard (1961) and Georgetown (1965). He has taught at Ohio State, Temple, and American University, and has been Senior Vice President and General Counsel of the National Association of Broadcasters since 1976.

THOMAS H. MARTIN joined the faculty of the School of Information Studies at Syracuse University in 1980. He was graduated from Dartmouth in 1963 and received a degree in law from Berkeley and a doctorate in communications from Stanford. He has been a Peace Corps volunteer and taught at Stanford and the Annenberg School at the University of Southern California.

JOHN MEISEL has been Chairman of the Canadian Radio-Television and Telecommunications Commission since 1980. He was born in Austria and holds a B.A. (1948) and M.A. (1950) from the University of Toronto and a Ph.D. from the London School of Economics. Before assuming his present position, he was head of the Department of Political Studies at Queen's University, where he also held the Hardy Chair in political science.

IAN PARKER is an Associate Professor in the Department of Economics at the University of Toronto. He received his Ph.D. in economics from Yale University. He is currently working on an edition of the papers of Harold Innis.

FRANK W. PEERS is Professor of Political Science at the University of Toronto, and is one of Canada's leading experts in communications policy. He has published extensively in the area of communications and is the author of The Politics of Canadian Broadcasting 1920-1951 and The Public Eye: Television and the Politics of Canadian Broadcasting 1952-1968.

GLEN O. ROBINSON holds the John C. Stennis Professorship at the University of Virginia School of Law. He graduated from Harvard in 1958 and received his law degree from Stanford in 1961. He was a Commissioner of the FCC, 1974-76, and led the U.S. delegation to the World Administrative Radio Conference in 1978-79.

STEPHEN A. SHARP was appointed a Commissioner of the FCC in 1982. He graduated from Washington and Lee in 1969 and holds a law degree from the University of Virginia. He has taught at George Mason University and at the University of Virginia and was in private practice from 1978 to 1981. He worked with the transition team of President-elect Reagan in 1980-81, and was named General Counsel of the FCC in 1981.